WORKBOOK

to accompany

SOCIAL PSYCHOLOGY *ALIVE*

FIRST CANADIAN EDITION

JAMES M. OLSON
STEVEN J. BRECKLER
ELIZABETH C. WIGGINS

ELIZABETH C. WIGGINS
FEDERAL JUDICIAL CENTER

MEGHAN A. DUNN
FEDERAL JUDICIAL CENTER

AND ELIZABETH RIDLEY
UNIVERSITY OF TORONTO

THOMSON
★
NELSON

Australia • Canada • Mexico • Singapore • Spain • United Kingdom • United States

Workbook to accompany
Social Psychology Alive
First Canadian Edition

by Elizabeth C. Wiggins, Meghan A. Dunn, and Elizabeth Ridley

Associate Vice President,
Editorial Director:
Evelyn Veitch

Editor-in-Chief,
Higher Education:
Anne Williams

Senior Marketing Manager:
Lenore Taylor-Atkins

Senior Developmental Editor:
Alwynn Pinard

Permissions Coordinator:
Indu Ghuman

Proofreader:
Carrie McGregor

Production Coordinator:
Ferial Suleman

Design Director:
Ken Phipps

Cover Design:
William Bache

Cover Image:
© Philip Wallick/Corbis

Printer:
Thomson West

Table of Contents

Acknowledgments

We gratefully acknowledge the following reviewers who commented on drafts of the workbook at various stages of the project. We thank them for their time and their good ideas, which undoubtedly allowed us to improve upon our initial work: Carolyn Adams-Price, Mississippi State University; Chris Anderson, Temple University; Roger Bailey, East Tennessee State University; Gordon Bear, Ramapo College; Anne Duran, CSU, Bakersfield; Wayne Harrison, University of Nebraska at Omaha; J. Andy Karafa, Ferris St University; Tim Ketelaar, New Mexico State University; Marcia Finkelstein, University of South Florida; Doug Krull, Northern Kentucky University; Helen Linkey, Marshall University; James McNulty, Ohio State University; Matt Newman, University of Texas at Austin; Jacqueline Pope-Tarrence, Western Kentucky University; Brian Shrader, Emporia State University; Karen Tinsley, Guilford College; Wayne Weiten, University of Nevada, Las Vegas, Bozena Zdaniuk, University of Pittsburgh.

At Wadsworth/Thomson, our developmental editor, Kristin Makarewycz, kept a clear sense of the end product as she guided us through drafts and redrafts. Her thoughtful suggestions, sincere encouragement, and friendly manner made for a better product, and for more fun along the way. We extend to her a heartfelt thanks. We also thank Marianne Taflinger, for helping us envision what the workbook could and should be, and Jennifer Wilkinson, for her invaluable work in shepherding the workbook through production and organizing countless details.

Introduction

Welcome to the *Social Psychology Alive* workbook. Our goal for the workbook is to bring social psychology *alive* for you—to help you appreciate the eloquence of its theories and research methods and its relevance to everyday life and world events.

The workbook is a study guide designed to reinforce concepts discussed in the text. The study tools include:

Learning Objectives

Within each chapter, the *Learning Objectives* include a series of open-ended questions to guide your study of the text.

Test Yourself

Test Yourself consists of multiple-choice, sentence completion, and matching questions to test your mastery of the material.

The workbook is more than a study guide, however. It also includes several types of exercises to help you to learn more about social psychological principles and their applications to the world around you. The types of exercises include:

Social Psychology Alive Journal exercises

As you learn about social psychological findings and concepts, you'll find that you begin to see evidence of them in your own life. You'll also find that you begin to see evidence of them everywhere—in the newspapers and magazine articles that you read, in news reports on TV, in commercials and print advertisements, and even in comic strips. *Social Psychology Alive* Journal exercises provide specific instructions and space for recording such experiences.

Try It Yourself exercises

Try It Yourself exercises describe step-by-step how to conduct simple experiments and demonstrations to illustrate social psychological processes, and give you all the resources you need to do them. Through these exercises, we hope you grow to appreciate the intricacies of research methods and discover that conducting social psychology research is interesting and fun.

Thinking Critically about Social Psychology exercises
Thinking Critically about Social Psychology exercises typically include a reading about an important world event or human phenomenon, and analytical questions to help you probe more deeply into how social psychology might offer an explanation or solution.

On the Web
Numerous websites offer links and content directly related to social psychology, or material waiting for psychological interpretation. *On the Web* exercises direct you to these sites and guide your use of them.

Social Psychology Online Lab
Finally, each workbook chapter includes an introduction to the *Social Psychology Online Labs* for the corresponding textbook chapter. The online labs—access to which is provided with your textbook—give you first-hand experience as a participant in more than a dozen studies on a variety of topics.

We hope you enjoy the workbook and that it does indeed bring social psychology alive for you.

The views expressed here are those of the authors and not those of the Federal Judicial Center.

Chapter 1
Introducing Social Psychology

Social Psychology Alive Journal
Personal Experiences

As you learn about social psychological findings and concepts, you'll find that you begin to see evidence of them in your personal life and the lives of your family, friends, and acquaintances. We suggest that you keep a journal of these experiences. Some exercises in the Workbook provide specific instructions and space for recording such experiences. In addition, space is provided in Appendix A of the Workbook to record entries beyond those related to a specific exercise.

To help get you started, here are four sample entries of personal experiences that relate to social psychology.

Entry #1

Downward and Upward Counterfactual Thoughts (Chapter 3). Last week, my two best friends tried out for the university hockey team. Both wanted to make the A (or top tier) team but they both made the B (second tier) team. My friend Ben was disappointed because he was nearly good enough for the A team, and kept saying, "If only I had practiced more in the off season, I would have made the A team" (upward counterfactual thinking). My friend Avi was ecstatic because, to be honest, he could barely skate. He kept saying, "It could have been worse—I could have been cut altogether" (downward counterfactual thinking).

Entry #2

Self-handicapping (Chapter 4). I am a psychology major but decided to take a full-year anatomy and physiology course. The course is really designed for students interested medicine but my advisor and I think it is important for psychology majors to know how the human body works too. The problem is that for the first test we had to memorize the location and name of ALL, well, nearly all, the bones in the body. I knew I couldn't do it so I made a point of taking a beach trip the weekend before the test. Everyone else spent the weekend studying but I let them know I wasn't going to put in so much time.

Entry #3

Cognitive Dissonance (Chapter 7). Like most students, I'm on a somewhat limited budget. Last month, I spent $100 (a lot of money, to me) to take a kayaking course. The course was a disaster—I felt completely uncoordinated and couldn't keep up with the other people in the class. Plus, it was scorching hot! During the lesson, I said to myself "I hate this. I can't wait for it to be over!" Funny thing, though. The following week I found myself telling my friends what a blast I'd had and that the course was well worth the money.

Entry #4

Norm of Social Responsibility and Norm of Reciprocity (Chapter 12). Last week I gave $50 to help low-income families who had lived in an apartment complex that burned down—it was just the right thing to do (norm of social responsibility). I also gave one of my good friends $20; she was broke and wanted to go out to dinner. I know that she'll return the favour when I need it (norm of reciprocity).

Social Psychology Alive **Journal**
Events in the Media

As you learn about social psychological findings and concepts, you'll also find that you begin to see evidence of them everywhere—in the newspapers and magazine articles that you read, in news reports on TV, in commercials and print advertisements, and even in comic strips.

Throughout the semester, we suggest that you keep a journal of events portrayed in the popular media that demonstrate social psychological phenomena. A typical journal entry would include a copy of the printed matter or a description of the article, radio, or television spot, and a brief description of the psychological phenomena that it demonstrates. Some exercises in the Workbook provide specific instructions and space for recording such events. In addition, space is provided in Appendix A of the Workbook to record events beyond those related to a specific exercise.

To get you started, here are three sample journal entries.

Entry #1

On Friday, September 15th, an article appeared in the *Globe and Mail* that suggested there is a link between the events of 9/11 and the incidence of the flu. The article stated that: "Researchers have long suspected that air travel fuels the rapid spread of infectious diseases around the world. But it took the tragic events of 9/11 to prove their assumption was, indeed, correct." According to the article, researchers identified the time period when deaths due to the flu peaked by examining records of the flu and related pneumonia death records from nine regions in the United States. Based on their findings that in the 2001–2002 flu season deaths peaked two weeks later than usual, the lead researcher claimed that "there can be little doubt that the cutback in air travel after 9/11 slowed the spread of the flu."

This article provides a good example of a correlational study using archival data. The statement that "there can be little doubt that the cutback in air travel after 9/11 slowed the spread of the flu" indicates some confusion between correlation and causality. It is important to recognize that correlation does not equal causation. In this case for example, there may be other reasons (or "third" factors) responsible for the reported decrease in flu deaths after 9/11.

Entry # 2

In the final match of the 2006 World Cup soccer tournament, Zinedine Zidane, a well-known and talented player on the French national team, gave a head-butt to a player on the opposing team. Following the incident, he was given a red-card and sent off the field for the remainder of the game. Many soccer fans around the world explained that Zidane's aggressive behaviour was the result of provocation by the opposing player. Indeed, there was much speculation on the content of what was said by the other player and what kind of insult would have provoked such an attack.

This event and the ensuing explanations for Zidane's behaviour can be used to understand the difference between a situational and personal attribution. Many fans explained that Zidane's behaviour was the result of provocation from the other player (a situational attribution) rather than as a result of an aggressive personality (a personal attribution). This attribution was interesting because using a situational attribution is not the typical choice for explaining the behaviour of others. Instead, more often we commit the fundamental attribution error and use personal attributions to explain other people's actions.

Entry # 3

Dilbert © Scott Adams/Dist. by United Feature Syndicate, Inc. Used by permission.

Dilbert is trying to justify doing something that will hurt other people. In doing this, he demonstrates two principles of social psychology. First, he says he was only acting under orders. Research on "obedience to authority" shows that people are willing to do bad things to others when they are ordered to do so by an authority figure. The cartoon also demonstrates the concept of "Belief in a Just World." To further avoid responsibility for doing harm to others, Dilbert places the blame on the victims as if they deserved their fate. In this light, the bad outcome can be explained as being "just."

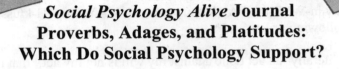

Social Psychology Alive Journal
Proverbs, Adages, and Platitudes:
Which Do Social Psychology Support?

Eugene Ehrlich has compiled two clever collections of Latin phrases that reflect inherent wisdoms and insights into the Roman civilization with the mischievous intention of helping you "conquer your enemies, [and] impress your friends with everyday Latin." In this exercise, we reproduce nine entries from his most recent collection, *Veni, Vidi, Vici* (1995). We do so to show how social psychology addresses many issues and problems with which regular folks are concerned. Below each entry, we refer you to the textbook chapter where the related social psychology is covered.

As you learn about social psychology, you'll find that you begin to hear "old sayings" in a new light. Be on the lookout for proverbs, adages, and platitudes—perhaps this time in English!—that relate to social psychology. Sometimes you will find that sayings are in conflict—such as "many hands make light work" and "too many cooks spoil the broth" or "birds of a feather flock together" and "opposites attract." Ask yourself whether one of the sayings in a pair is better supported by social psychological research or whether the truth lies somewhere in the middle.

Record below five sayings about human nature and social interaction you have heard. If, as the semester progresses, you learn of a psychological concept or finding that supports or disabuses the saying, come back to this exercise and briefly describe what you have learned.

Saying	Related Social Psychology Concept or Finding

The following entries are taken from: Ehrlich, E. (1995). *Veni, Vidi, Vici*. New York: HarperCollins. The bracketed words are the workbook authors' definitions of uncommon words and references to related textbook chapters.

1. **"actus me invito factus non est meus actus"**
   AH-ktuss may in-WEE-toh FAHK-tuus nohn est MAY-uus AH-ktuss
   I was only following orders.

"A legal phrase, literally 'an act done against my will is not my act,' that makes life difficult for police officers and prosecuting attorneys. In conformity with this principle, if a person is coerced into signing an agreement, committing a crime, or confessing guilt, the law does not hold the person responsible." (p. 11)

[See the discussion of "obedience to authority" in Chapter 8, Conformity, Compliance, and Obedience.]

2. **"aliena vitia in oculis habemus, a tergo nostra sunt"**
   ah-lee-AY-nah WIH-tee-ah in AWK-uu-lihs hah-BAY-muus, ah TEHR-goh NAW-strah suunt
   Oh wad some power the giftie give us
   To see ourselves as others see us!

"In these lines Robert Burns told us that while we are quick to recognize shortcomings of character in other people, we are blind to our own. Seneca expressed the same thought in *aliena vitia in oculis habemus, a tergo nostra sunt*, literally 'another's faults are before our eyes, our own are behind us.'" (p. 24)

[Learn more about "self-serving judgments" in Chapter 3, Social Cognition and Chapter 4, Social Perception.]

3. **"asinus asino, et sus sui pulcher"**
   AH-sih-nuus Ah-sih-noh et soos SOO-ee PUUL-kehr
   There's somebody for everybody

"This observation, 'an ass is beautiful to an ass, and a pig to a pig,' may not appear to be a felicitous [i.e., appropriate] way of alluding to people and the way they appear to one another, but it is comforting to believe that beauty may really be in the eyes of the beholder." (p. 39)

[Learn more about the role of similarity in interpersonal attraction in Chapter 13, Liking, Loving, and Close Relationships.]

4. **"simile simili gaudet"**
   SIH-mih-leh SIH-mih-lih GOW-det
   birds of a feather flock together

"Literally, 'like delights in like.'" (p. 231)

[Again, see the material about the role of similarity in interpersonal attraction in Chapter 13, Liking, Loving, and Close Relationships.]

5. **"beneficium invito non datur"**
   beh-neh-FIH-kee-uum in-Wee-toh nohn DAH-tuur
   I thought it was just a gift.

"This maxim, literally 'a benefit cannot be bestowed on an unwilling person,' advises us to question whether an exceptional act of generosity carries with it an unstated expectation that something—perhaps something illicit—is expected in return, that is, **quid pro quo** (kwid-proh-kwoh), literally 'something for something.'" (pp. 46–47)

[This is the "norm of reciprocity" that you will learn about in Chapter 8, Conformity, Compliance, and Obedience.]

6. **"manus manum lavat"**
   MAH-nuus MAH-nuum LAH-what
   One hand washes the other

"You help me, I help you." (p. 153)

[This is the "norm of reciprocity" too, found in Chapter 8, Conformity, Compliance, and Obedience.]

7. **"exemplo plus quam ratione vivimus"**
   ek-SEM-ploh ploos kwahm rah-tih-OH-neh WEE-wih-muus
   Do what I do, not what I say.

"A maxim, literally 'we live more by example than by reason,' suggesting that we are influenced less by moral precepts [i.e., principles]—taught usually by teachers, parents, or ministers—than by what we see these same people do." (p. 106)

[See the discussion of conformity and social validation in Chapter 8, Conformity, Compliance, and Obedience, and modeling of aggression in Chapter 11, Aggression and Violence.]

8. **"iniquum petas ut aequum feras"**
   in-EE-Kwuum PEH-tahs uut I-kwuum FEH-rahs
   The gentle art of haggling.

"Insurance lawyers and literary agents surely have learned this Latin phrase, literally 'ask for what is unreasonable so that you may obtain what is just.'" (p. 136)

[The Romans apparently knew how to use the "door in the face" technique that you'll learn about in Chapter 8: Conformity, Compliance, and Obedience.]

9. **"multorum manibus magnam levatur onus"**
   muul-TAWR-uum MAH-nih-buus MAH-gnahm leh-WAH-tuur AW-nuus
   Many hands make light work.

"Literally 'by the hands of many a great load is lightened.' As long as all the hands don't think they are in charge of the operation. Recall the English proverb "too many cooks spoil the broth." (p. 161)

[See which of these maxims social psychology supports by reading about "social loafing" in Chapter 10, Group Dynamics and Intergroup Conflict, and diffusion of responsibility in Chapter 12, Helpful Social Behaviour.]

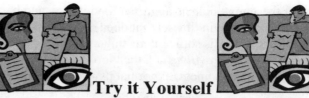

Try it Yourself

How Does Social Psychology Compare to Other Areas of Psychology and Other Disciplines?

In the textbook, we compare social psychology to other disciplines in the social and behavioural sciences. Fields such as sociology, political science, and cultural anthropology address many of the same problems as social psychology. Within psychology, the sub-fields of developmental, cognitive, and abnormal intersect in interesting and important ways with social psychology. Yet, each specialty offers its own unique conceptual approach and methods. One way to understand the similarities and differences is by examining the tables of contents of introductory textbooks.

In Appendix B on page 394 of the Workbook, we have reproduced the tables of contents of the following textbooks:

Olson, J. M., Breckler, S. J., & Wiggins, E. C. (2008). *Social psychology alive* (1st Canadian edition). Toronto, ON: Thomson Nelson.

Shaffer, D. R. (2005). *Social and personality development* (5th ed.). Belmont, CA: Wadsworth.

Barlow, D. H., Durand, V. M., & Stewart, S. H. (2006). *Abnormal psychology: An integrative approach* (1st Canadian ed.). Toronto, ON: Thomson Nelson.

Brym, R. J., Lie, J., & Nelson, A. (2005). *Sociology: Your compass for a new world* (Brief ed., 1st Canadian ed.). Toronto, ON: Thomson Nelson.

Haviland, W. A., Fedorak, S. A., Crawford, G. W., & Lee, R. B. (2005). *Cultural anthropology* (2nd Canadian ed.). Toronto, ON: Thomson Nelson.

Dyck, R. (2008). *Studying politics* (2nd ed). Toronto, ON: Thomson Nelson.

Can you see the similarities and differences among the disciplines they represent?

Even a quick perusal of these tables of contents reveals a number of interesting similarities and differences among the disciplines. As you would expect, they vary in the topics they cover. But most of them address some topics in common. One striking difference is in the "level of analysis." Psychology books all tend to focus at the level of the individual person. In some cases, the emphasis is almost entirely on the intrapsychic life of people (abnormal psychology), and in others the emphasis is on the interaction between individuals and their social contexts (social psychology, social and personality development). The other books (sociology, cultural anthropology, political science) all tend to focus at a broader, societal level. They describe theories of how social, cultural, and political institutions develop and change over time. These are all human-made institutions, and the books emphasize how and why people created them, and their effects on human behaviour. Still, the focus is more on the dynamics of those institutions and less on the individual people who interact with them.

One topic addressed in most of these textbooks is aggression, violence, and harmful actions. Indeed, the cognitive psychology book is the only one in this set that does not address this topic in some way. A closer look at the other types of texts reveals some interesting and important differences in how this topic is covered. We start with *Social Psychology Alive*, and then look at the tables of contents from current textbooks on social and personality development, abnormal psychology, sociology, cultural anthropology, and political science.

Social Psychology. This topic receives the most attention in Chapter 9 on stereotypes, prejudice, and discrimination and Chapter 11 on aggression and violence. These chapters review theories of how and why people engage in prejudice, discrimination, and intentional acts of harm-doing. Research in this area relies on both laboratory and field methods. Clearly, the focus is on the dynamics of individuals' harmful actions.

Social and Personality Development. This topic receives the most attention in Chapter 9 on aggression and antisocial conduct. The organization of material is very similar to social psychology, although the emphasis is more on developmental trends in aggression, family influences on aggression, and interventions aimed at reducing aggression in children. The focus is still on the dynamics of individuals' harmful actions.

Abnormal Psychology. Unlike the other psychology books, material on harmful actions is spread throughout the book on abnormal psychology. Also, the focus is clearly on harmful actions that are directed inward rather than outward. This book covers such topics as the causes and harmful consequences of alcohol and drug abuse (Chapter 11), eating disorders (Chapter 8), and mood disorders (Chapter 7). Thus, there is some similarity between abnormal psychology and social psychology in focusing on the role of emotions (mood) in aggressive behaviour, and in looking at the effects of modifying variables (such as alcohol) on aggressive behaviour.

Sociology. Here we begin to see the difference in the "level of analysis" applied to a problem. In the sociology book, harmful social behaviour is most directly addressed in Chapter 6 on deviance and crime. It comes up again in Chapters 7, 8, and 9 which all address facets of social inequality (socioeconomic, racial, ethnic, and gender). In sociology, these are treated as problems at the societal level rather than the individual level. Stepping back, we can see that harm-doing is a more unifying theme that cuts across chapters, rather than receiving focused attention in one or two chapters (as it does in social psychology).

Cultural Anthropology. In cultural anthropology we see an even clearer difference in the "level of analysis" compared to psychology. Here, the social group (family, tribe, nation) occupies the main focus of attention. In Chapter 11 ("Political Organization and the Maintenance of Order") we find an extended discussion of war and tribal warfare. Chapter 15 ("Cultural Change and the Future of Humanity") addresses problems of "structural violence" (violence exerted by situations, institutions, and social, political, and economic structures).

Political Science. In political science, most of the coverage of harm-doing has to do with "structural violence" of the sort described in cultural anthropology. For example, Chapter 5 "Political Theory and Ideology" describes various political ideologies, including fascism and how it rejects the concept of social equality, advocating racism instead.

Try It Yourself

The above example should give you a sense of how the various disciplines cover the same general topic in different ways. Can you spot other similarities and differences? Pick one of the following topics (or another of your choosing) and compare and contrast how the various disciplines and areas of psychology vary in their treatment of it. If you have difficulty with this exercise, don't worry. As the semester progresses (and as you take additional courses), the similarities and differences will become much clearer.

- The benefits of social support and close interpersonal relationships
- Cooperation and competition
- Decision making
- Effects of the mass media on attitudes and opinions

Your Topic: _____

	Is the topic covered in the textbook? Yes/No/Can't Tell	How is the treatment of the topic different or the same from social psychology?
Social Psychology		
Social and Personality Development		
Abnormal Psychology		
Sociology		
Cultural Anthropology		
Political Science		

 **Learning Objectives**

What Is Social Psychology?

1. Briefly explain the four key aspects of the definition of social psychology. (pp. 6–8)
Influenced by others, thoughts/feelings/behavior, Individual beliefs, Scientific study.

2. Briefly describe three ways individuals are influenced by other people. (pp. 8–11)
Interpret events, feel about the self, Affect behaviour.

3. What is the value of conducting social psychology research on a topic you think can be explained by intuition or common sense? (pp. 11–12)
Intuition is not always right, usually vague & contradicting.

4. What are three benefits of studying social psychology? Describe two real-world situations or problems to which social psychology is relevant. (pp.13–14)
Shed light on social problems, Relevant to life, learn about the self.

5. How is social psychology similar to and different from developmental, cognitive, and clinical counselling psychology? (pp.14–16)

6. How is social psychology similar to and different from the related disciplines of sociology, anthropology, and political science? (pp. 16–17)

Historical Background of Social Psychology

7. Describe two or more social psychological concepts that can be traced back to philosophy. (pp. 17–18)
The Social Contract, Identity and the essence of human existence.

8. Contrast behaviourism and Gestalt theory and their implications for social psychology. (pp. 19–20)

Test Your Knowledge

Multiple Choice Questions

1. Which of the following is not a component of Allport's definition of social psychology?
    A. It is a scientific study.
    B. It takes individual's perspectives into account.
    C. It traces the evolution of cultures over millennia.
    D. It involves how we are influenced by others.

2. The study in which several bystanders fail to assist a man lying on the ground is a classic one in social psychology, and it demonstrated how
    A. we rely on other people to interpret our world.
    B. we compare ourselves to other people.
    C. groups can exhibit aggressive behaviour.
    D. historical data can help explain social behaviour.

3. Mullen's study of lynchings demonstrated how
    A. we rely on other people to interpret our world.
    B. we compare ourselves to other people.
    C. groups can exhibit aggressive behaviour.
    D. historical data can help explain social behaviour.

4. Which statement best describes the relationship between social psychology and common sense (or folk wisdom)?
    A. Social psychology can be vague and simplistic, whereas common sense is more specific.
    B. Social psychology offers more than common sense or folk wisdom.
    C. Social psychology findings are validated by all of our common sense intuitions.
    D. Social psychology and common sense are interchangeable.

5. Which of the following is not an example of how social psychology can be applied to real life?
    A. a politician designing a media campaign
    B. a chemist developing a new arthritis drug
    C. a teacher mediating a dispute
    D. a student trying to make a good first impression on a blind date

6. The study of how traits help explain behaviour is known as
    A. clinical psychology.
    B. cognitive psychology.
    C. developmental psychology.
    D. personality psychology.

13

7. The study of how the human mind remembers information is known as
   A. clinical psychology.
   B. cognitive psychology. *(circled)*
   C. developmental psychology.
   D. personality psychology.

8. What is the primary difference between social psychology and sociology?
   A. Sociology focuses on groups; social psychology focuses on individuals. *(circled)*
   B. Sociology focuses on individuals; social psychology focuses on groups.
   C. Sociology manipulates factors in experiments; social psychology studies existing conditions.
   D. Sociology studies government systems; social psychology studies individual's perceptions of those systems.

9. The term that is often used to refer to individuals' perceptions of a situation is
   A. Social influence.
   B. Social cognition.
   C. Social construal. *(circled)*
   D. Social comparison.

10. The earliest sources of social psychology can be found in
    A. philosophy. *(circled)*
    B. biology.
    C. sociology.
    D. anthropology.

11. Kurt Lewin is often considered the father of modern social psychology, and his theoretical background was based on the idea that a person's overall, subjective interpretations of objects are more important than the physical features of that object. This approach is known as
    A. self-perception theory.
    B. behaviourism.
    C. Gestalt theory. *(circled)*
    D. social facilitation.

Sentence Completion

1. Social psychology is the ___scientific___ study or how individuals' ___thoughts___, ___feelings___, and ___behaviours___ are influenced by ___other___ ___people.___

2. ___Social___ ___Contract___ refers to the idea that to survive and prosper, human groups had to develop some basic rules of social and moral conduct.

3. ___Behaviouralism___ attempts to explain behaviour purely in terms of stimulus-response connections established through experience and reinforcement.

4. According to ___Gestalt Theory'___, people's overall subjective interpretations of objects are more important than the object's physical features.

5. By the end of the ___Second World War___, social psychology was emerging as a distinct area of psychology.

Matching I – Key Terms

E	1.	social psychology
A	2.	social contract
B	3.	behaviourism
C	4.	Gestalt theory
D	5.	social construals

A. the idea that human societies have developed basic rules of social and moral conduct, which members of the societies implicitly agree to follow

B. an approach in psychology that assumes that behaviour can be explained purely in terms of stimulus-response connections established through experience and reinforcement

C. an approach in psychology that assumes that people's overall, subjective interpretations of objects are more important than the object's physical features, and that objects are perceived in their totality, as a unit, rather than in terms of their individual features

D. how individuals personally interpret or perceive a social situation

E. the scientific study of how individuals' thoughts, feelings, and behaviours are influenced by other people

Answers to Test Your Knowledge

Multiple Choice Questions

1. C	6. D	11. C
2. A	7. B	
3. D	8. A	
4. B	9. C	
5. B	10. A	

Sentence Completion

1. scientific, thoughts, feelings, behaviours, other people
2. social contract
3. behavourism
4. Gestalt theory
5. Second World War

Matching I – Key Terms

1. E
2. A
3. B
4. C
5. D

Chapter 2
The Methods of Social Psychology

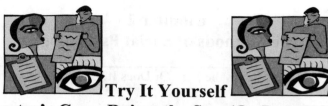

Try It Yourself
The Rooster's Crow Raises the Sun (Or Does It?): Part 1

There's no limit to how complicated things can get, on account of one thing leading to another.
(E.B. White, Title Chapter, *Quo Vadimus*, 1939)

Below are five statements each describing a causal relationship between two things. To most people, some of statements will seem blatantly false, and others will appear at least somewhat plausible. A correlation between the two things in each statement actually exists, but the causal statement is not necessarily true. For each statement, try to think of another explanation for the correlation. Does the statement reflect the incorrect causal direction? Does the statement treat a distal cause as if it is a proximal cause? (A proximal cause is the most immediate cause of an effect—it is the thing that most directly and closely produces an effect. A distal cause is a more remote cause—something that happens earlier in a chain of events to produce an effect.) Is an extraneous third factor actually responsible for the correlation? If you get stumped, take a look at the hints at the end of the exercise.

1. The rooster's crow raises the sun.

What is another explanation for the correlation between the rooster crowing and the sun rising?

2. Growing a beard makes a man happy.

What is another explanation for the correlation between happiness in men and their growing beards?

3. Children with bigger feet spell better.

What is another explanation for the correlation between big feet and good spelling in children?

4. In eastern provinces, a higher divorce rate leads to a lower death rate.

What is another explanation for the correlation between a high divorce rate and a low death rate?

5. Watching television causes children to develop AD/HD.

What is another explanation for the correlation between watching TV and children having AD/HD?

Hints:

1. The sun coming up wakes up the rooster who then crows.

2. Happy relaxed men (on vacation) grow beards.

3. Children with bigger feet are older and so spell better. Age is an extraneous variable that is related to both size of feet and spelling ability.

4. The implication of the causal statement is that people who stay married are more likely to kill one another. What's really at work? The median age of a province's population is related to both the divorce rate and the death rate. That is, people who are younger are more likely to divorce and also less likely to die compared to people who are older.

5. Watching television is more attractive to children who have AD/HD; that is, having AD/HD leads children to watch TV rather than the other way around. Also, AD/HD is inherited, so children with AD/HD are more likely to have parents with AD/HD, and those parents are more likely to allow their children to watch TV.

19

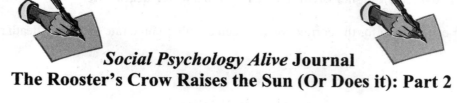

Social Psychology Alive Journal
The Rooster's Crow Raises the Sun (Or Does it): Part 2

Statements of causation abound in the media. During the next few days, identify two or three causal statements in the newspaper or news magazines, and explain whether you think it is justified. What additional information, if any, do you need to make this determination?

Statement of Causation and Source of the Statement	Do you think the statement of cause and effect is justified? Why or why not? What additional information, if any, do you need to make this determination?
1.	
2.	
3.	

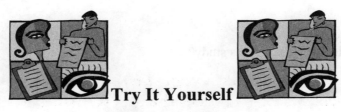

Try It Yourself

What's in a Design?

Three studies and their results are briefly described below. For each study, we ask several questions about the research design and the results depicted in the graph.

Study 1

Four equally attractive women, working with the researchers, enrolled in an undergraduate course on personality psychology—a large class of almost 200 students. On the days that they attended, the women entered the lecture room a few minutes before the class was to begin, walked slowly down the stairs to a front row, and sat where they could be seen by everyone. During the class, they listened and took notes quietly. At the end of the class, they rose, walked slowly up the stairs to the back of the room and left without speaking to any other students. One of the women attended 15 of 40 lectures in the course, another attended 10 lectures, another attended 5 lectures, and another did not attend any lectures at all. Only one of the women attended any given lecture. After the course was over, students in the course were shown photos of each of the four women's faces and were asked to rate how much they liked her. An "index of attraction" was created by averaging across 10 ratings on dimensions such as unattractive/attractive, cold/warm, and boring/interesting. The index can range in value from 1 to 7. The results are presented in the next figure. (Adapted from Moreland and Beach, 1992).

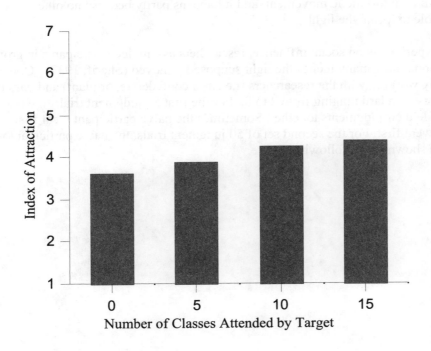

Questions:

1. What is the independent variable in this study?

2. What is the dependent variable in this study?

3. Based on the graph, what general conclusion can you draw between the level of exposure to a person and the degree to which the person is judged as attractive?

Study 2

In a darkened room, a point of light projected on the wall will appear to move, even though it is not really moving at all. This is known as auto-kinetic movement, and it happens partly because no other visual frame of reference is available to locate the light.

In one of the classic early experiments on social influence, researchers assembled participants in groups of two to make judgments about how many inches the light supposedly moved (Sherif, 1937). One of the two participants was actually working with the researchers (i.e., as a confederate, or plant) and varied his judgments around an arbitrary standard ranging from 2 to 8. For the first 50 judgment trials, the two participants in each pair made their judgments together. Sometimes the naïve participant went first; sometimes the confederate went first. For the second set of 50 judgment trials, the naïve participant was tested alone. The results are shown in the following figure.

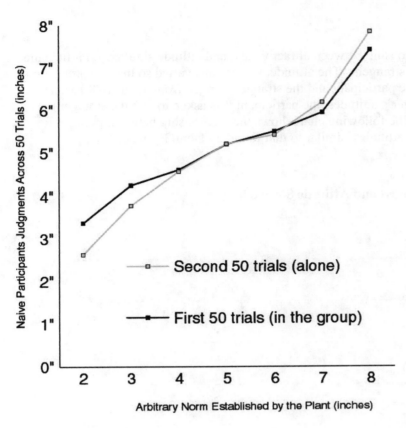

Naïve Participants Judgments Across 50 Trials (inches)

Arbitrary Norm Established by the Plant (inches)

Second 50 trials (alone)

First 50 trials (in the group)

Questions:

1. What is the independent variable in this study? In other words, what are the experimental conditions?

2. What is the dependent variable in this study?

3. Based on the graph: (a) When in the presence of the confederate, did the naïve participants follow the confederate's lead when judging how much the light moved? (b) Did the norm established in the first 50 trials carry over to the naïve participants' judgements when they were alone?

Study 3

A researcher was interested in the relationship between attractiveness and attitude similarity. Participants were told about the attitudes of various strangers. The attitude descriptions varied so that the proportion of attitudes held in common between the participant and the strangers ranged from about 10% to nearly 100%. After learning about each stranger's attitudes, the participant was asked to rate the stranger on a scale of attractiveness (from 2 to 14). The following chart shows the relationship between ratings of attractiveness and proportion of similar attitudes, similar to that found by Donn Byrne (1971).

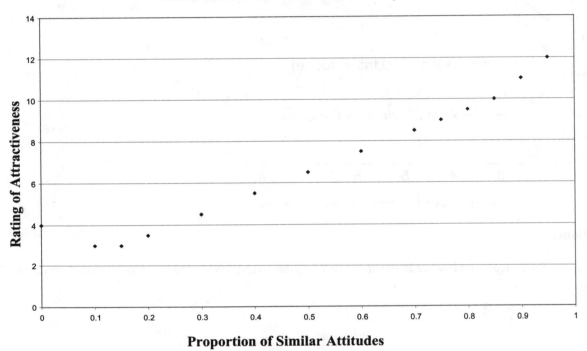

Attractiveness and Attitude Similarity

Questions:

1. Does the graph depict a positive or negative correlation between attractiveness and attitude similarity?

2. Based on the graph, what general conclusions can you draw about the relationship between attractiveness and attitude similarity?

Thinking Critically about Social Psychology
The Protection of Research Participants

On the next pages you will read about two events that raise important ethical considerations regarding the protection of participants in research: (1) the medical experiments conducted by physicians and medical researchers associated with the German Reich during World War II, and (2) a notorious medical study of syphilis carried out in the United States from 1932 to 1972 with black men as participants.

The human rights violations in these events are particularly egregious. But violations are not always so heinous and easy to identify. In later chapters of the workbook, the rights and protection of research participants will be considered again within the context of specific social psychology studies. Although these studies do not involve physical harm, the psychological effects they have on research participants are considerable.

As you read these excerpts, think about what basic human rights the research violated, and then answer the following questions.

Questions:

1. In what ways are the human rights violations by the researchers in the Tuskegee Study different from the violations of the doctors in the German Reich? In what ways are they the same?

2. Based on what happened in the Tuskegee Study, what rules might you adopt to protect participants in medical research?

3. Should the rules for medical research also apply in psychological research? Why or why not?

The Doctors Trial at Nuremberg

The following is a transcription of the indictment dated October 25, 1946 against physicians and medical researchers and officials associated with the German Reich during World War II. The transcription comes from the official trial record: *Trials of War Criminals before the Nuremberg Military Tribunals under Control Council Law No. 10. Nuremberg, October 1946–April 1949.* Washington, D.C.: U.S. G.P.O, 1949–1953.

COUNT TWO—WAR CRIMES

6. Between September 1939 and April 1945 all of the defendants herein unlawfully, willfully, and knowingly committed war crimes, as defined by Article II of Control Council Law No. 10, in that they were principals in, accessories to, ordered, abetted, took a consenting part in, and were connected with plans and enterprises involving medical experiments without the subjects' consent, upon civilians and members of the armed forces of nations then at war with the German Reich and who were in the custody of the German Reich in exercise of belligerent control, in the course of which experiments the defendants committed murders, brutalities, cruelties, tortures, atrocities, and other inhuman acts. Such experiments included, but were not limited to, the following:

(A) High-Altitude Experiments. From about March 1942 to about August 1942 experiments were conducted at the Dachau concentration camp, for the benefit of the German Air Force, to investigate the limits of human endurance and existence at extremely high altitudes. The experiments were carried out in a low-pressure chamber in which atmospheric conditions and pressures prevailing at high altitude (up to 68,000 feet) could be duplicated. The experimental subjects were placed in the low-pressure chamber and thereafter the simulated altitude therein was raised. Many victims died as a result of these experiments and others suffered grave injury, torture, and ill treatment. The defendants Karl Brandt, Handloser, Schroeder, Gebhardt, Rudolf Brandt, Mrugowsky, Poppendick, Sievers, Ruff, Romberg, Becker-Freyseng, and Weltz are charged with special responsibility for and participation in these crimes.

(B) Freezing Experiments. From about August 1942 to about May 1943 experiments were conducted at the Dachau concentration camp, primarily for the benefit of the German Air Force, to investigate the most effective means of treating persons who had been severely chilled or frozen. In one series of experiments the subjects were forced to remain in a tank of ice water for periods up to 3 hours. Extreme rigor developed in a short time. Numerous victims died in the course of these experiments. After the survivors were severely chilled, rewarming was attempted by various means. In another series of experiments, the subjects were kept naked outdoors for many hours at temperatures below freezing. The victims screamed with pain as their bodies froze. The defendants Karl Brandt, Handloser, Schroeder, Gebhardt, Rudolf Brandt, Mrugowsky, Poppendick, Sievers, Becker-Freyseng, and Weltz are charged with special responsibility for and participation in these crimes.

(C) Malaria Experiments. From about February 1942 to about April 1945 experiments were conducted at the Dachau concentration camp in order to investigate immunization for and treatment of malaria. Healthy concentration-camp inmates were infected by mosquitoes or by injections of extracts of the mucous glands of mosquitoes. After having contracted malaria the subjects were treated with various drugs to test their relative efficacy. Over 1,000 involuntary subjects were used in these experiments. Many of the victims died and others suffered severe pain and permanent disability. The defendants Karl Brandt, Handloser, Rostock, Gebhardt, Blome, Rudolf Brandt, Mrugowsky, Poppendick, and Sievers are charged with special responsibility for and participation in these crimes.

(D) Lost (Mustard) Gas Experiments. At various times between September 1939 and April 1945 experiments were conducted at Sachsenhausen, Natzweiler, and other concentration camps for the benefit of the German Armed Forces to investigate the most effective treatment of wounds caused by Lost gas. Lost is a poison gas that is commonly known as mustard gas. Wounds deliberately inflicted on the subjects were infected with Lost. Some of the subjects died as a result of these experiments and others suffered intense pain and injury. The defendants Karl Brandt, Handloser, Blome, Rostock, Gebhardt, Rudolf Brandt, and Sievers are charged with special responsibility for and participation in these crimes.

(E) Sulfanilamide Experiments. From about July 1942 to about September 1943 experiments to investigate the effectiveness of sulfanilamide were conducted at the Ravensbrueck concentration camp for the benefit of the German Armed Forces. Wounds deliberately inflicted on the experimental subjects were infected with bacteria such as streptococcus, gas gangrene, and tetanus. Circulation of blood was interrupted by tying off blood vessels at both ends of the wound to create a condition similar to that of a battlefield wound. Infection was aggravated by forcing wood shavings and ground glass into the wounds. The infection was treated with sulfanilamide and other drugs to determine their effectiveness. Some subjects died as a result of these experiments and others suffered serious injury and intense agony. The defendants Karl Brandt, Handloser, Rostock, Schroeder, Genzken, Gebhardt, Blome, Rudolf Brandt, Mrugowsky, Poppendick, Becker-Freyseng, Oberheuser, and Fischer are charged with special responsibility for and participation in these crimes.

(F) Bone, Muscle, and Nerve Regeneration and Bone Transplantation Experiments. From about September 1942 to about December 1943 experiments were conducted at the Ravensbrueck concentration camp, for the benefit of the German Armed Forces, to study bone, muscle, and nerve regeneration, and bone transplantation from one person to another. Sections of bones, muscles, and nerves were removed from the subjects. As a result of these operations, many victims suffered intense agony, mutilation, and permanent disability. The defendants Karl Brandt, Handloser, Rostock, Gebhardt, Rudolf Brandt, Oberheuser, and Fischer are charged with special responsibility for and participation in these crimes.

(G) Sea-water Experiments. From about July 1944 to about September 1944 experiments were conducted at the Dachau concentration camp, for the benefit of the German Air Force and Navy, to study various methods of making sea water drinkable. The subjects were deprived of all food and given only chemically processed sea water. Such experiments caused great pain and suffering and resulted in serious bodily injury to the victims. The defendants Karl Brandt, Handloser, Rostock, Schroeder, Gebhardt, Rudolf Brandt, Mrugowsky, Poppendick, Sievers, Becker-Freyseng, Schaefer, and Beiglboeck are charged with special responsibility for and participation in these crimes.

(H) Epidemic Jaundice Experiments. From about June 1943 to about January 1945 experiments were conducted at the Sachsenhausen and Natzweiler concentration camps, for the benefit of the German Armed Forces, to investigate the causes of, and inoculations against, epidemic jaundice. Experimental subjects were deliberately infected with epidemic jaundice, some of whom died as a result, and others were caused great pain and suffering. The defendants Karl Brandt, Handloser, Rostock, Schroeder, Gebhardt, Rudolf Brandt, Mrugowsky, Poppendick, Sievers, Rose, and Becker-Freyseng are charged with special responsibility for and participation in these crimes.

(I) Sterilization Experiments. From about March 1941 to about January 1945 sterilization experiments were conducted at the Auschwitz and Ravensbrueck concentration camps, and other places. The purpose of these experiments was to develop a method of sterilization that would be suitable for sterilizing millions of people with a minimum of time and effort. These experiments were conducted by means of X-ray, surgery, and various drugs. Thousands of victims were sterilized and thereby suffered great mental and physical anguish. The defendants Karl Brandt, Gebhardt, Rudolf Brandt, Mrugowsky, Poppendick, Brack, Pokorny, and Oberheuser are charged with special responsibility for and participation in these crimes.

(J) Spotted Fever (Fleckfieber) Experiments. [It was definitely ascertained in the course of the proceedings, by both prosecution and defense, that the correct translation of "Fleckfieber" is typhus. A finding to this effect is contained in the judgment. A similar initial inadequate translation occurred in the case of "typhus" and "paratyphus" which should be rendered as typhoid and paratyphoid.] From about December 1941 to about February 1945 experiments were conducted at the Buchenwald and Natzweiler concentration camps, for the benefit of the German Armed Forces, to investigate the effectiveness of spotted fever and other vaccines. At Buchenwald numerous healthy inmates were deliberately infected with spotted fever virus in order to keep the virus alive; over 90 percent of the victims died as a result. Other healthy inmates were used to determine the effectiveness of different spotted fever vaccines and of various chemical substances. In the course of these experiments 75 percent of the selected number of inmates were vaccinated with one of the vaccines or nourished with one of the chemical substances and, after a period of 3 to 4 weeks, were infected with spotted fever germs. The remaining 25 percent were infected without any previous protection in order to compare the effectiveness of the vaccines and the chemical substances. As a result, hundreds of the persons experimented upon died. Experiments with yellow fever, smallpox, typhus, paratyphus [It was definitely ascertained in the course of the proceedings, by both prosecution and defense, that the correct translation of "Fleckfieber" is typhus. A finding to this effect is contained in the judgment. A similar initial inadequate translation occurred in the case of "typhus" and "paratyphus" which should be rendered as typhoid and paratyphoid] A and B, cholera, and diphtheria were also conducted. Similar experiments with like results were conducted at Natzweiler concentration camp. The defendants Karl Brandt, Handloser, Rostock, Schroeder, Genzken, Gebhardt, Rudolf Brandt, Mrugowsky, Poppendick, Sievers, Rose, Becker-Freyseng, and Hoven are charged with special responsibility for and participation in these crimes.

(K) Experiments with Poison. In or about December 1943, and in or about October 1944, experiments were conducted at the Buchenwald concentration camp to investigate the effect of various poisons upon human beings. The poisons were secretly administered to experimental subjects in their food. The victims died as a result of the poison or were killed immediately in order to permit autopsies. In or about September 1944 experimental subjects were shot with poison bullets and suffered torture and death. The defendants Genzken, Gebhardt, Mrugowsky, and Poppendick are charged with special responsibility for and participation in these crimes.

(L) Incendiary Bomb Experiments. From about November 1943 to about January 1944 experiments were conducted at the Buchenwald concentration camp to test the effect of various pharmaceutical preparations on phosphorous burns. These burns were inflicted on experimental subjects with phosphorous matter taken from incendiary bombs, and caused severe pain, suffering, and serious bodily injury. The defendants Genzken, Gebhardt, Mrugowsky, and Poppendick are charged with special responsibility for and participation in these crimes.

The Tuskegee Syphilis Study: A Hard Lesson Learned
[Source: Center for Disease Control; http://www.cdc.gov/nchstp/od/tuskegee/time.htm]

The Tuskegee Syphilis Study, carried out in Macon County, Alabama, from 1932 to 1972, is an example of medical research gone horribly wrong. The United States Public Health Service, in trying to learn more about syphilis and justify treatment programs for blacks, withheld adequate treatment from a group of poor black men who had the disease, causing needless pain and suffering for the men and their loved ones.

In the wake of the Tuskegee Study and other studies, the U.S. government took a closer look at research involving human subjects and made changes to prevent the moral breaches that occurred in Tuskegee from happening again.

The Study Begins

In 1932, the Public Health Service, working with the Tuskegee Institute, began a study in Macon County, Alabama, to record the natural history of syphilis in hopes of justifying treatment programs for blacks. It was called the "Tuskegee Study of Untreated Syphilis in the Negro Male."

The study involved 600 black men—399 with syphilis and 201 who did not have the disease. Researchers told the men they were being treated for "bad blood," a local term used to describe several ailments, including syphilis, anemia, and fatigue. In truth, they did not receive the proper treatment needed to cure their illness. In exchange for taking part in the study, the men received free medical exams, free meals, and burial insurance. Although originally projected to last 6 months, the study actually went on for 40 years.

What Went Wrong?

In July 1972, a front-page *New York Times* story about the Tuskegee Study caused a public outcry that led the Assistant Secretary for Health and Scientific Affairs to appoint an Ad Hoc Advisory Panel to review the study. The panel had nine members from the fields of medicine, law, religion, labour, education, health administration, and public affairs.

The panel found that the men had agreed freely to be examined and treated. However, there was no evidence that researchers had informed them of the study or its real purpose. In fact, the men had been misled and had not been given all the facts required to provide informed consent.

The men were never given adequate treatment for their disease. Even when penicillin became the drug of choice for syphilis in 1947, researchers did not offer it to the subjects. The advisory panel found nothing to show that subjects were ever given the choice of quitting the study, even when this new, highly effective treatment became widely used.

The Study Ends and Reparation Begins

The advisory panel concluded that the Tuskegee Study was "ethically unjustified"—the knowledge gained was sparse when compared with the risks the study posed for its subjects. In October 1972, the panel advised stopping the study at once. A month later, the Assistant Secretary for Health and Scientific Affairs announced the end of the Tuskegee Study.

In the summer of 1973, a class-action lawsuit filed by the National Association for the Advancement of Colored People (NAACP) ended in a settlement that gave more than $9 million to the study participants. As part of the settlement, the U.S. government promised to give free medical and burial services to all living participants. The Tuskegee Health Benefit Program was established to provide these services. It also gave health services for wives, widows, and children who had been infected because of the study. The Centers for Disease Control and Prevention was given responsibility for the program, where it remains today in the National Center for HIV, STD, and TB Prevention.

Commentary:

The trial at Nuremberg led to the adoption of the first international standard for the conduct of research— the Nuremberg Code. This Code set forth ten basic principles that must be observed to morally, ethically, and legally safeguard human research participants. Among these principles are that:

- the voluntary consent of the participants is absolutely essential;

- the degree of risk to be taken should never exceed that determined by the humanitarian importance of the problem to be solved by the experiment;

- the experiment should be conducted so as to avoid all unnecessary physical and mental suffering and injury; and

- participants should be free to terminate their participation.

The Nuremberg Code has formed the basis of many ethical codes and research regulations throughout the world.

In response to public concern about the Tuskegee Study and other similar research abuses, the U.S. Congress established the National Commission for the Protection of Human Subjects of Biomedical and Behavioural Research. The purpose of this Commission was to identify the ethical principles that would guide all research involving humans. In 1979, the Commission issued the Belmont Report, Ethical Principles and Guidelines for the Protection of Human Subjects, on which the current federal regulations for the protection of human research participants are premised. The Belmont Report can be found at the following site: http://ohsr.od.nih.gov/guidelines/belmont.html.

There are similar ethical regulations for the protection of human participants in Canada. Ethical regulations regarding human research in Canada are dictated by the *Tri-Council Policy Statement: Ethical Conduct for Research Involving Humans*. This document outlines the policies of three important research agencies in Canada: the Canadian Institutes of Health Research (CIHR), the Natural Sciences and Engineering Research Council of Canada (NSERC) and the Social Sciences and Humanities Research Council of Canada (SSHRC). The *Tri-Council Policy Statement: Ethical Conduct for Research Involving Humans* can be found on the Interagency Advisory Panel's website at http://www.pre.ethics.gc.ca/english/index.cfm.

To Learn More

The Government of Canada's Interagency Advisory Panel on Research Ethics offers researchers an online tutorial on the *Tri-Council Policy Statement (TCPS)* in order to educate researchers on the TCPS and enable researchers to interpret and implement the guidelines in the TCPS. The tutorial consists of an introduction, conclusion, and five sections including: Ethics Review (including information on Research Ethics Board (REB)), Free and Informed Consent, Privacy and Confidentiality, Conflict of Interest, and

Inclusion in Research. The tutorial can be accessed at http://www.pre.ethics.gc.ca/english/tutorial/ and takes approximately two hours to complete. The following is a list of the learning objectives for each section:

Introduction:

By the end of this section, you should be able to:

- identify when the TCPS applies to a research project involving humans
- describe the goals and rationale of the TCPS
- describe the guiding principles underlying the TCPS
- apply ethical principles to the conduct of research involving human subjects in the context of a research project.

Section 1 Ethics Review:

By the end of this section, you should be able to:

- determine when the REB should be consulted
- describe the role of the REB
- explain what the REB has authority to do
- list the minimum REB membership requirements
- recognize the TCPS standards and procedures for REB administration
- describe the concept of minimal risk and its relationship to a proportionate approach to ethics assessment
- indicate when scholarly review of research is required
- describe the TCPS standards and procedures for on-going review
- analyze the harms and benefits associated with a research project
- apply the TCPS ethics review process in the context of a research project.

Section 2 Free and Informed Consent:

By the end of this section, you should be able to:

- define free and informed consent
- describe the TCPS requirement for free and informed consent
- identify when the free and informed consent procedure may be modified or waived
- explain procedures to ensure consent is voluntary
- explain procedures to ensure consent is fully informed
- define competence to give free and informed consent
- describe the type of situations in which individuals who are not legally competent may be asked to be research subjects
- describe the free and informed consent requirements in a situation where an authorized third party provides consent

- identify when an individual who is not legally competent should be given the opportunity to assent to or dissent from research participation
- apply the TCPS standards and procedures for obtaining free and informed consent in the context of a research project.

Section 3 Privacy and Confidentiality:

By the end of this section, you should be able to:

- define identifiable personal information
- describe how privacy and confidentiality are protected in research
- discuss the limits of privacy and confidentiality protections
- describe the TCPS requirements for personal interviews
- describe the TCPS requirements for surveys, questionnaires, and the collection of data
- describe the TCPS requirements for secondary use of data
- describe the TCPS requirements for data linkage
- apply the TCPS standards and procedures for protecting the privacy and confidentiality of subjects in the context of a research project.

Section 4 Conflict of Interest:

By the end of this section, you should be able to:

- describe how a conflict of interest arises
- describe the impact of actual, potential, or perceived conflicts of interest on the research process
- describe the TCPS reporting requirements for conflicts of interest involving researchers
- explain how the REB manages conflicts of interest involving researchers
- describe the TCPS reporting requirements for conflicts of interest involving REB members
- explain how the REB manages conflicts of interest involving REB members
- discuss the importance of REB independence in the avoidance and management of institutional conflicts of interest
- apply the TCPS standards and procedures for managing conflicts of interest in the context of a research project.

Section 5 Inclusion in Research:

By the end of this section, you should be able to:

- describe the TCPS requirement concerning just distribution of the benefits of research across all groups in society
- describe the TCPS requirement concerning inclusion of women in research
- describe the TCPS requirement concerning non-exclusion of those not capable of providing free and informed consent in research

- apply the TCPS standards and procedures that promote just distribution of the benefits of research subjects in the context of a research project.

To learn even more about ethics in Canada and internationally, visit the Government of Canada's Interagency Advisory Panel on Research Ethics and click on the "Links and Resources" link or go directly to http://www.pre.ethics.gc.ca/english/links/links.cfm. Here you will find an extensive list of links to ethics policies, laws, and guidelines from governmental and non-governmental organizations as well as other organizations involved in research ethics.

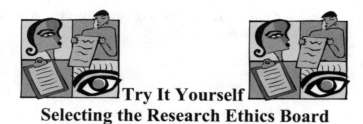

Try It Yourself
Selecting the Research Ethics Board

Imagine that you have the task of selecting persons to serve on the Research Ethics Board (REB) at the University of Toronto. Using the ethics review guidelines from Section 1 of the *Tri-Council Policy Statement: Ethical Conduct for Research Involving Humans* (TCPS), select five of the people listed below to serve. Demographic information about each person is shown in parentheses following his or her name and occupation. Make sure that the guidelines are followed and justify your selection.

V. Chow is a professor of psychology at the University of Toronto (Asian-Canadian, female, married to C. Folk)
C. Wong is employed by the University of Toronto as an attorney (Asian-Canadian, male, married to V. Greaud)
B. Shapiro is an attorney in private practice in Toronto (White, female, married to M. Shapiro)
M. Shapiro is a professor of psychology at the University of Toronto (White, male, married to B. Shapiro)
M. Hamilton is a professor of sociology at the University of Toronto (White, female)
C. Adoni is a professor of political science at the University of Toronto (Aboriginal, female)
S. Wheatman is a professor of psychology at York University in Toronto (White, female)

Your selections:

1. _____

2. _____

3. _____

4. _____

5. _____

Questions:

1. Explain your choices and how they help meet the requirements for REB composition found in the TCPS.

2. Why do you think the REB require the assortment of persons they do?

Section 1

B2. Membership of the REB

Article 1.3

The REB shall consist of at least five members, including both men and women, of whom:

a. **a. At least two members have broad expertise in the methods or in the areas of research that are covered by the REB;**

b. **At least one member is knowledgeable in ethics;**

c. **For biomedical research, at least one member is knowledgeable in the relevant law; this is advisable but not mandatory for other areas of research; and**

d. **At least one member has no affiliation with the institution, but is recruited from the community served by the institution.**

These basic membership requirements are designed to ensure the expertise, multidisciplinarity, and independence essential to competent research ethics review by REBs. The concept of independence implies that members of the REB under Article 1.3(a-c) should contain a majority of those whose main responsibilities are in research or teaching. The institution may need to exceed these minimum requirements in order to ensure an adequate and thorough review. The Agencies consider it essential that effective community representation be maintained. Thus, as the size of an REB increases beyond the minimum of five members, the number of community representatives should also increase.

The majority of members of an REB should have both the training and the expertise to make sound judgements on the ethics of research proposals involving human subjects. The terms of REB appointments should be arranged to balance the need to maintain continuity with the need to ensure diversity of opinion and the opportunity to spread knowledge and experience gained from REB membership throughout the institution and community.

Because the REB should reflect the ethical values of this Policy in the context of the society within which it operates, its membership should be broad enough to reflect that society. The members of the REB therefore play different but complementary roles. Article 1.3(a) indicates that general expertise in the relevant sciences or research disciplines is essential. Article 1.3(b) requires a member knowledgeable in ethics, so as to alert the REB to potential ethics issues and options.

The role of the member who is knowledgeable in the applicable law is to alert REBs to legal issues and their implications, not to provide formal legal opinions nor to serve as legal counsel for the REB. An understanding of relevant legal issues and contexts is advisable for all REBs, although for non-biomedical research such insights may be sought from someone who sits on the REB only for specific research projects. The institution's legal counsel should not be a member of the REB.

The community member requirement of Article 1.3(d) is essential to help broaden the perspective and value base of the REB beyond the institution, and thus advance dialogue with, and accountability to, local communities.

REBs should husband their resources and expertise prudently. For example, in the event that the REB is reviewing a project that requires particular community or research subject representation, or a project that requires specific expertise not available from its regular members, the REB Chair should nominate appropriate *ad hoc* members for the duration of the review. Should this occur regularly, the membership of the REB should be modified.

Institutions should consider the nomination of substitute REB members so that Boards are not paralysed by illness or other unforeseen eventualities. The use of substitute members should not, however, alter the membership structure as outlined in Article 1.3.

# Try It Yourself
Evaluating the Adequacy of Informed Consent

A social psychologist (Professor Benjamin Best, University of Yekcoh) is planning a study of people's attitudes toward a variety of political and social issues. Participants will complete two attitude questionnaires. The entire study will take 50 minutes. The risk to participants is minimal. The study will further scientific knowledge but will not directly benefit participants. Participants' names and other identifying information will not go beyond Professor Best's records and will not be used when reporting the results of the study. Data obtained in the study will be identified only by anonymous code numbers.

On page 38 is a draft of the consent form that Professor Best plans to have participants sign, and on page 39 are the regulations setting out the requirements of informed consent from section 2 of the TCPS. Evaluate whether the draft consent form complies with each of the articles in section 2D in the following table. First state, whether the consent form complies with each article, and then, if it does not comply, indicate the specific changes you would make. For example, if you think a sentence should be added, write that sentence. If you think a sentence should be deleted or modified, indicate which sentence should be deleted or how it should be modified.

	Does the Form Comply? Yes or No	Suggested change
Article 2.4 (a)		
Article 2.4 (b)		
Article 2.4 (c)		
Article 2.4 (d)		
Article 2.4 (e)		

Consent to Participate

Participants in this study will complete two questionnaires.

If you decide to participate, your participation is confidential and anonymous. Your name and other identifying information will not go beyond the original researcher's records and will not be used when reporting the results of the study. Information obtained in the study will be identified only by anonymous code numbers.

You may not withdraw from the study once you have agreed to participate. Once you have completed the study, you must not contact the researcher for any reason.

If you decide to participate, please print and sign your name, and date the form below. Thank you in advance for your participation.

PARTICIPANT'S NAME AND SIGNATURE

Name (please print) _____

Signature _____

Date _____

EXPERIMENTER'S NAME AND SIGNATURE

Name (please print) _____

Signature _____

Date _____

Section 2

D1. General Conditions

Article 2.4

Researchers shall provide, to prospective subjects or authorized third parties, full and frank disclosure of all information relevant to free and informed consent. Throughout the process of free and informed consent, the researcher must ensure that prospective subjects are given adequate opportunities to discuss and contemplate their participation. Subject to the exception in Article 2.1(c), at the commencement of the process of free and informed consent, researchers or their qualified designated representatives shall provide prospective subjects with the following:

   a. **Information that the individual is being invited to participate in a research project;**

   b. **A comprehensible statement of the research purpose, the identity of the researcher, the expected duration and nature of participation, and a description of research procedures;**

   c. **A comprehensible description of reasonably foreseeable harms and benefits that may arise from research participation, as well as the likely consequences of non-action, particularly in research related to treatment, or where invasive methodologies are involved, or where there is a potential for physical or psychological harm;**

   d. **An assurance that prospective subjects are free not to participate, have the right to withdraw at any time without prejudice to pre-existing entitlements, and will be given continuing and meaningful opportunities for deciding whether or not to continue to participate; and**

   e. **The possibility of commercialization of research findings, and the presence of any apparent or actual or potential conflict of interest on the part of researchers, their institutions or sponsors.**

Learning Objectives

The Scientific Method

1. What is a theory and what are hypotheses? (pp. 33–34)
    Theory - explanation of event/outcome — Hypotheses - Prediction.
2. Provide an example of a concept and its operational definition. (pp. 35–36)
    Depression - number of times you feel down/sad everyday.
3. What are the advantages and disadvantages of self-report measures? of behavioural measures?
    (pp.36–37) *Pro - easy answers,*
    Con - Demand characteristics. or social desirability responding
4. What does it mean to say a measure is reliable? What are two distinct ways of thinking about
    reliability? (pp. 38–39) *Consistent & stable.*
    Over time & across judges.
5. What does it mean to say a measure is valid? (pp. 39–40)
    Assesses the right thing.

Correlational Research

6. What are the three major types of correlational research? What is the major limitation of correlational
    studies? (pp. 40–46) *No cause/effect generalizations.*
    Surveys, Archival Research, Observational Studies.

Experimental Research

7. Describe the basic logic of an experiment and the three categories of variables that may be active in
    an experiment. (pp. 47–48) *Concept is manipulated to observe impact.*
    Independent, Dependent, Extraneous
8. Explain how standardized procedures and random assignment help minimize the extraneous variable
    problem. (pp. 49–50)
    Spreads them across equally.
9. What are demand characteristics and how do researchers try to minimize them? (pp. 50–51)

10. What is meant by internal validity? external validity? (pp. 51–52)
    Int - Clear causal info   Ext - Generalized beyond the sample
11. Describe the logic of a single-factor experiment and provide an example. (pp. 52–53)

12. What is the purpose of conducting experiments with more than one independent variable? What is the
    name of the experimental design used in such studies? (pp. 53–55)

13. What is meant by experimental realism? mundane realism? (pp. 55–57) *Increases ext. V.*
    Exp. R - feels realistic & involving. Mun. R - feels like outside world.
14. What are the advantages and disadvantages of conducting social psychological research via the
    Internet? (pp. 57–58)

15. Describe two new technological tools for studying social psychology. (pp. 58–60)

Ethical Issues in Social Psychology

16. What three procedures have been established to protect human participants? (pp. 60–61)

Research ethics board, Informed Consent, Debriefing.

17. What are the basic elements of informed consent? (p. 60)

Told about the study, allowed to withdraw

Test Your Knowledge

Multiple Choice Questions

1. Which statement best describes the relationship between theories and hypotheses?
   A. Theories provide a means of testing hypotheses.
   B. Hypotheses provide a means of testing theories.
   C. Theories provide a means of predicting hypotheses.
   D. Hypotheses provide a means of predicting theories.

2. In Milgram's teacher/learner study, the concept of obedience to authority was operationally defined as the
   A. speed with which participants responded to the newspaper ad.
   B. number of errors the learner made.
   C. severity of the shock the participant delivered.
   D. extent of discomfort the participants reported feeling.

3. Which of the following is *not* generally considered a disadvantage to using most self-report measures?
   A. They are often difficult for researchers to score.
   B. They may not elicit an honest response.
   C. They often require precise wording.
   D. They are subject to socially desirable responding.

4. You are anxious to avoid an exam, and feel you may be getting sick. You take your temperature and are amazed to find you don't have a fever. You take it again, with the same results. Desperate, you go to the infirmary and use their thermometer, only to find that you definitely do not have a fever. This is an example of which characteristic of a measure?
   A. psychometrics
   B. response time
   C. validity
   D. reliability

5. Correlational studies have several drawbacks. Which of the following is the most serious?
   A. They are subject to socially desirable responding.
   B. They can only be used with a small subset of issues.
   C. They do not show causal relationships.
   D. They are often used in artificial settings.

6. Which of the following issues is relevant to surveys but not to other correlational methods of research?
   A. hypothesis specificity
   B. representative samples
   C. independent variables
   D. naturalistic settings

42

7. Which of the following statements is an example of a hypothesis?
   A. The belief that one can personally be successful causes individuals to be inspired by a superstar.
   B. The belief that one can succeed should directly increase how much a person is inspired by a superstar.
   C. The belief that one is a superstar causes people to be productive.
   D. Participants exposed to information about a superstar felt better about themselves.

8. What is the difference between independent and dependent variables?
   A. Independent variables are manipulated by the experimenter; dependent variables are measured by the experimenter.
   B. Independent variables are controlled by the experimenter; dependent variables are measured by the experimenter.
   C. Independent variables are measured by the experimenter; dependent variables are manipulated by the experimenter.
   D. Independent variables are manipulated by the experimenter; dependent variables are controlled by the experimenter.

9. Which two strategies are used to eliminate extraneous variables?
   A. Random assignment and operational definitions.
   B. Random sampling and standardized procedures.
   C. Random sampling and demand characteristics.
   D. Random assignment and standardized procedures.

10. The extent to which research results can be generalized to the real world is known as
    A. internal validity.
    B. external validity.
    C. internal reliability.
    D. external reliability.

11. You are interested in testing how different types of contact (cooperative or competitive) and different amounts of contact (minimal or daily) can influence a person's perceptions of a minority group. What sort of experimental design should you use?
    A. single-factor design
    B. correlational design
    C. factorial design
    D. covariational design

12. Your text describes a study by Bochino and Insko on the effects of source credibility (YMCA director or Nobel laureate) and message extremity (people need 7 hours of sleep or 1 hour of sleep) on the effectiveness of a persuasive message. In that experiment, they found that the effects of source credibility depended on the extremity of the message. What is this finding an example of?
    A. a single factor
    B. a correlation
    C. a main effect
    D. an interaction

13. What is the difference between experimental and mundane realism?
    A. Experimental realism refers to the extent to which the experimental situation feels real to the participants; mundane realism refers to the extent to which the experimental situation looks like the real world.
    B. Experimental realism refers to the extent to which the experimental situation looks like the real world; mundane realism refers to the extent to which the experimental situation feels real to the participants.
    C. Experimental realism refers to the extent to which the experimental situation looks like the real world; mundane realism refers to the extent to which participants respond in a socially acceptable manner.
    D. Experimental realism refers to the extent to which participants respond in a socially acceptable manner; mundane realism refers to the extent to which the experimental situation looks like the real world.

Sentence Completion

1. A _____ is a scientist's framework for explaining an event or outcome and a _____ is a specific prediction about what should occur if that framework is valid.

2. Responding to self-report measures to create a positive impression of one self is called _____ _____ responding.

3. _____ refers to whether scores on a measures represent the underlying concept they are supposed to represent.

4. _____ refers to the consistency or stability of scores on a measure across _____ and over _____.

5. When conducting a survey, _____ _____ can be used to obtain a representative sample of respondents.

6. A _____ variable is a concept that is measured by the experimenter because it might be affected by a manipulation. It is the _____ in cause-effect sequences.

7. An _____ occurs when the effect of one experimental manipulation depends on the level of another experimental manipulation.

8. When an experimental situation feels realistic to research participants and elicits their spontaneous behaviour, _____ realism has been achieved. When an experiment looks and feels like the outside world, _____ has been achieved.

9. Almost all research in universities, research institutes, and companies must first be reviewed by a _____ _____ _____.

10. Three procedures that help protect human participants in research are _____ _____ _____, (2) _____ _____, and (3) _____.

Matching I – Key Terms

_D_	1.	theory
_I_	2.	hypothesis
_F_	3.	operational definition
_C_	4.	socially desirable responding
_J_	5.	unobtrusive measures
_E_	6.	psychometrics
_B_	7.	reliability
_H_	8.	validity
_G_	9.	correlational research
_A_	10.	survey

A. a correlational study in which the researcher asks questions to respondents, either in a printed questionnaire, on a computer, over the telephone, or during an interview

B. the extent to which a measure is free of "random" fluctuations, both over time and across judges

C. a form of responding that involves giving answers that portray the respondent in a positive light

D. an explanation of why an event or outcome occurs; it identifies the underlying causes of an event or phenomenon

E. a sub-discipline within psychology that is devoted to understanding and refining methods for psychological measurement

F. a specific, observable response that is used to measure a concept

G. studies in which investigators measure two or more concepts and see whether the concepts are associated with one another

H. the extent to which a measure really assesses what it is supposed to assess — whether scores on the measure actually reflect the assumed underlying concept

I. a specific prediction about what should occur if a theory is valid; it provides the means by which a theory can be tested

J. assessments that are taken without the realization of participants, thereby minimizing socially desirable responding

Matching II – Key Terms

_F_ 11.	representative sample	A. investigations in which the researcher manipulates one concept (or more than one) and assesses the impact of the manipulation on one or more other concepts
_I_ 12.	random sampling	B. correlational investigations that are based on pre-existing information obtained by researchers, such as historical records, newspaper articles, or other forms of public data
_B_ 13.	archival research	
_J_ 14.	observational studies	C. a special type of observational study in which a researcher actually joins an ongoing group to observe the members' behaviour
_C_ 15.	participant-observation research	D. a concept that is measured by the researcher after the manipulation(s) in an experiment; it is typically expected to be affected by the manipulation(s)
_A_ 16.	experimental research	E. a procedure by which each participant in an experiment is equally likely to take part in any of the experimental conditions; it controls extraneous variable problems coming from characteristics of the participants
_H_ 17.	independent variable	
_D_ 18.	dependent variable	F. a group of respondents that accurately reflects a larger population from which it was drawn and to which the researcher wants to generalize the results
_G_ 19.	extraneous variables	G. potential sources of error in the experiment that should be controlled; they encompass everything in the experiment except the independent and dependent variables
_E_ 20.	random assignment	H. a concept or factor that is manipulated by the researcher in an experiment; its causal impact on one or more other variables is assessed in the experiment
		I. a recruitment process in which every person in a particular population has exactly the same probability of being in the study; it produces a representative sample
		J. correlational investigations in which researchers watch participants and code measures from the observed behaviour, either "live" or from videotapes

46

Matching III – Key Terms

_L_ 21. **demand characteristics**

_H_ 22. **internal validity**

_J_ 23. **external validity**

_C_ 24. **single-factor experiment**

_A_ 25. **factorial design experiment**

_I_ 26. **interaction**

_G_ 27. **main effect**

_D_ 28. **experimental realism**

_F_ 29. **mundane realism**

_B_ 30. **field experiment**

_M_ 31. **immersive virtual environments technology**

_N_ 32. **Research Ethics Board (REB)**

_E_ 33. **informed consent**

_K_ 34. **debriefing**

A. an experimental study that involves two or more independent variables

B. an experimental study that is conducted in a setting outside the laboratory; it tends to produce high mundane realism and external validity

C. an experimental study that involves only one independent variable

D. the extent to which the study's setting feels realistic and involving to participants and elicits spontaneous behaviour

E. a procedure by which participants are told beforehand what to expect in the study and are reminded that they can withdraw at any time

F. the extent to which the study's setting looks and feels like the outside world; it increases the external validity of research results

G. the effect of one experimental manipulation on the dependent variable, averaged across all levels of other experimental manipulations

H. the extent to which research yielded clear causal information; it tends to be low in correlational research and high in experimental research

I. result showing that the effect of one experimental manipulation depends on the level of another experimental manipulation; it can only be observed in a factorial design experiment

J. the extent to which research results can be generalized beyond the current sample, setting, and other characteristics of the study

K. a post-experimental procedure in which participants are given a full and complete description of the study's design, purpose, and expected results; if there has been any deception during the study, it must be identified and explained in the debriefing

L. cues in a study that suggest to participants how they are supposed to respond

M. computer programs that construct an imaginary setting in which participants behave; the computer controls the visual and auditory information and allows participants to respond as if the scene was real

N. a committee that must approve all studies before they can be started; it ensures that the procedures will not cause unacceptable harm to participants

Answers to Test Your Knowledge

Multiple Choice Questions

1. B	6. B	11. C
2. C	7. B	12. D
3. A	8. A	13. A
4. D	9. D	
5. C	10. B	

Sentence Completion

1. theory, hypothesis
2. socially desirable
3. validity
4. reliability, judges, time
5. random sampling

6. dependent, effect
7. interaction
8. experimental, mundane
9. Research Ethics Board (REB)
10. Research Ethics Board, informed consent, debriefing

Matching I – Key Terms

1. D	6. E
2. I	7. B
3. F	8. H
4. C	9. G
5. J	10. A

Matching II – Key Terms

11. F	16. A
12. I	17. H
13. B	18. D
14. J	19. G
15. C	20. E

Matching III – Key Terms

21. L	28. D
22. H	29. F
23. J	30. B
24. C	31. M
25. A	32. N
26. I	33. E
27. G	34. K

Chapter 3
Social Cognition: Thinking About People

Thinking Critically about Social Psychology
The Sports Illustrated Jinx: Does Appearance on the Cover Doom the Featured Athlete to a Terrible Fate?

The weekly sports magazine *Sports Illustrated* regularly features athletes and teams on its cover. Since the magazine's inception in 1954, many people have believed that appearing on its cover is linked to subsequent poor performance, the so-called "Sports Illustrated Cover Jinx." Over the years, the jinx has allegedly affected a wide variety of athletes and teams: men and women, professional and amateur, team competitors and individual competitors, even horses.

Anecdotal evidence appears in an article written in *Sports Illustrated* on January 21, 2002 to support the existence of a jinx. The article lists numerous examples in which the featured cover athlete or team was negatively impacted by the cover appearance — a loss, an injury, or even death. For example: "Swimmer Carin Cone, unbeaten in the 100-meter backstroke for four years leading up to the '60 Olympic trials, failed to qualify for the Games after her cover," "Two months after Steve Cauthen's cover in '77, the leg of his mount, Baystreak, was broken in a three-horse pileup, and Cauthen suffered multiple fractures and required 25 stitches," and "Skater Laurence Owen appeared on the cover in '61, billed as AMERICA'S MOST EXCITING GIRL SKATER; two days after the cover date Owen and the rest of the U.S. skating team perished in a plane crash."

According to the article, two *Sports Illustrated* researchers analyzed the fate of 2456 subjects who had appeared on the cover of *Sports Illustrated* to determine whether the jinx really exists. They identified six categories of misfortune, and found an overall "jinx rate" of 37%, with the majority of the misfortunes being losses or bad performances by a team. They also found that individual-sport athletes appeared to be more vulnerable to the jinx than team-sport athletes.

Obviously, *Sports Illustrated* has a vested interest in demonstrating that the jinx is nothing more than a statistical anomaly, and several alternate explanations are offered for the phenomenon. Several of the explanations are rooted in social and research psychology, including the idea of the illusory correlation. The illusory correlation, similar to what the magazine article calls post-hoc reasoning, is the mistaken belief that if two things occur together, one must have caused the other.

There are, however, explanations given in the article for the "jinx" that take into account the idea that the cover appearance may alter the athlete's experiences immediately following the cover. A sports psychologists is quoted who suggests that "being on the cover changes the way people see themselves, and they have to metabolize a different set of conditions. They're supposed to be superstars now, and if they don't live up to that, they've somehow failed. This changing perception causes many athletes to feel pressure and have a much harder time achieving their ideal performance." While this may explain sudden drops in batting averages, or failures to win expected Olympic medals, it is more of a stretch to apply this explanation to injuries or deaths that follow a cover appearance.

Questions:

1. The results of the quasi-scientific study conducted by the authors of the *Sports Illustrated* article discussed above seemed somewhat supportive of the anecdotal evidence of athletes who have met with bad fate after being featured on the cover of the magazine. Throughout social psychology, however, there are many instances in which anecdotal evidence is not borne out by empirical data.

From the chapters you have read so far, can you think of research findings that contradict anecdotal evidence? Why it is necessary to verify anecdotal evidence with more empirical methods?

2. As mentioned above, the researchers found that 37% of people who had appeared on the cover suffered some verifiable misfortune. Do you think this is evidence of a jinx? Based on what you have learned about the concept of illusory correlations, do you think that the *SI* jinx is a good example of the phenomenon? Why or why not?

3. One of the interesting aspects of this story is that a wide variety of people place stock in the idea of the cover jinx. It's not just the individual athlete, but also entire teams, coaches, and fans. Can you think of other instances in sports in which superstitions, and the illusory correlation, occur? For example, when a pitcher is working on a no-hitter, certain superstitious conventions are observed. One of many is that the announcers will not directly say the words "no-hitter" when discussing the game in progress, but will instead rely on euphemisms (i.e., saying "no batters have reached base"). When these conventions are broken, and the pitcher gives up a hit, fans and players may blame it on the announcer prematurely speaking about the no-hitter. These trends are powerful – even though people may rationally know that the announcer's words have no effect on the outcome of the game, it still may seem as though he is to blame. What does that tell you about the nature of athletics in our society? About the importance of superstition? To explore these issues further, see the item on the "hot hand" phenomenon in this workbook chapter.

4. Another explanation posited for the jinx is that increased pressure on the athlete undermines their confidence. Can you think of any other alternate explanations for the supposed "jinx?"

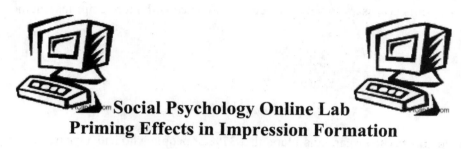

Social Psychology Online Lab
Priming Effects in Impression Formation

The online lab, Impression Formation, allows you to demonstrate how priming can influence the interpretation of ambiguous information and affect your impression of a person. In the lab, you will first do a sentence completion task. The computer will present groups of four words, and instruct you to select as quickly as possible any of the three words in each group that could form a sentence. In one condition, some of the word groups (e.g., "leg break arm his") result in sentences with hostile, aggressive meanings (e.g., break his arm). In the other condition, all word groupings and sentences are neutral (e.g., "her found knew I"). You will then read a paragraph about a young man, which will include several actions that are ambiguous with respect to hostility — that is, the actions can be interpreted as hostile or as assertive (e.g., refusing to pay rent to his landlord until his apartment is repainted). After reading the paragraph, you will be asked to rate the target person on several dimensions.

For each participant, the program uses the trait ratings to calculate (1) an index of how hostile the participant viewed the young man, and (2) an index of how favourable the participant viewed the young man. The computer will calculate and show the average scores on the indexes for people in "hostility" condition and those in the "neutral" condition, and give you some guidance about how to interpret the results.

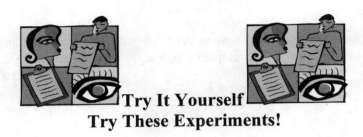 **Try It Yourself**
Try These Experiments!

Experiment A: What traits are chronically accessible to your friends, family members, and roommates?

E. Tory Higgins and his colleagues (1982) demonstrated that the extent to which certain traits are chronically accessible to us (that is, those traits that are easily activated or brought to mind) influences the impressions we form about others, and what we remember about others. You can try a version of their experiment on your own, and see which traits are chronically accessible for the people closest to you.

Using the form on page 56, ask three friends or family members to write a brief description of themselves, using no more than 10 traits in the description. Then ask them to describe four friends, again using no more than 10 traits. Look at the lists generated by your three friends or family members, and see whether you can see which traits are chronically accessible them.

Questions:

1. For each friend or family member, do some traits appear on several lists? What traits appear to be chronically accessible to the friend or family member?

2. Are the traits that are chronically accessible to your friends or family members the ones that you would use to describe them?

Experiment B: WE are individuals but THEY are all alike: A demonstration of the outgroup homogeneity effect.

The outgroup homogeneity effect refers to the tendency for people to overestimate the similarity within social groups that they do not belong to. You can see this effect in action all around you.

To demonstrate this effect, first ask a friend to complete the scales on page 57 by circling a number between "1" and "5" to indicate how similar or diverse members of each group are. Then ask the friend to place checks beside each group to which he or she belongs.

Questions:

1. Did your friend rate the groups to which he or she belonged as more diverse than the groups to which he or she did not belong? This is an example of the outgroup homogeneity effect.

2. Share you results with your classmates. Do their results demonstrate the outgroup homogeneity effect?

Experiment C: Is your fate really in the stars? A demonstration of an illusory correlation.

Early research on the illusory correlation suggests that people are more likely to notice if something congruent with their horoscope happens than if something incongruent with their horoscope happens. The vagueness of horoscopes makes it particularly likely that something that can be interpreted as congruent will occur that day. You can conduct your own test of the accuracy of horoscopes by keeping a journal. Monitor your astrological forecast for about a week and record in the chart below whether the events of the day support the forecast or not. Be sure to do this everyday, to capture both "hits" and "misses."

Day of the Week	Was the astrological forecast a "hit," a "miss," or somewhere "in between"?
Day 1	
Day 2	
Day 3	
Day 4	
Day 5	
Day 6	
Day 7	

Questions:

1. How many "hits" do you have? How many "in between" ratings (or "near hits") do you have?

2. Explain why the occasional "hit" or "near hit" may produce an illusory correlation.

Form for Experiment A

1. First, using no more than 10 trait terms (e.g., athletic, short, outgoing) write a brief description of yourself.

2. Now, write a brief description of four friends, again using no more than 10 trait terms for each friend.

Friend 1:

Friend 2:

Friend 3:

Friend 4:

Form for Experiment B

Instructions: Circle a number between 1 and 5 to indicate how similar or diverse members of the following groups are.

	Very Similar	Somewhat similar	About as similar as diverse	Diverse	Very Diverse
Psychology majors	1	2	3	4	5
Engineering majors	1	2	3	4	5
University Students	1	2	3	4	5
Men	1	2	3	4	5
Women	1	2	3	4	5
Athletes	1	2	3	4	5
Musicians	1	2	3	4	5
Members of a student club (e.g., debating, drama)	1	2	3	4	5
Members of a youth gang	1	2	3	4	5
Students who are not in a club	1	2	3	4	5
Youth who are not in a gang	1	2	3	4	5
Redheads	1	2	3	4	5
City dwellers	1	2	3	4	5
Catholics	1	2	3	4	5

Thinking Critically about Social Psychology
Should "Seeing" Always Equate to "Believing"?
The Fallibility of Eyewitness Testimony

Canadian wrongful conviction cases:

David Milgaard
Sentence: 1970 – life imprisonment for murder
Time in prison: 23 years
Outcome: cleared by DNA evidence in 1997

Donald Marshall
Sentence: 1971 – life imprisonment for murder
Time in prison: 11 years
Outcome: aquitted in 1983

Thomas Sophonow
Sentence: 1983 – life imprisonment for murder
Time in prison: 45 months
Outcome: cleared by DNA evidence in 2000

Commission of Inquiry into the wrongful conviction of Thomas Sophonow
One of the mechanisms in place within the Canadian justice system for addressing and understanding wrongful convictions is called a commission of inquiry. One of the mandates of a commission of inquiry is to make recommendations in order to prevent future wrongful convictions. In the Commission of Inquiry into the wrongful conviction of Thomas Sophonow, recommendations were made with regard to the proper collection and use of eyewitness testimony.

Recommendations for eyewitnesses from the Sophonow inquiry:

Live line-up

- The third officer who is present with the prospective eyewitness should have no knowledge of the case or whether the suspect is contained in the line-up.

- The officer in the room should advise the witness that he does not know if the suspect is in the line-up or, if he is, who he is. The officer should emphasize to the witness that the suspect may not be in the line-up.

- All proceedings in the witness room while the line-up is being watched should be recorded, preferably by videotape but, if not, by audiotape.

- All statements of the witness on reviewing the line-up must be both noted and recorded verbatim and signed by the witness.

- When the line-up is completed, the witness should be escorted from the police premises. This will eliminate any possibility of contamination of that witness by other officers, particularly those involved in the investigation of the crime itself.

- The fillers in the line-up should match as closely as possible the descriptions given by the eyewitnesses at the time of the event. It is only if that is impossible, that the fillers should resemble the suspect as closely as possible.

- At the conclusion of the line-up, if there has been any identification, there should be a question posed to the witness as to the degree of certainty of identification. The question and answer must be both noted and recorded verbatim and signed by the witness. It is important to have this report on record before there is any possibility of contamination or reinforcement of the witness.

- The line-up should contain a minimum of 10 persons. The greater the number of persons in the line-up, the less likelihood there is of a wrong identification.

Photo pack line-up

- The photo pack should contain at least 10 subjects.

- The photos should resemble as closely as possible the eyewitnesses' description. If that is not possible, the photos should be as close as possible to the suspect.

- Everything should be recorded on video or audiotape from the time that the officer meets the witness, before the photographs are shown through until the completion of the interview. Once again, it is essential that an officer who does not know who the suspect is and who is not involved in the investigation conducts the photo pack line-up.

- Before the showing of the photo pack, the officer conducting the line-up should confirm that he does not know who the suspect is or whether his photo is contained in the line-up. In addition, before showing the photo pack to a witness, the officer should advise the witness that it is just as important to clear the innocent as it is to identify the suspect. The photo pack should be presented by the officer to each witness separately.

- The photo pack must be presented sequentially and not as a package.

- In addition to the videotape, if possible, or, as a minimum alternative, the audiotape, there should be a form provided for setting out in writing and for signature the comments of both the officer conducting the line-up and the witness. All comments of each witness must be noted and recorded verbatim and signed by the witness.

- Police officers should not speak to eyewitnesses after the line-ups regarding their identification or their inability to identify anyone. This can only cast suspicion on any identification made and raise concerns that it was reinforced.

- It was suggested that, because of the importance of eyewitness evidence and the high risk of contaminating it, a police force other than the one conducting the investigation of the crime should conduct the interviews and the line-ups with the eyewitnesses. Ideal as that procedure might be, I think that it would unduly complicate the investigation, add to its cost and increase the time required. At some point, there must be a reasonable degree of trust placed in the police. The interviews of eyewitnesses and the line-up may be conducted by the same force as that investigating the crime, provided that the officers dealing with the eyewitnesses are not involved in the investigation of the crime and do not know the suspect or whether his photo forms part of the line-up. If this were done and the other recommendations complied with, that would provide adequate protection of the process.

Trial instructions

- There must be strong and clear directions given by the Trial Judge to the jury emphasizing the frailties of eyewitness identification. The jury should as well be instructed that the apparent confidence of a witness as to his or her identification is not a criteria of the accuracy of the identification. In this case, the evidence of Mr. Janower provides a classic example of misplaced but absolute confidence that Thomas Sophonow was the man whom he saw at the donut shop.

- The Trial Judge should stress that tragedies have occurred as a result of mistakes made by honest, right-thinking eyewitnesses. It should be explained that the vast majority of the wrongful convictions of innocent persons have arisen as a result of faulty eyewitness identification. These instructions should be given in addition to the standard direction regarding the difficulties inherent in eyewitness identification.

- Further, I would recommend that judges consider favourably and readily admit properly qualified expert evidence pertaining to eyewitness identification. This is certainly not junk science. Careful studies have been made with regard to memory and its effect upon eyewitness identification. Jurors would benefit from the studies and learning of experts in this field. Meticulous studies of human memory and eyewitness identification have been conducted. The empirical evidence has been compiled. The tragic consequences of mistaken eyewitness identification in cases have been chronicled and jurors and Trial Judges should have the benefit of expert evidence on this important subject. The expert witness can explain the process of memory and its frailties and dispel myths, such as that which assesses the accuracy of identification by the certainty of a witness. The testimony of an expert in this field would be helpful to the triers of fact and assist in providing a fair trial.

- The Trial Judge must instruct and caution the jury with regard to an identification which has apparently progressed from tentative to certain and to consider what may have brought about that change.

- During the instructions, the Trial Judge should advise the jury that mistaken eyewitness identification has been a significant factor in wrongful convictions of accused in the United States and in Canada, with a possible reference to the Thomas Sophonow case.

For more information on the Thomas Sophanow Inquiry you can go to the website for the inquiry at http://www.gov.mb.ca/justice/publications/sophonow/recommendations/english.html

For More Information and Study

Association in Defense of the Wrongfully Convicted (AIDWYC). For other wrongful case profiles you can go to the website for the Association in Defense of the Wrongfully Convicted (www.aidwyc.org). According to their website:

> "AIDWYC is a Canadian volunteer organization dedicated to preventing and rectifying wrongful convictions. AIDWYC has two broad objectives: first, eradicating the conditions that can cause miscarriages of justice; and second, participating in the review and, where warranted, correction of wrongful convictions. AIDWYC was founded in 1993. It is the direct successor to the *Justice for Guy Paul Morin Committee,* a grassroots organization that formed to support Guy Paul Morin immediately following his wrongful conviction in 1992. When Guy Paul Morin was released on bail in February 1993 pending his appeal, this Committee reconstituted itself as AIDWYC, with the goal of acting in defence of all persons who have been wrongly convicted."

"Ivan the Terrible": A Case Study. In September 1986, John Demjanjuk was charged in a Jerusalem court with crimes against humanity committed during World War II. Relying heavily on the eyewitness testimony of concentration camp survivors, the court concluded that Denjanjuk, a former Cleveland autoworker, was "Ivan the Terrible," a cruel and sadistic guard and gas chamber operator at Tremblinka where over 870,000 Jews were killed between 1942 and 1943. He was sentenced to death.

A detailed account of Denjanjuk's 18-month trial, including the eyewitness evidence, is provided in the book, *The Trial of Ivan the Terrible: The State of Israel vs. John Demjanjuk* authored by Tom Teicholoz (New York: St. Martin's Press, 1990). Consider reading this book with an eye to whether the procedures used to elicit the eyewitness testimony are consistent with the recently promulgated Sophonow report. More specifically, you might ask yourself:

- Were the photo spreads conducted to minimize the danger of a false identification?

- Were showups, either live or by use of a single photo, used? Were appropriate procedures used to reduce their suggestiveness?

You may want to check your analyses with those of Willem Wagenaar, a defense witness at Demjanjuk's trial, who testified as an expert about the problems of eyewitness identification. He has documented his testimony in the book, *Identifying Ivan: A Case Study in Legal Psychology* (Cambridge, Massachusetts: Harvard University Press, 1988).

You will find that Wagenaar was quite critical of the identification procedures used in the Demjanjuk case. He took care, however, not comment critically on the court's ultimate verdict recognizing that the "combination of all relevant facts which form a final judgment is a complex task that goes beyond" the insights of one expert witness.

If you find yourself critical of the identification procedures, you too may need to remind yourself that in reading these books, as detailed as they are, you do not have the benefit of actually hearing the witnesses testify and seeing other documentary evidence.

Question:

1. Compare the research findings on eyewitness testimony presented in your textbook to the recommendations made in the Sophonow report. Are there any recommendations that you would add based on psychological research to date?

On the Web

Is It a Hot Hand or an Illusory Correlation?

Many basketball players and fans believe that players shoot in streaks — that is, a player is more likely to make a shot if they just made a previous shot than if they missed the previous shot. And if you have ever played on a basketball team, you know that some coaches also subscribe to this belief and instruct teammates to get the ball to a player who has made a high percentage of his or her shots in the game. This hypothesis of the "hot hand" is widely accepted in sports, perhaps especially in basketball.

Do you think that athletes can get "hot" or go "cold" in their performance? Do basketball players sometimes have a "hot hand" such that they just can't miss in a particular game? Do baseball players go on streaks where they hit the ball well for an extended period of time? Do tennis players have streaks of good and bad performance in serving the ball?

To learn more on the "hot hand" theory, visit Dr. Alan Reifman's blog at http://thehothand.blogspot.com/. Here Dr. Reifman continually updates his blog with new studies and within the sidebar, lists various researchers and websites on the subject. See his "Tools for Conducting and Teaching About Hot Hand Analysis" for various calculators/tests, activities, tips, etc. where you can confirm (or disconfirm) your own favourite athlete's hot hand."

Question:

1. There is no doubt that streaks in sports performance sometimes occur. Now that you have learned more, do you think that they occur by chance or because some athletes really have a "hot hand" and an inherent ability to perform in streaks?

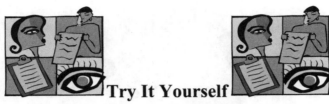

Try It Yourself
The Perseverance Effect:
Implications for the Ethical Treatment of Research Participants

Some social psychologists study how mood affects people's perception of themselves and others and how it affects their processing of social information. In a typical study, participants complete a test purporting to measure a valued skill or attribute (e.g., intelligence). To induce either a positive or negative mood, the experimenter gives the participants false feedback about their performance on the test, either telling them they did much better or much worse than average. Then the participants are asked to make some sort of social judgement. At the end of the experiment, the experimenter tells participants that the feedback they were given about their performance on the test was false and that it did not really reflect their performance.

Imagine that you are a member of your university's Research Ethics Board (REB). (See Workbook Chapter 2 for more information about REBs and the review process.) Below we set out some hypothetical experiments of this sort for you to consider in this role, and pose some related questions for you to answer.

Experiment A:

The research is studying the effect of mood on people's self-esteem. Participants take a practice MCAT, the test that all applicants to medical school must take. To induce positive or negative mood, the experimenter tells participants that they either performed very well or very poorly on the test. Then, participants rate themselves on a number of measures, including measures of self-esteem. At the end of the experimental session, the experimenter tells the participants that the feedback they received was not based on their actual performance on the test.

Questions:

1. Given what you learned in the text about the perseverance effect, what concerns would you have about this experiment?

2. What else should the experimenter tell participants after the experiment?

Experiment B:

Experiment B follows the same procedure as Experiment A, but is conducted in two sessions held one week apart. At the first session, participants take the practice MCAT, are given false feedback, and complete self-esteem measures. At the second session, participants complete the self-esteem measure again and then the experimenter debriefs them (e.g., tells them that the feedback was false).

Questions:

1. What additional concerns does this experiment raise?

2. Does debriefing participants at the second session adequately minimize their risk of receiving false feedback?

3. Would you be more or less concerned to learn that the study was conducted at a university renowned for its highly-competitive pre-medical program rather than at a university with more varied academic majors? At a community college rather at a university with varied academic majors? Would positive false feedback be more detrimental than negative false feedback under some circumstances?

Experiment C:

Experiment C follows the same procedure as Experiment A, but participants take a test that presumably measures social skills instead of taking the MCAT, and complete measures concerning their popularity and friendships instead of completing measures of self-esteem.

Question:

1. Is this experiment of more or less concern than Experiment A? Why?

Experiment D:

Experiment D is the same as Experiment C, but it takes place in two sessions held one-month apart. Participants are given false feedback during the first session and are debriefed during the second.

Question:

1. What additional concerns does this experiment raise? Does the debriefing procedure adequately address these concerns?

Social Psychology Alive Journal
Have You and Your Friends Experienced
These Social Cognition Phenomena?

For about a week, keep your eyes and ears open for examples in your personal life of the social cognition phenomena listed in the following chart and record your observations. Here's an example of downward and upward counterfactual thoughts to get you started.

Downward and Upward Counterfactual Thoughts. Last week, I studied for an advanced biology test with a classmate. We both wanted to receive an A but we both received a B. My classmate was disappointed because he nearly scored high enough for an A and kept saying "If only I had studied more, I would have made the A" (upward counterfactual thinking). I, on the other hand, was happy because, to be honest, I'm not very good in biology. I kept thinking to myself "It could have been worse—I could have made a C" (downward counterfactual thinking).

Phenomena	Your Observation
availability heuristic	
representiveness heuristic	
illusory correlation	
hindsight bias	
downward counterfactual thoughts	
upward counterfactual thoughts	
self-serving trait definitions	
self-serving perceptions of others	
self-serving activation of stereotypes	
mood influenced perceptions of stereotypes	

Learning Objectives

How Does the Mind Work?

1. What are schemas and how do they help us to make sense of the world around us? How do they affect the information that we notice and the interpretation we give to it? (pp. 67–70)

    increased likelihood of schema easily activated.

2. Explain how priming and chronic accessibility can affect the activation of a schema, and give an example of each. What are the basic findings on priming by Carver et al. (1983) and on chronic accessibility by Higgins et al. (1982)? (pp. 70–72)

3. Explain with reference to Forgas and Bond (1985) one way the chronic accessibility of schemas may differ between cultures. (pp. 72–73)

    cultural schemas — Western individuality vs. Eastern community

4. What is a stereotype and how do stereotypes affect our judgments of our ingroups and outgroups? What is the outgroup homogeneity effect? (pp. 73–74)

    Sim. of groups we're not in.

5. Explain how stereotypes lead to selective processing of information, by guiding our attention to particular information and biasing our interpretation of ambiguous behaviour. (pp. 74–75)

6. Describe the differences between automatic and controlled mental processes, and how they affect our use of stereotypes. (pp. 75–76)

Reconstructive Memory

7. Explain how reconstructive memory cues can be used to retrieve and reconstruct autobiographical memories. Generally describe the findings and implications of the Ross and Wilson studies. (p. 76–80)

    - student ratings of themselves more positive than fact.

8. With reference to Lindsay and his colleagues (2004), explain how false memories might be reconstructed. What are the implications for the accuracy of eyewitness reports? (pp.79–80)

9. What is the relationship between confidence in a memory and the accuracy of that memory? What has proved under some circumstances to be a better indicator of accuracy than confidence? (pp. 82–83)

    speed of identification

10. What might the legal system do to reduce eyewitness error and jurors' over-reliance on eyewitness testimony? (pp. 83–84)

    blank or sequential lineup

Heuristics and Biases in Everyday Judgments

11. Describe the role of heuristics in the cognitive miser model of information processing. (p. 85)

12. What is the availability heuristic? Relying on the Tversky and Kahneman (1973) study and the Schwarz et al. (1991) study, explain how the availability heuristic is influenced by the total number of examples a person can recall and also by the ease with which a person can recall the examples. (pp. 85–87) *How easily relevant examples come to mind*

13. What is the representativeness heuristic? With reference to the Kahneman and Tversky (1983) study, explain how it might lead to errors in judgment. (pp. 87–88) *Group target with category (based on looks).*

14. What is an illusory correlation and how does it help explain the "hot hand" phenomena? What is an alternative explanation for the phenomena? (pp. 88–90) *notice streaks* *Two variables are related belief streaks occur when events are independent.*

15. What is the planning fallacy? Explain a possible cause of the planning fallacy according to research conducted by Buehler and his colleagues at the University of Waterloo (1994) (pp. 91–93)

What Might Have Been: Counterfactual Thinking

16. Explain the difference between upward and downward counterfactual thinking. Explain the emotional consequences of each type of thought. (pp. 94–97)

Hot Cognition: Adding Motives and Mood to the Cognitive Mix

17. Describe how the motive to see the self positively can lead to self-serving judgments, that is: self-serving trait definitions, self-serving perceptions of others, and self-serving activation of stereotypes. (pp. 97–100)

18. How does mood influence people's perceptions of stereotypes, their recall of positive or negative information, and their manner of processing information? (pp. 100–103)

Test Your Knowledge

Multiple Choice Questions

1. Dogs are furry, walk on four legs, and have a tendency to bark at doorbells. This statement is an example of a
   A. memory.
   B. controlled process.
   C. schema.
   D. category.

2. The theory of spreading activation would predict that, when asked to recall the most recent book you've read, the order in which schemas would be activated likely be
   A. books in general; the most recent book you read; specific types of books (novels/mysteries, non-fiction).
   B. specific types of books (novels/mysteries, non-fiction); books in general; the most recent book you read.
   C. books in general; specific types of books (novels/mysteries, non-fiction); the most recent book you read.
   D. the most recent book you read; books in general; specific types of books (novels/mysteries, non-fiction).

3. Early one evening, Kevin watched a movie full of violent language and acts. Later that evening, he and his friend, Tony, witnessed a young man jostling another man on the street. Kevin thought the young man was assaulting the other man, but Tony thought he was just kidding around with him. This is an example of
   A. perseverance effect.
   B. illusory correlations.
   C. self-serving judgments.
   D. priming.

4. Chronically accessible traits
   A. influence what you remember about and how you describe people.
   B. are stable over a person's lifetime.
   C. differ between Eastern and Western cultures.
   D. both A and C.

5. A prospective student asks you to compare the students who attend your university to the students who attend your biggest rival, City College. According to the outgroup homogeneity effect, how would you answer?
   A. All of the students at our university are very similar, as are all of the students at City College.
   B. The students at our school are quite diverse, but the students at City College are all the same.
   C. The students at our school are all very similar, but the students at City College are quite diverse.
   D. The students at both our university and City College are very diverse.

6. Autobiographical memories
    A. are susceptible to suggestion.
    B. are immune to alteration.
    C. describe how we view acquaintances.
    D. are infallible.

7. People generally rate their current selves more favourably than their past selves. What is the most plausible explanation for this effect?
    A. Most people actually do improve in key ways over time.
    B. Most of us believe that people generally improve over time on most characteristics.
    C. Most of us desire to see the current self positively.
    D. Most of us see our past self in a negative light.

8. Why is empirical research on recovered memories problematic?
    A. There is no agreed upon criteria for distinguishing true memories from false ones.
    B. Physical evidence to support the recovered memory rarely exists.
    C. Ethical standards prevent empirical study of recovered memories.
    D. All of the above.

9. Which eyewitness is most likely to be accurate?
    A. one who is highly confident
    B. one who picked the perpetrator quickly
    C. one who picked the perpetrator from a simultaneous lineup rather than a sequential lineup
    D. all of the above – eyewitnesses are all accurate

10. If you are a cognitive miser, you
    A. dislike thinking about making charitable donations.
    B. use heuristics to make judgments the majority of the time.
    C. always engage in deliberate information processing.
    D. consciously activate related schemas in memory.

11. Many people believe that traveling by airplane is more dangerous than travelling by car, when in fact the reverse is true: fatal car accidents far outnumber plane crashes. This is an example of
    A. hindsight bias.
    B. the representativeness heuristic.
    C. the availability heuristic.
    D. an illusory correlation.

12. A person who bases a judgment on the following rationale, "it looks like a dog, it must be a dog," is demonstrating
    A. hindsight bias.
    B. the representativeness heuristic.
    C. the availability heuristic.
    D. illusory correlation.

13. A youth hockey team in Florida eagerly awaited the arrival of a Canadian boy to serve as their goalie. The team was certain that he was an excellent player when he was in fact average. The team judgment reflects
   A. hindsight bias.
   B. the representativeness heuristic.
   C. the availability heuristic.
   D. illusory correlation.

14. A soccer player scores a goal after eating sushi for breakfast. For the rest of the season, she goes out of her way to have sushi for breakfast before each game. This is an example of
   A. hindsight bias.
   B. the representativeness heuristic.
   C. the availability heuristic.
   D. illusory correlation.

15. Which of the following statements is NOT true of the perseverance effect?
   A. It occurs when a person continues to make self-evaluations consistent with discredited information.
   B. The effect of false negative feedback can be reduced by asking people to think of positive feedback.
   C. It presents an ethical issue in conducting certain types of psychology experiments.
   D. None of the above; all of the above statements are true.

16. In one study, Olympic bronze medalists were judged to be happier than Olympic silver medalists. One possible explanation for this finding is that the bronze medalists are engaging in
   A. downward counterfactual thinking.
   B. upward counterfactual thinking.
   C. self-serving judgments.
   D. hindsight bias.

17. What are the effects of upward counterfactual thinking after a negative event?
   A. It helps people avoid similar negative outcomes in the future.
   B. It causes negative emotions, such as dissatisfaction or unhappiness.
   C. It makes people feel better.
   D. Both A and B.

18. Which of the following is generally considered to be a characteristic of "cold" cognition?
   A. emotion
   B. moods
   C. motives
   D. categorization

19. According to the research of Esses and Zanna (1994), how does mood influence stereotypes about minority groups?
   A. Positive moods lead to more positive stereotypes.
   B. Negative moods lead to more positive stereotypes.
   C. Negative moods lead to more negative stereotypes.
   D. Mood has no effect on stereotypes.

20. Being in a good mood can
    A. increase your tendency to use detailed information to make decisions.
    B. decrease your tendency to use detailed information to make decisions.
    C. reduce the accessibility of positive information in memory.
    D. none of the above.

Sentence Completion

1. _____ are mental representations of objects or categories of objects.

2. Activation of a schema _____ the likelihood that the schema will be activated again in the future.

3. A group to which a perceiver belongs is one of his or her _____, whereas a group to which a perceiver does not belong is one of his or her _____.

4. John Darley and Paget Gross (1983) demonstrated that stereotypes can change how people interpret _____ behaviour.

5. Recognizing and identifying a common object is an example of _____ processing whereas thinking carefully about why someone behaved in a certain way is an example of _____ processing.

6. With a _____ lineup, the eyewitness sees each person in the lineup separately; this type of lineup generally leads to _____ eyewitness identification errors compared to simultaneous lineups.

7. MacLoad and Campbell (1992) asked research participants to generate an example of certain types of events in their own lives. Participants who could generate an example quickly were _____ likely to predict they would experience the event again. This demonstrates the _____ heuristic.

8. When someone starts a conversation with the phrase, "I should have known that that would happen," he or she is probably engaging in _____ bias.

9. When people believe that they will interact with or be dependent on another individual, they tend to view that individual more positively; these perceptions are _____.

Matching I – Key Terms

_C_ 1. **categorization**	A. the degree to which schemas are easily activated for an individual across time and situations
_E_ 2. **social cognition**	B. the process by which the activation of a schema increases the likelihood that the schema will be activated again in the future
_D_ 3. **schemas**	C. the process of recognizing and identifying something
_F_ 4. **accessibility**	D. mental representations of objects or categories, which contain the central features of the object or category as well as assumptions about how the object or category works
_B_ 5. **priming**	E. the study of how information about people is processed and stored
_A_ 6. **chronic accessibility**	F. the ease with which a schema comes to awareness

Matching II – Key Terms

F	7.	**stereotype**
I	8.	**outgroup homogeneity effect**
B	9.	**automatic process**
J	10.	**controlled process**
C	11.	**reconstructive memory**
A	12.	**autobiographical memory**
H	13.	**blank lineup**
D	14.	**sequential lineup**
G	15.	**heuristic**
E	16.	**cognitive miser model**

A. stored information about the self, such as goals, personality traits, past experience, and other qualities

B. a judgment or thought that we cannot control, which occurs without intention, very efficiently, and sometimes beneath our awareness

C. the process of trying to rebuild the past based on cues and estimates

D. the procedure of showing an eyewitness each individual in the group separately rather than together in a simultaneous line

E. a view of information processing that assumes people usually rely on heuristics to make judgments and will only engage in careful, thoughtful processing when necessary

F. a set of characteristics that a perceiver associates with members of a group

G. an informal rule or shortcut that is used to make everyday judgments

H. a group of individuals that does not include the suspect; everyone in the lineup is known to be innocent

I. the tendency for people to overestimate the similarity within groups to which they do not belong

J. a judgment or thought that we command that is intentional, requires significant cognitive resources, and occurs within our awareness

Matching III – Key Terms

_H_ 17.	availability heuristic	A. the tendency for people to overestimate the predictability of known outcomes
_J_ 18.	representativeness heuristic	B. reflections on how past events might have turned out worse
_C_ 19.	illusory correlation	C. the belief that two variables are related to one another when, in fact, they are not
_A_ 20.	hindsight bias	D. reflections on how past events might have turned out differently
_I_ 21.	perseverance effect	E. the idea that positive feelings will activate positive memories and negative feelings will activate negative memories
_D_ 22.	counterfactual thoughts	F. reflections on how past events might have turned out better
_B_ 23.	upward counterfactual thoughts	G. perceptions or comparisons that enhance the perceived worth of the self
_F_ 24.	downward counterfactual thoughts	H. the tendency to base a judgment on how easily relevant examples can be generated
_G_ 25.	self-serving judgments	I. the tendency for people to make self-evaluations that are consistent with information that has been discredited
_E_ 26.	mood-congruent recall	J. the tendency to judge the likelihood that a target belongs to a category based on how similar the target is to the typical features of the category

Answers to Test Your Knowledge

Multiple Choice Questions

1. C	6. A	11. C	16. A
2. C	7. C	12. B	17. D
3. B	8. D	13. B	18. D
4. D	9. B	14. D	19. C
5. B	10. B	15. D	20. B

Sentence Completion

1. schemas
2. increases
3. ingroups, outgroups
4. ambiguous
5. automatic, controlled

6. sequential, fewer
7. more, availability
8. hindsight
9. self-serving

Matching I – Key Terms

1. C
2. E
3. D
4. F
5. B

6. A

Matching II – Key Terms

7. F
8. I
9. B
10. J
11. C

12. A
13. H
14. D
15. G
16. E

Matching III – Key Terms

17. H
18. J
19. C
20. A
21. I

22. D
23. F
24. B
25. G
26. E

Chapter 4
Social Perception: Perceiving the Self and Others

Social Psychology Alive Journal
The Intuitive Scientist

Either consciously or unconsciously, we all make many judgments every day about why people behave in particular ways and why certain events occur. We make many such judgments almost in passing (e.g., assessing why a friend skipped his or her Friday morning classes, why he or she choose a certain food, why he or she choose to attend a certain movie, or why he or she received an extremely low grade) while other judgments are more deliberative (e.g., interpreting the comments of a teacher, especially about your ability or performance).

Record some of the judgments that you make in the course of a week below. Describe the behaviour or event and your judgment about its cause, and explain the reasoning you used to ascertain the cause.

Behaviour or event	Cause	How did you ascertain the cause?
1.		
2.		
3.		
4.		
5.		
6.		
7.		
8.		
9.		
10.		

Harold Kelly suggested that we sometimes make causal judgments in much the same way as scientists. According to his covariation model of attribution, when we have multiple observations of an event across several individuals and across several settings, we try to determine whether the event is associated with a person, a situation, or some combination of the two. That is, we systematically test its cause. For example, we might attribute a friend's negative evaluation of a professor to the professor's teaching ability or personality, if many other people in the professor's class also negatively evaluate the professor. On the other hand, we might attribute the friend's negative evaluation of the professor to something about the friend's own personality if he always complains about his professors.

Questions:

1. Did reasoning similar to the covariation model of attribution underlie any of the judgments you recorded above?

2. Did any of your judgments demonstrate the false consensus effect? The discounting principle? The augmentation principle? Correspondence bias or the fundamental attribution error?

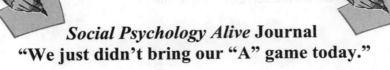

Social Psychology Alive Journal
"We just didn't bring our "A" game today."

Attributions are everywhere, and perhaps no more visible than in the world of sports. Every day, the sports section of the newspaper is filled with the attributions of athletes, praising the work of their teammates after wins, and blaming the calls of officials after disappointing losses. Now that you've learned about attributions and the correspondence bias, are you more aware of these attributions in daily life?

For the next few days, read the sports section of your daily local and/or school newspaper, paying particular attention to the quotes given by athletes and coaches in post-game interviews. Use the table below to record any attributions about the game's outcome that you see. If possible, try to identify attributions made by opposing teams for the outcome of the same game.

Statement	Was player on the winning or losing team?
1.	
2.	
3.	
4.	
5.	
6.	
7.	
8.	

Try to apply the correspondence bias to statements made after both wins and losses. According to the correspondence bias, you might expect that after a loss, a player or team might make more situational attributions (i.e., "We were unused to the high altitude", or "The umpire wasn't giving me the strike zone that I am used to") than dispositional attributions (i.e., "We just couldn't get the puck past the goalie today"). Similarly, you might expect more dispositional attributions after a victory ("We played really well as a team, and everyone contributed") than situational attributions (i.e., "The weather really helped the ball travel out of the ballpark").

Questions:

1. Which of the statements reflect the correspondence bias?

2. Do opposing teams make differing attributions about the same outcome? Do their attributions match with the correspondence bias?

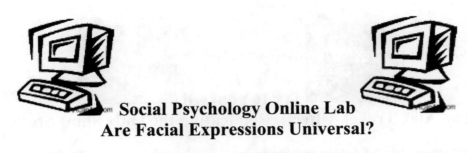

Social Psychology Online Lab
Are Facial Expressions Universal?

As described in the text, Charles Darwin proposed that facial expressions in humans are biologically-based and universal. He believed that facial expressions evolved from more primitive behaviours (e.g., the expression for disgust is a simplified derivative of vomiting or spitting) and all humans expressed their emotions similarly. Paul Ekman and a large number of collaborators (Ekman et al., 1987) tested this hypothesis, in part, with a cross-cultural study involving 10 countries. University-aged participants were shown 18 facial photographs of Caucasian men and women expressing one of six emotions. For each photograph, participants were asked to select which emotion was being expressed. Although there were some variations across cultures, all of the emotions were correctly identified by the majority of participants from each culture.

You can test this hypothesis yourself using the Social Psychology Online Lab, Facial Expressions. In the lab, you will be shown a series of 56 photographs of human faces; each face will be expressing an emotion. The models displaying the emotions will come from diverse ethnic/racial backgrounds (e.g., Asian, Caucasian, African), and you will be asked to indicate your own ethnic background. You will be asked to choose the correct emotion for each face from a list of six emotions (anger, disgust, happiness, sadness, contempt, and fear). The prediction is that most faces will be similarly identified by most students, irrespective of the models' and students' ethnic backgrounds. After you complete the lab, answer the following questions.

Questions:

1. Are positive emotions more recognizable than negative emotions?

2. Are female faces easier to judge than male faces? Are faces of your own ethnic/racial background easier to judge? Do you think men or woman are better at judging facial expressions of emotion?

3. Would there be as much agreement in labelling the emotions if people had to generate a label rather than select it from a list?

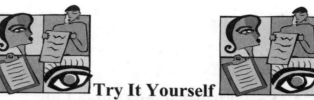

Try It Yourself
The Alex Trebek Effect: Replicating the Quiz Show Study

The "quiz show" study (Ross, Amabile, and Steinmetz, 1977) has always been one of the authors' favourites, and is an easy one to replicate on your own. This classic study demonstrated the correspondence bias—the tendency for people to attribute someone else's poor performance to internal characteristics (i.e., "he must not be very smart") rather than external characteristics (i.e., "he was assigned the role of the contestant"). The correspondence bias may also account for why thousands of people think Alex Trebek, host of television's "Jeopardy!" is extremely smart. He does, after all, know the answer to every question that is asked!

You can see the Alex Trebek effect by replicating the quiz show study with some of your friends. Recruit three friends, and randomly assign them to the role of questioner, contestant, or observer. Tell the questioner to think up 10 challenging, but not impossible, trivia questions and to ask the contestant to answer those questions. Keep track of the answers, so you will know how many the contestant got right. The person assigned the role of observer will simply watch the question and answer session.

After all 10 questions have been answered, ask all three participants (questioner, contestant, and observer) to rate the intelligence of the questioner and the contestant on a scale of 1 to 10, with 1 meaning "very unintelligent", 5 meaning "of average intelligence", and 10 meaning "very intelligent." You can use the form on the next page to do this.

Be sure to explain the correspondence bias to your friends at the end of the study, and tell them that this study in no way means that the contestant friend is less intelligent than the questioner friend (otherwise, you may have problems recruiting that friend again for more studies!). You can tell them how important situational factors (such as being assigned the role of questioner) are in evaluations of behaviour, and that generating trivia questions to which you alone know the answer is almost a guarantee of being seen as more knowledgeable in this situation. It may reassure your friends to know that the original questioner would have appeared less intelligent if he or she had been assigned the role of contestant.

Questions:

1. In the original experiment, both the contestant and the observer rated the contestant as less knowledgeable than the questioner. Did you see the same results?

2. Did the questioner rate himself as more intelligent, or did he recognize the power given him by the role of questioner?

Scales for the Quiz Show Study

On a scale from 1 to 10, how intelligent is the contestant?

1	2	3	4	5	6	7	8	9	10
Very unintelligent				Of average intelligence					Very intelligent

On a scale from 1 to 10, how intelligent is the questioner?

1	2	3	4	5	6	7	8	9	10
Very unintelligent				Of average intelligence					Very intelligent

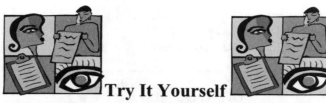

Try It Yourself
Encouraging Children to Read: Is Money the Answer?

> Reading has always been my home, my sustenance, my great invincible companion. 'Book love,' Trollope called it. 'It will make your hours pleasant as long as you live.' . . . I did not read from a sense of superiority, or advancement, or even learning. I read because I loved it more than any other activity on earth.
> from Anna Quindlen, *How Reading Changed My Life* (1998), p. 8.

In this era of Internet technology, innovative strategies are being used to market and sell books. In one such innovative twist on the traditional novel, a man by the name of Michael Stadther has written and published several children's books that offer children all over the world the chance of solving clues to find real (and very valuable) hidden treasure.

Websites accompany the novels: http://www.atreasurestrove.com/Public/Home/index.cfm and http://www.alchemistdar.com/Public/Home/index.cfm offering children, their parents, educators, and anybody that chooses to visit, extensive information on the progress of the treasure hunt, activites, and an online shop to buy related paraphernalia.

Visit these websites and think about the information presented in terms of what you have learned in the chapter about intrinsic motivation, the over-justification effect, self-efficacy, the illusion of control, and the false hope syndrome.

Questions:

1. Promotional material for the book (found at: http://www.atreasurestrove.com/documentFiles/4.pdf) includes the following statement:

   > "Asking most kids to pick up a book during July or August is like asking them to clean their room or eat their Brussels sprouts. Fortunately, there's a simple solution to the quandary of summer reading lists: stock them with titles that are fun, challenging, and encourage kids to look beyond a book's covers."

   In addition, a link on the the CBC radio's website, http://www.cbc.ca/ontariotoday/rings.html, leads you to information about the "treasures" and states that:

   > "Getting your kids to read might not be a struggle if they are tempted by a story with a treasure hunt leading to $2 million dollars in diamonds."

   Based on your knowledge of the social psychological principles presented in chapter four, discuss some potential flaws with the reasoning in the statements above.

2. Based on your knowledge of the social psychological factors involved in motivating and explaining our own behaviour, what advice would you give someone wishing to design a program to encourage children to read?

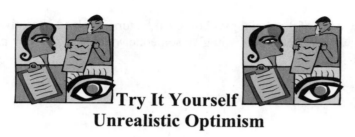

Try It Yourself
Unrealistic Optimism

In the chapter, you read about how people are more optimistic about their own futures than about the futures of other people like them. How pervasive is this effect? Using the chart below, ask your friends to estimate the likelihood that certain events will happen to them and to other students.

Instructions

What do you think is the likelihood that each of the following events will happen to you, and what is the likelihood that they will happen to other students at your university? Choose a percentage between 0% and 100% to show the probability that the events will happen to you or to other students, where 0% represents no chance at all, 50% represents an equal chance that it will happen or it won't happen, and 100% represents a sure thing.

	SELF	OTHERS
1. Having a heart attack		
2. Being happy with your romantic or marital partner in later life		
3. Being physically healthy in middle age		
4. Being refused a bank loan		
5. Having a mentally gifted child or niece or nephew		
6. Being killed in a car accident		
7. Becoming alcoholic		
8. Developing arthritis		
9. Having your work recognized with an award		
10. Being actively involved in a charitable organization		

Question:

1. According to the theory of unrealistic optimism, percentages for "self" should be higher than "others" for positive things (i.e., being happy with your romantic partner), but lower than "others" for negative things (i.e., having a heart attack). Compare the percentages for "self" and "others." Do you see evidence of unrealistic optimism?

Social Psychology Alive Journal
School Spirit

Basking in reflected glory is a term that refers to feelings of pride when someone close to you does well. Bragging to your roommates about your brother's promotion as a foreign diplomat is one example of basking in reflected glory. Making sure everyone knows you go to the university with the debate team that won a national honour is another example. You can also see the phenomenon on a larger scale with school loyalty, by taking the following steps. Share your results with your classmates and see if others found similar results.

1. Look around your classes today – how many students are wearing clothing declaring the name of your college or university?

2. Then, the next time an athletic team from your college or university celebrates a big win, again count the number of students you see wearing "school spirit" clothing – T-shirts, sweatshirts, baseball caps. Did the number increase? Is the school basking in the reflected glory of the athletic team?

3. What other situations can you think of in which this process might be at work?

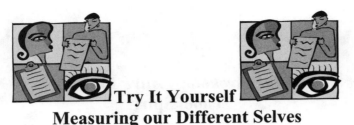

Try It Yourself
Measuring our Different Selves

The actual, ideal and ought selves represent the various ways we view ourselves. The *actual self* is how we believe we really are, the *ideal self* is how we would like to be, and the *ought self* is how we think we should be. Any discrepancies between these different conceptions of ourselves has implications for our emotions and self-esteem. For example, you may be unhappy if you see yourself as shy and introverted but would ideally like to be outgoing and extroverted. You may feel agitated if you see yourself as untrustworthy but believe that you ought to be trustworthy.

You can measure your different selves with the following exercise. First, list 10 attributes that you actually possess (i.e., procrastinating, shy, selfish); this is a representation of your actual self. Then list 10 attributes that you would like to possess (i.e., extraverted, punctual) – a representation of your ideal self. Finally, list 10 attributes that you think you should possess (i.e., generous, moral). This is a representation of your ought self, or your conscience.

Actual Attributes	Ideal Attributes	Ought to Possess Attributes
1.	1.	1.
2.	2.	2.
3.	3.	3.
4.	4.	4.
5.	5.	5.
6.	6.	6.
7.	7.	7.
8.	8.	8.
9.	9.	9.
10.	10.	10.

Questions:

Now examine your lists of attributes and answer the following questions.

1. Do you see the same attributes in all three lists? Are there any discrepancies?

2. Are the discrepancies predominantly between the actual and ideal selves, or between the actual and the ought selves? How do those discrepancies make you feel?

3. Do you agree with E. Tory Higgins' theory that we feel sad and dejected when the actual and ideal selves do not match, but feel agitated and anxious when the actual and the ought selves do not match?

Learning Objectives

What We See in Others: Social Perception

1. Explain Harold Kelley's covariation model of attribution, using a concrete example of an attribution you have made yourself. (pp. 110–111)

2. What is the false consensus effect and why does it occur? (pp. 111–113)

3. Explain the discounting and augmentation principles, and provide a concrete example of each. (pp. 113–114)

4. What were the basic findings of the Ross, Amabile, and Steinmetz (1977) "quiz show" experiment, and what attribution error do they demonstrate? What are three possible reasons this type of error is so common? (pp. 114–117)

5. Explain the importance of nonverbal cues in interpreting the meaning of a message when such cues conflict with the substance of what has been said. Do children use nonverbal cues in the same way as adults? Why are nonverbal cues so useful in judging the emotion of a speaker? (pp. 119–120)

6. Describe the evidence accumulated by Paul Ekman and others for the universality of facial expressions and the recognition of emotion. (pp. 120–121)

7. Explain how nonverbal behaviour varies by gender and by culture. (pp. 121–122)

What We See in Ourselves: Self-Perception

8. What types of social comparisons are stimulated by the desire to accurately assess one's abilities? By the desire to improve? By the desire to feel better? Describe the diverse consequences of upward social comparisons. How does the use of social comparison vary between cultures? (pp. 123–127)

9. What is the basic thesis of Daryl Bem's self-perception theory? What modification to this thesis is supported by the 1981 study by Shelly Chaiken and Mark Baldwin? (pp. 128–130)

10. Explain the over-justification effect, describing the results of the 1983 study by Mark Lepper, David Greene, and Richard Nisbett that demonstrates it. (pp. 130–132)

11. Describe the phenomena of unrealistic self-evaluation and unrealistic optimism and be familiar with the studies that demonstrate them. Are these self-serving biases adaptive or maladaptive? Generally, how do these phenomena vary across cultures? (pp. 132–138)

12. Describe the phenomena of self-efficacy, illusion of control, learned helplessness, and the false hope syndrome. (pp. 138–140)

13. What is meant by the actual, ideal, and ought conceptions of the self? According to self-discrepancy theory, what are the consequences of perceived discrepancies between the actual self and either the ideal or ought self? (pp. 140–143)

What Others See in Us

14. According to Ned Jones and Thane Pittman (1982), what are the two most common goals of impression management? (p. 144)

15. What is meant by self-handicapping and why do people engage in it? What are its benefits and downsides? (pp. 145–148)

16. What is the actor-observer difference in attribution and why does it occur? (pp. 148–149)

Test Your Knowledge

Multiple Choice Questions

1. The theory that people are intuitive scientists refers to the idea that
    A. People make casual attributions in a scientific way.
    B. People want to be scientific in their approach to others.
    C. Scientists can predict the future using astrology.
    D. People can explain the past based on their judgments of other people.

2. A volunteer for a local politician's campaign is confident that his candidate will win, estimating the candidate will receive 75% of the vote. On election day, the candidate loses, much to the dismay of the volunteer. The volunteer was a victim of
    A. illusory correlation.
    B. hindsight bias.
    C. false consensus.
    D. fundamental attribution error.

3. The discounting principle states that the perceived role of an internal cause will be _____ because an external cause is present.
    A. decreased
    B. increased
    C. eliminated
    D. unaffected

4. Your friend excitedly announces "I aced my physiology test. I knew I had what it takes to get into medical school." You know almost everyone in the class scored very well and think to yourself, "it's not his smarts, it's the test." This demonstrates
    A. augmentation principle.
    B. discounting principle.
    C. false hope syndrome.
    D. illusory correlation.

5. The researcher given credit for initially identifying the correspondence bias is
    A. Harold Kelley.
    B. Ziva Kunda.
    C. William James.
    D. Edward Jones.

6. According to the correspondence bias, which of the following best describes how we make judgments about other people?
   A. We tend to accurately assess the role of the person but overestimate the role of the situation.
   B. We tend to overestimate the role of the situation and underestimate the role of the personality.
   C. We tend to overestimate the role of personality and underestimate the role of the situation.
   D. We tend to disregard both the role of the situation and the role of the personality.

7. Which are the following statements best describes the use of nonverbal cues to judge emotion by children and adults when the nonverbal cues are inconsistent with verbal content?
   A. Young children (4-5 years) as well as older children (9-10) rely almost exclusively on nonverbal cues, whereas adults almost always rely on the verbal content.
   B. Young children rely almost exclusively on nonverbal cues whereas older children and adults rely on the verbal content.
   C. Young children rely almost exclusively on verbal content whereas adults rely almost exclusively on nonverbal cues.
   D. Young children, older children, and adults rely almost exclusively on the nonverbal cues.

8. According to Elfenbein and Ambady's (2003) research on facial expressions, all of the following emotions can be accurately recognized across various cultures **except**
   A. disgust.
   B. weariness.
   C. surprise.
   D. contempt.

9. Although some nonverbal behaviours appear to be almost universal, interpretations of other nonverbal behaviours can vary depending on all of the following **except**
   A. gender.
   B. culture.
   C. age.
   D. intelligence.

10. As part of a New Year's resolution, you decide to eat more vegetables. To get ideas on how to fulfill your resolution, you try to model your behaviour after that of your vegetarian roommate. This is an example of
    A. upward social comparison.
    B. downward social comparison.
    C. looking glass self.
    D. overjustification.

11. Suppose you and a close friend both very much wanted to gain admittance to law school upon graduation. According to the self-evaluation maintenance model, how would you feel if your friend was admitted but you were not?
    A. You would feel like a failure and be jealous of your friend's success.
    B. You would be happy about your friend's success and be proud of your friendship.
    C. You would feel like a failure but be proud of your friendship.
    D. You would feel both happy and jealous about your friend's success.

12. According to Bem's theory of self-perception, which statement best explains the effect of attitude strength and external causes on judgments of one's own internal state?
    A. People with weak attitudes and no clear external cause will rely on past behaviour to judge internal state.
    B. People with weak attitudes and a clear external cause will rely on past behaviour to judge internal state.
    C. People with strong attitudes and no clear external cause will rely on past behaviour to judge internal state.
    D. People with strong attitudes and a clear external cause will rely on past behaviour to judge internal state.

13. What is the best way to encourage a love of reading in a child?
    A. require the child to read for 1 hour before he can play a video game.
    B. praise the child for his effort.
    C. praise the child for his intelligence.
    D. reward the child for reading a book he would have read anyway.

14. CEOs for large companies were asked to rate their ability as below average, average, or above average compared to their peers. How do you think they rated themselves?
    A. Nearly all of them rated themselves as average.
    B. Nearly all of them rated themselves as either below or above average; no one rated themselves as average.
    C. Nearly all of them rated themselves as below average.
    D. Nearly all of them rated themselves as above average.

15. Self-enhancement is maladaptive in which of the following situations?
    A. coping with serious illness
    B. maintaining a dating relationship
    C. making a first impression
    D. being successful in achievement situations

16. Which of the following best describes the cross-cultural research on unrealistic self-evaluation?
    A. Members of collectivist societies tend to engage in more unrealistic self-evaluation than members of individualist societies.
    B. Members of individualist societies tend to engage in more unrealistic self-evaluation than members of collectivist societies.
    C. Members of collectivist societies never engage in unrealistic self-evaluation, whereas members of individualist societies always do.
    D. There are no differences in the extent to which members of individualist societies and members of collectivist societies engage in unrealistic self-evaluation.

17. According to E. Tory Higgins' self-discrepancy theory, a discrepancy between the *actual* self and the *ideal* self will produce feelings of
    A. helplessness.
    B. surprise.
    C. anxiety.
    D. depression.

18. According to E. Tory Higgins' self-discrepancy theory, a discrepancy between the *actual* self and the *ought* self will produce feelings of .
   A. helplessness.
   B. surprise.
   C. anxiety.
   D. depression.

19. Jack's parents want him to go to law school, but Jack is nervous about how well he'll perform on the required entrance examination, the LSAT. The night before the exam, Jack goes out partying with his rugby teammates instead of reviewing for the test. At the LSAT the following morning, he is fighting a vicious hangover. Jack's behaviour is an example of
   A. self-perception.
   B. self-aggrandizement.
   C. fundamental attribution error.
   D. self-handicapping.

Sentence Completion

1. If a student performs very well on a test that yielded a class average of 45%, observers will typically conclude the student is very smart. This is an example of the _____ _____.

2. In studies of gender differences, researchers have found that _____ are better judges of people's emotions than are _____.

3. In studies of gender differences, researchers have found that _____'s facial expressions of emotion are easier to identify than are _____'s facial expressions.

4. I conclude that I am an active community volunteer because I volunteer about 15 hours a week whereas most people I know do not volunteer at all. This inference is based on _____ _____.

5. If you want to assess yourself accurately, you should compare yourself to people who are _____ on dimensions relevant to the performance.

6. Rather than making social comparisons, older people tend to make more _____ comparisons.

7. According to the phenomenon of self-enhancement, people usually estimate that they are _____ likely that the average person to experience positive events and _____ likely to experience negative events.

8. In _____ cultures, people are seen as independent beings who possess stable abilities, traits, and attitudes whereas in _____ cultures, people are seen as interdependent beings who should contribute to harmonious group functioning.

9. Making and breaking the same New Year's resolution every year is an example of the _____ _____ _____.

10. The _____ self is a conception of the self describing our perception of how we really are, the _____ is a conception of the self describing our perception of how we would ideally like to be,

and the _____ is a conception of the self describing our perception of how we think we should or ought to be.

Matching I – Key Terms

D	1.	attributions
J	2.	intuitive scientists
A	3.	covariation model of attribution
H	4.	false consensus effect
C	5.	discounting principle
G	6.	augmentation principle
F	7.	correspondence bias
B	8.	nonverbal behaviour
I	9.	display rules
E	10.	looking glass self

A. an attribution theory proposing that we make causal judgments by determining whether a particular behaviour correlated with a person, a situation, or some combination of persons and situations

B. actions and cues that communicate meaning in ways other than by words

C. a rule of attribution stating that the perceived role of a cause will be discounted (reduced) if other plausible causes are also present

D. causal judgments about why an event or behaviour occurred

E. the tendency to internalize other people's judgments about us into our self-concept

F. the tendency to assume that people's actions and words reflect their personality, their attitudes, or some other internal factor, rather than external or situational factors

G. a rule of attribution stating that the perceived role of a cause will be augmented (increased) if other factors are present that would work against the behaviour

H. the tendency to assume that other people share our own attitudes and behaviours to a greater extent than is actually the case

I. norms in a culture for how and when emotions should be expressed

J. untrained scientists who try to make causal judgments in a rational, scientific manner

Matching II – Key Terms

_____ 11.	social comparison	A.	a theory proposing that we often judge our own internal states by reviewing our past behaviour and inferring internal states consistent with our behaviour unless there were clear external causes of our behaviour
_____ 12.	upward social comparison	B.	the belief that we are capable of performing a particular behaviour that is required for a certain goal
_____ 13.	downward social comparison	C.	social comparison with people who are better off or more skilled than we are
E 14.	relative deprivation	D.	the tendency to overestimate our control of situations and events
_____ 15.	individualist cultures	E.	a feeling of anger or resentment about our outcomes based on comparisons with better-off others
_____ 16.	collectivist cultures	F.	cultures in which people are seen as independent beings who possess stable abilities, traits, and attitudes
A 17.	self-perception theory	G.	the tendency to think that biases and errors in judgments are more common in others than in ourselves
J 18.	overjustification effect	H.	the process of comparing ourselves to others in order to judge the self
G 19.	bias blind spot	I.	social comparison with people who are worse off or less skilled than we are
B 20.	self-efficacy	J.	an inference that we performed a potentially enjoyable activity for external reasons (e.g., for a reward) rather than because we enjoyed it
D 21.	illusion of control	K.	cultures in which people are seen as interdependent beings who should contribute to harmonious group functioning

Matching III – Key Terms

_____ 22.	learned helplessness	A. the tendency to try repeatedly but unsuccessfully to achieve a goal because of unrealistic expectations about the likelihood of success
_____ 23.	false hope syndrome	B. a pattern of differences in attributions in which actors tend to make external attributions for their own behaviour, whereas observers tend to make internal attributions for the same actions
_____ 24.	ideal self	C. behaviour designed to make someone respect us
_____ 25.	actual self	D. the tendency to seek, create, or claim inhibitory factors that interfere with performance and thus provide an explanation for potential failure
_____ 26.	ought self	E. a theory proposing that perceived differences between the actual self and the ideal self produce depression, and perceived differences between the actual self and the ought self produce anxiety
E 27.	self-discrepancy theory	F. the deliberate control of our public behaviour to create a certain impression
F 28.	impression management	G. a scale that measures how often people engage in self-handicapping behaviour
H 29.	self-presentation	H. impression management
L 30.	ingratiation	I. a conception of the self describing our perception of how we would ideally like to be
_____ 31.	self-promotion	J. a state of apathy in which we simply give up trying to achieve our goals
_____ 32.	self-handicapping	K. a conception of the self describing our perception of how we really are
_____ 33.	self-handicapping scale	L. behaviour designed to make someone like us
B 34.	actor-observer difference	M. a conception of the self describing our perception of how we think we should or ought to be

Answers to Test Your Knowledge

Multiple Choice Questions

1. A	6. C	11. A	16. B
2. C	7. C	12. A	17. D
3. A	8. B	13. B	18. C
4. B	9. D	14. D	19. D
5. D	10. A	15. C	

Sentence Completion

1. augmentation principle
2. women, men
3. women, men
4. social comparison
5. similar
6. temporal
7. more, less
8. individualist, collectivist
9. false hope syndrome
10. actual, ideal, ought

Matching I – Key Terms

1. D
2. J
3. A
4. H
5. C
6. G
7. F
8. B
9. I
10. E

Matching II – Key Terms

11. H
12. C
13. I
14. E
15. F
16. K
17. A
18. J
19. G
20. B
21. D

Matching III – Key Terms

22. J
23. A
24. I
25. K
26. M
27. E
28. F

29. H
30. L
31. C
32. D
33. G
34. B

Chapter 5
The Person in the Situation: Self-Concept, Gender, and Dispositions

Thinking Critically about Social Psychology
Did Martha Get Shafted?

In 2004, Martha Stewart, the owner of the extremely successful company *Martha Stewart Living Omnimedia* was convicted of conspiracy and obstruction of justice and spent five months in prison.

An article appeared on March 12, 2004 in the *Pittsburgh Business Times* discussing the role of gender in the Martha Stewart case. The local president of the National Association of Women Business Owners, Selena Schmidt, is quoted in the article as saying, gender "played a key role" in the case because Martha Stewart's business has to do with "women's things" such as "cooking, designs, keeping stripes from clashing with plaids." According to Ms. Schmidt, these are things "that a lot of people, especially men, might think are less important in the economy than companies that deal in high technology, telecommunication or energy." According to the article, it is Ms. Schmidt's position that "because Ms. Stewart combined both celebrity status and nonessential woman's work, she became an easy target for the Bush administration." Stewart's gender is also discussed as a reason for her negative treatment by the media: "the parodies of Ms. Stewart, the late-night jokes on television and radio and now the focus on how she will have to clean jailhouse bathrooms and cook in prison kitchens each has a sexist, gender bias."

Questions:

1. Martha Stewart has been a successful businesswoman for decades. In her role as CEO of Martha Stewart Omnimedia, her assertive leadership style has been the focus of much criticism. How do traditional gender stereotypes (i.e., women as nurturing, men as aggressive) influence how we evaluate women in leadership positions? Has Stewart been unjustly criticized for behaviour that would have been praised in a male leader? Would Martha Stewart be more accepted if her leadership style was more nurturing?

2. Stewart has built her empire around domestic activities – celebrating the traditional role of the woman in the household. Does that violate gender stereotypes or conform to them? Do you think that if her business were based on more typically male domains (such as finance) she would engender the same hostility?

3. In violating traditional gender stereotypes as a female leader with a male leadership style, Stewart has aroused hostility from both men and women. Do you think both groups are upset about the same aspects of Stewart's career? For example, is it possible that Stewart is a threat to men because they feel unable to match her business acumen but that she is a threat to women because they feel unable to measure up to her domestic achievements?

4. What is the role of social comparison with regard to Martha Stewart? As you learned in Chapter 4, we use others as a basis of comparison to make ourselves feel better. Is Martha Stewart a good target for upward social comparison? Can you explain the glee with which many greeted the news of Stewart's setback in terms of social comparison?

5. Do you think Martha Stewart would have been found guilty if she were a man? Why or why not?

Commentary:

Almost nobody feels neutral about Martha Stewart—people either admire her business acumen or hate everything she represents. When she was convicted in conjunction with a questionable stock deal, many wondered whether the jury would have convicted a man of the same crime. Indeed, as this book goes to press, many male CEOs have yet to be punished for arguably worse behaviour. Was Stewart's gender really her downfall?

Traditional gender stereotypes in America dictate that men are aggressive and dominant, whereas women are emotional and nurturing. As a hard charging, successful businesswoman, Martha Stewart violates many of these stereotypes and challenges our perceptions of female leaders. One consequence of this stereotype violation is hostility towards Martha Stewart herself.

Why does the violation of these stereotypes make us so uncomfortable? How much of a role does culture play in these stereotypes? Western society is a patriarchal one; do you think that Martha Stewart would have been treated differently in a society that was more traditionally accustomed to women in leadership roles?

Martha Stewart's story is just one example of how women in leadership positions may be held to a different standard than men in leadership positions. As you read the newspapers and magazines, be aware of these portrayals. Notice how many times a man's treatment of his family, for example, is mentioned as compared to the number of times a woman's relationship with her family is discussed. What does that tell you about the acceptance of women as leaders? of the persistence of gender stereotypes?

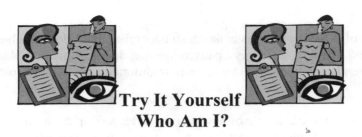

Try It Yourself
Who Am I?

One of the central themes of this chapter is identity—the characteristics that define you and describe your most important qualities. You can get a good assessment of your own identity by completing the following simple exercise.

Complete each of the ten sentences below as if you were talking to yourself and not paying attention to logic.

1. I am _____

2. I am _____

3. I am _____

4. I am _____

5. I am _____

6. I am _____

7. I am _____

8. I am _____

9. I am _____

10. I am _____

Questions:

1. What sorts of characteristics have you listed? Did you list primarily traits (such as shy, or optimistic) or attitudes (pro-choice)? Did you identify your gender or your membership in a group? What do these items tell you about how you see yourself?

2. Researchers have shown that people prefer to maintain a moderate or intermediate level of distinctiveness from other people—enough to have our own identity but not so much that we feel disconnected. Do your responses reflect a balance between your uniqueness and your interconnections with others? Do your responses reflect a bias toward individualism or collectivism?

3. Research on the self-serving bias has demonstrated that people generally want to see themselves in a favourable light. Did you engage in the self-serving bias? Are most of your responses positive ones?

Try It Yourself
Self-Monitoring and Finding Mr. or Ms. Right

One of the personality dimensions described in your text is self-monitoring – the extent to which people rely on internal or external cues to guide their behaviour. Social psychologists have shown that self-monitoring, like other personality characteristics, can affect a person's behaviour in many ways. Scores on the self-monitoring scale are even related to whom people choose to date. In 1985, Mark Snyder and his colleagues demonstrated that high self-monitors were more likely to choose attractive but unpleasant dates, whereas low self-monitors were more likely to choose pleasant but unattractive dates. Sound unbelievable? You can check this out for yourself by doing a simple replication of the study, using your friends as participants.

Method

1. Recruit about five willing friends as participants, and ask them to complete the following self-monitoring scale.

2. Present them with the two descriptions of potential dates that appear on the page after the scale, and ask them, which of the two people they would most likely pick as a date.

3. Score each friend's self-monitoring scale and put their score on the summary sheet, along with the choice of date.

    To score the self-monitoring scale, give one point for each of the following answers:

    > True: 5, 6, 7, 8, 10, 11, 13, 15, 16, 18, 19, 24, 25
    > False: 1, 2, 3, 4, 9, 12, 14, 17, 20, 21, 22, 23

    Higher scores indicate higher self-monitors.

4. It is more likely that the pattern of results found by Mark Synder will emerge with a larger number of participants, so you may want to combine and then review your results with those of your classmates.

Participant	Self-Monitoring Score	Date Choice (A or B)
1.		
2.		
3.		
4.		
5.		
6.		
7.		
8		
9.		
10.		

Questions:

1. Did you get the same results as Mark Snyder and his colleagues? Did your high self-monitoring friends choose to date Person A? Did your friends who had lower self-monitoring scores choose Person B?

2. Are these the results you would have expected, based on your understanding of self-monitoring? Why or why not?

Instructions for Completing the Scale[1]

Please indicate whether each of the following sentences is more true or more false about you by placing a T or an F next to the statement.

True or False?	
	1. I find it hard to imitate the behavior of other people.
	2. My behavior is usually an expression of my true inner feelings, attitudes and beliefs.
	3. At parties and social gatherings, I do not attempt to do or say things that others will like.
	4. I can only argue for ideas which I already believe.
	5. I can make impromptu speeches even on topics about which I have almost no information.
	6. I guess I put on a show to impress or entertain people.
	7. When I am uncertain how to act in a social situation, I look to the behavior of others for cues.
	8. I would probably make a good actor.
	9. I rarely need the advice of my friends to choose movies, books, or music.
	10. I sometimes appear to others to be experiencing deeper emotions than I actually am.
	11. I laugh more when I watch a comedy with others than when alone.
	12. In a group of people I am rarely the center of attention.
	13. In different situations and with different people, I often act like very different persons.
	14. I am not particularly good at making people like me.
	15. Even if I am not enjoying myself, I often pretend to be having a good time.
	16. I'm not always the person I appear to be.
	17. I would not change my opinions (or the way I do things) in order to please someone else or win their favor.
	18. I have considered being an entertainer.
	19. In order to get along and be liked, I tend to be what people expect me to be rather than anything else.
	20. I have never been good at games like charades or improvisational acting.
	21. I have trouble changing my behavior to suit different people and different situations.
	22. At a party, I let others keep the jokes and stories going.
	23. I feel a bit awkward in company and do not show up quite so well as I should.
	24. I can look anyone in the eye and tell a lie with a straight face (if for a right end).
	25. I may deceive people by being friendly when I really dislike them.

---

[1] Snyder, M. (1974). Self-monitoring of expressive behavior. *Journal of Personality and Social Psychology, 30,* 526-537; Snyder, M. (1987). *Public appearances, private realities: The psychology of self-monitoring.* New York: Freeman; Snyder, M., & Gangestad, S. (1986). On the nature of self-monitoring: Matters of assessment, matters of validity. *Journal of Personality and Social Psychology, 51,* 125-139.

Select a Date

If you were sent the following two descriptions of potential dates from an Internet dating service, which one of the two would you be most likely to pick as a date?

A is very good-looking and people on the street often turn their heads to watch as A walks past. A has even done some modelling in the past. However, A tends to be reserved towards strangers, and is sometimes moody. Friends of A acknowledge that A can be self-centred, and a less than sympathetic listener.

B is very outgoing and a great listener. B was voted by high-school classmates as All-Around Nicest Person. B has a wonderful sense of humour, and appreciates the same qualities in others. However, B is overweight and has some acne.

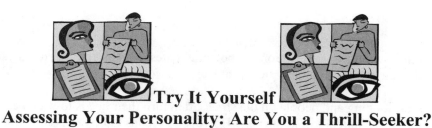

Try It Yourself
Assessing Your Personality: Are You a Thrill-Seeker?

Life is either a daring adventure or nothing.
Helen Keller, Let Us Have Faith *(1940).*

Send me out into another life. But get me back
for supper.
Faith Popcorn, The Popcorn Report *(1991)*

There are two kinds of adventurers: those who go
truly hoping to find adventure and those who go
secretly hoping they won't.
William Least Heat-Mood, Blue Highways: A
Journey into America *(1982)*

A life without adventure is likely to be
unsatisfying, but a life in which adventure is
allowed to take whatever form it will is sure to
be short.
Bertrand Russell, "Social Cohesion and
Human Nature," Authority and the Individual
(1949)

Psychologists have developed scales to measure many types of personality traits. Many of those scales are summarized in the table at the end of this exercise: Individual Difference Variables That Have Been Shown to Influence Social Behaviour: Trait, Definition, Sample Finding, References. One scale, the Sensation-Seeking Scale, is reproduced below. It is designed to measure the extent to which people seek out a high level of stimulation or sensation. Marvin Zuckerman (1979), who developed the scale, believes that the thirst for sensation is a general personality trait that leads people to seek thrills, adventures, and new experiences.

Instructions

For each of the 34 pairs of statements, indicate which whether statement A or statement B best describes your likes or the way you feel. It is important that you respond to each pair with only one choice. If you find that both choices describe what you like or feel, choose the one that describes your likes and feelings more often. If you find that neither choice describes your likes and feelings, mark the choice you dislike least. There are no right or wrong answers. Be frank and give an honest appraisal of yourself.

The Scale[2]

Your Choice: A or B		
	1.	A. I would like a job which would require a lot of traveling.
		B. I would prefer a job in one location.
	2.	A. I am invigorated by a brisk, cold day.
		B. I can't wait to get indoors on a cold day.
	3.	A. I find a certain pleasure in routine kinds of work.

---

[2] Zuckerman, M. (1979). Sensation seeking: Beyond the optimal level of arousal. Hillsdale, NJ: Erlbaum. Reprinted by permission of Lawrence Erlbaum Associates, Inc.

			B. Although it is sometimes necessary, I usually dislike routine kinds of work.
		4.	A. I often wish I would be a mountain climber.
			B. I can't understand people who risk their necks climbing mountains.
		5.	A. I dislike all body odors.
			B. I like some of the earthy body smells.
		6.	A. I get bored seeing the same old faces.
			B. I like the comfortable familiarity of everyday friends.
		7.	A. I like to explore a strange city or section of town by myself, even if it means getting lost.
			B. I prefer a guide when I am in a place I don't know well.
		8.	A. I find the quickest and easiest route to a place and stick to it.
			B. I sometimes take different routes to a place I often go, just for variety's sake.
		9.	A. I would not like to try any drug that might produce strange and dangerous effects on me.
			B. I would like to try some of the new drugs that produce hallucinations.
		10.	A. I would prefer living in an ideal society where everyone is safe, secure, and happy.
			B. I would have preferred living in the unsettled days of our history.
		11.	A. I sometimes like to do things that are a little frightening.
			B. A sensible person avoids activities that are dangerous.
		12.	A. I order dishes with which I am familiar, so as to avoid disappointment and unpleasantness.
			B. I like to try new foods that I have never tasted before.
		13.	A. I can't stand riding with a person who likes to speed.
			B. I sometimes like to drive very fast because I find it exciting.
		14.	A. If I were a salesperson, I would prefer a straight salary rather than the risk of making little or nothing on a commission basis.
			B. If I were a salesperson, I would prefer working on a commission if I had a chance to make more money than I could on a salary.
		15.	A. I would like to take up the sport of water skiing.
			B. I would not like to take up the sport of water skiing.
		16.	A. I don't like to argue with people whose beliefs are sharply divergent from mine, since such arguments are never resolved.
			B. I find people who disagree with my beliefs more stimulating than people who disagree with me.
		17.	A. When I go on a trip, I like to plan my route and timetable fairly carefully.
			B. I would like to take off on a trip with no preplanned or definite routes or timetables.
		18.	A. I enjoy the thrills of watching car races.
			B. I find car races unpleasant.
		19.	A. Most people spend entirely too much money on life insurance.
			B. Life insurance is something that no one can afford to be without.
		20.	A. I would like to learn to fly an airplane.
			B. I would not like to learn to fly an airplane.
		21.	A. I would not like to be hypnotized.
			B. I would like to have the experience of being hypnotized.
		22.	A. The most important goal of life is to live it to the fullest and experience as much of it as you can.

		B. The most important goal of life is to find peace and happiness.
	23.	A. I would like to try parachute jumping.
		B. I would never want to try jumping out of a plane, with or without a parachute.
	24.	A. I enter cold water gradually, giving myself time to get used to it.
		B. I like to dive or jump right into the ocean or a cold pool.
	25.	A. I do not like the irregularity and discord of most modern music.
		B. I like to listen to new and unusual kinds of music.
	26.	A. I prefer friends who are excitingly unpredictable.
		B. I prefer friends who are reliable and predictable.
	27.	A. When I go on a vacation, I prefer the comfort of a good room and bed.
		B. When I go on a vacation, I would prefer the change of camping out.
	28.	A. The essence of good art is in its clarity, symmetry of form, and harmony of colors.
		B. I often find beauty in the "clashing" colors and irregular forms of modern painting.
	29.	A. The worst social sin is to be rude.
		B. The worst social sin is to be a bore.
	30.	A. I look forward to a good night of rest after a long day.
		B. I wish I didn't have to waste so much of a day sleeping.
	31.	A. I prefer people who are emotionally expressive even if they are a bit unstable.
		B. I prefer people who are calm and even-tempered.
	32.	A. A good painting should shock or jolt the senses.
		B. A good painting should give one a feeling of peace and security.
	33.	A. When I feel discouraged, I recover by relaxing and having some soothing diversion.
		B. When I feel discouraged, I recover by going out and doing something new and exciting.
	34.	A. People who ride motorcycles must have some kind of unconscious need to hurt themselves.
		B. I would like to drive or ride on a motorcycle.

Scoring the Scale

Use the scoring key below to obtain your score on the Sensation Seeking scale. Circle your response of A or B each time it corresponds to the keyed response below. For example, if you selected statement A for Question 1, you would circle "1. A" below; if you selected statement B for Question 1, you would circle nothing for Question 1. To get your score, add up the number of responses you circled.

1. A	8. B	15. A	22. A	29. B
2. A	9. B	16. B	23. A	30. B
3. B	10. B	17. B	24. B	31. A
4. A	11. A	18. A	25. B	32. A
5. B	12. B	19. A	26. A	33. B
6. A	13. B	20. A	27. B	34. B
7. A	14. B	21. B	28. B	

Your score: _____

Interpreting Your Score

Marvin Zuckerman provided the following guide to interpreting the scores of the average-age college or university student (17–23). The higher your score, the more of a sensation-seeker you purportedly are.

Low Score: 0–10
Intermediate Score: 11–20
High Score: 21–34

Male students tend to score higher than female students on the scale, but the differences are small enough to use the above guide for both genders. If you are older than the average-aged college or university student, however, a somewhat lower score may indicate a relatively higher level of sensation-seeking.

Questions:

1. Do the results of the scale match your own opinion of the extent to which you are a sensation seeker?

2. Do the results of the scale match how others see you? Ask your friends how they view you, and see if their descriptions correspond to the results of the scale.

3.   If your own personal evaluation and your friends' descriptions do not map on to the description of yourself provided by the scale, which are you more likely to believe?

4.   Businesses often use individual difference or personality inventories to screen employee applicants. In the table starting on the next page, you can see a number of individual difference behaviours that have been shown to influence social behaviour. Based on your experience with the Sensation Seeking Scale and your review of the table, do you think such inventories are likely to paint an accurate portrait of the applicant? Can you see some of the advantages to using personality inventories in this manner? Disadvantages?

Individual Difference Variables That Have Been Shown to Influence Social Behaviour: Trait, Definition, Sample Finding, References

Affiliation Motivation

>   Definition: individuals who are high in affiliation motivation (affiliation-oriented) seek interactions with others and are comfortable in social settings.

>   Finding: people who are affiliation-oriented excel in group performance situations, whereas people who are low in affiliation motivation "choke" in group performance situations.

>   References: Atkinson (1964); Sorrentino & Sheppard (1978)

Authoritarianism

>   Definition: individuals who are high in authoritarianism are obedient to authority, endorse anti-democratic and fascistic ideologies, are conventional, and tend to reject members of outgroups.

>   Finding: high authoritarians report more prejudice toward ethnic and religious minority groups than do low authoritarians.

>   References: Altemeyer (1988); Krauss (2002)

Belief in a Just World

>   Definition: individuals who are high in the belief in a just world believe that the world is a fair place where people get what they deserve—good people prosper and bad people suffer.

>   Finding: strong believers in a just world are more likely to blame victims (people who have suffered a misfortune) than are weak believers in a just world.

>   References: Hafer & Olson (1993); Montada & Lerner (1998)

Need for Cognition

>   Definition: individuals who are high in the need for cognition enjoy thinking and frequently engage in effortful cognitive activities.

>   Finding: people who are high in the need for cognition think carefully about the information in persuasive messages and have better subsequent memory for that information than do people who are low in the need for cognition.

>   References: Cacioppo & Petty, 1982; Cacioppo, Petty, Feinstein, & Jarvis, 1996

Need for Cognitive Closure

>   Definition: individuals who are high in the need for cognitive closure are motivated to come up with an answer, *any* answer, to a given question so as to avoid confusion and ambiguity.

>   Finding: people who are high in the need for cognitive closure are more likely to use information presented early in a sequence to make a judgment (a primacy effect) than are people who are low in this need.

>   References: Webster & Kruglanski (1994); Kruglanski & Webster (1996)

Need to Evaluate

>   Definition: individuals who are high in the need to evaluate are likely to form evaluations (good-bad judgments) of people, issues, and objects in the environment.

>   Finding: people who are high in the need for evaluation are more likely to report having attitudes toward a variety of social and political issues than are people who are low in this need.

>   References: Jarvis & Petty (1996); Tuten & Bosnjak (2001)

Self-Consciousness

    Definition: individuals who are high in self-consciousness are very aware of their internal states, such as their feelings, sensations, and thoughts (labelled *private* self-consciousness), and very aware of how they appear to others (labelled *public* self-consciousness).

    Finding: people who are high in self-consciousness (especially in *private* self-consciousness) possess more extensive and more accurate knowledge about themselves than do people who are low in self-consciousness.

    References: Fenigstein, Scheier, & Buss (1975); Hull, Sloan, Meteyer, & Matthews (2002)

Self-Handicapping Scale

    Definition: self-handicapping refers to deliberately doing something (e.g., ingesting a drug) that will hurt performance on a task in order to give an excuse for possible failure (see Chapter 4 on *Social and Self-Perception*). Some individuals engage in self-handicapping more often than do other individuals.

    Finding: people who score high on the self-handicapping scale spend less time practicing a task before being tested than do people who score low on the scale.

    References: Rhodewalt (1990); Deppe & Harackiewicz (1996)

Social Comparison Orientation

    Definition: individuals who are high in social comparison orientation often compare their own abilities and outcomes to other people's abilities and outcomes.

    Finding: people who score high in social comparison orientation spend more time inspecting information about other people's performance on a test they have taken than do people who are low in social comparison orientation.

    References: Gibbons & Buunk (1999); Buunk, Oldersma, & de Dreu (2001)

Social Dominance Orientation

    Definition: individuals who are high in social dominance orientation believe that competition between groups is natural, that hierarchies of dominance are appropriate, and that their ingroup is superior to outgroups.

    Finding: people who are high in social dominance orientation report more negative attitudes toward subordinate groups in society (e.g., the poor, racial minorities) and consider subordinate groups' disadvantaged status to be more fair than do people who are low in social dominance orientation.

    References: Sidanius, Pratto, & Bobo (1994); Van Hiel & Mervielde (2002)

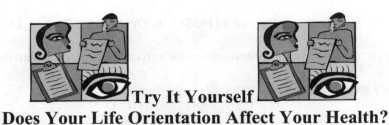

Try It Yourself
Does Your Life Orientation Affect Your Health?

As you learned from the textbook, many studies have suggested that some personality traits may be linked to health and well-being. Another workbook exercise explores the Type A personality attributes that have been found to be associated with coronary disease. This exercise explores how another personality trait, optimism, may be associated with better health.

Method

1. Recruit several friends to participate in a demonstration that should take them about 20 minutes each.

2. Ask each friend to complete the following Life Orientation Test (LOT).

3. Once the friend has completed the Life Orientation Test, ask him or her to record any physical complaints or illnesses (such as muscle soreness, headaches, fatigue, and dizziness) he or she has experienced in the previous week. Use the sheet provided on the page following the Life Orientation Test to do this.

4. Score each friend's Life Orientation Test. Items 1, 3, 4, and 7 are scored from 0 to 4, whereas items 2, 5, 6, and 8 are reverse-scored. To obtain the scores on numbers 2, 5, 6 and 8, subtract the number your friend circled from 4. Thus, if he or she circled 3 on Question 2, your reverse coded answer will be 4 minus 3, or 1. Add up the scores to obtain the Life Orientation Score. The higher the total score, the stronger your friend's level of optimism.

5. Examine the relationship between your friends' LOT scores and the degree to which they experienced physical complaints or illnesses. Do you notice a pattern?

6. It is more likely that the pattern of results found by Scheier and Carver (1985) will emerge with a larger number of participants, so you may want to combine and then review your results with those of your classmates.

Question:

1. According to Scheier and Carver (1985), people who score higher on the Life Orientation Test should have recorded fewer complaints than those who had lower scores. What factors could account for this pattern of results? What explanation does the research described in your text support?

Instructions. Circle the number that best represents your agreement with each statement.

1. In uncertain times, I usually expect the best.

0	1	2	3	4
Strongly Disagree	Disagree	Neutral	Agree	Strongly Agree

2. If something can go wrong for me, it will.

0	1	2	3	4
Strongly Disagree	Disagree	Neutral	Agree	Strongly Agree

3. I always look on the bright side of things.

0	1	2	3	4
Strongly Disagree	Disagree	Neutral	Agree	Strongly Agree

4. I'm always optimistic about my future.

0	1	2	3	4
Strongly Disagree	Disagree	Neutral	Agree	Strongly Agree

5. I hardly ever expect things to go my way.

0	1	2	3	4
Strongly Disagree	Disagree	Neutral	Agree	Strongly Agree

6. Things never work out the way I want them to.

0	1	2	3	4
Strongly Disagree	Disagree	Neutral	Agree	Strongly Agree

7. I'm a believer in the idea that "every cloud has a silver lining."

0	1	2	3	4
Strongly Disagree	Disagree	Neutral	Agree	Strongly Agree

8. I rarely count on good things happening to me.

0	1	2	3	4
Strongly Disagree	Disagree	Neutral	Agree	Strongly Agree

[3] Scheier, M. F., & Carver, C. S. (1985). Optimism, coping and health: Assessment and implications of generalized outcome expectancies, *Health Psychology*, 4, 219–247. Reprinted by permission of Lawrence Erlbaum Associates, Inc.

Record of Physical Complaints and Illnesses

Below, record any physical complaints or illnesses (such as muscle soreness, headaches, fatigue, and dizziness) you have experienced in the previous week. If you can remember, also note how frequently these symptoms/ailments occurred.

Physical Complaint	Frequency

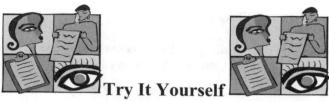

Try It Yourself
Assessing Your Personality: Are You Type A?

> **JOHN**
> **The Human Volcano**
>
> John is a 55-year-old business executive, married, with two teenage children. For most of his adult life, John has smoked about a pack of cigarettes each day. Although he maintains a busy and active schedule, John is mildly obese, partly from regular meals with business partners and colleagues. He has been taking several medications for high blood pressure since age 42. John's doctor has warned him repeatedly to cut down on his smoking and to exercise more frequently, especially because his father died of a heart attack. Although John has episodes of chest pain, he continues his busy and stressful life-style. It is difficult for him to slow down, because his business has been doing extremely well during the past 10 years.
>
> Moreover, John believes that life is so short that there is no time to slow down. He sees relatively little of his family and works late most evenings. Even when he's at home, John typically works into the night. It is very difficult for him to relax; he feels a constant urgency to get as much done as possible and prefers to work on several tasks simultaneously. For instance, John often proofreads a document, engages in a phone conversation, and eats lunch at all the same time. He attributes much of the success of his business to his working style. John is not well-liked by his peers, who often find him to be overbearing, easily frustrated, and, at times, hostile. His subordinates in particular claim he is overly impatient and critical of their performance.
>
> D. H. Barlow and V. M. Durand (2005), *Abnormal Psychology* (4th ed). Belmont, CA: Thomson/Wadsworth, p. 316.

Most of us recognize that John's behaviours and attitudes are classic symptoms of a Type A personality and that his attitudes and behaviours are associated with health risks, including increased blood pressure and increased risk of heart disease. The popular media often portrays Type A personalities as highly-driven, sometimes frustrated, middle-aged men who are driven to success and who may fly off the handle when confronted with life stresses. An exaggerated and pathological portrayal is the character, William Foster, played by Michael Douglas in the 1993 movie, *Falling Down*. William is a laid-off, divorced defense worker who life takes a turn for the worse. It is his daughter's birthday and he and his car with its personalize license plate, D-FENS, are stuck in traffic. Impatiently, he steps out on foot to find a present, and along the way, he aggressively deals with anyone and anything that gets in his way – from a grocer who refuses to give him phone change without a purchase, to gang members who take umbrage at where he chose to rest, and a fast food restaurant that has just stopped serving breakfast.

However, just like middle-aged men, women and younger or older people may also have a Type A personality; it just may exhibit itself in somewhat different behaviours and attitudes. Generally, Type A individuals have been described as people who tend to:

- Perceive time passing quickly;
- Show a deteriorating performance on tasks that require delayed responding;
- Work near maximum capacity even when there is not a time deadline;
- Arrive early for appointments;
- Become aggressive and hostile when frustrated;
- Report less fatigue and fewer physical symptoms; and
- Are intensely motivated to master their physical and social environments to maintain control. (Glass, 1977).

More specifically, some examples of interview questions that are used to identify Type A individuals are:

4. Does your job carry heavy responsibility?
   a. Is there any time when you feel particularly rushed or under pressure?
   b. When you are under pressure, does it bother you?

6. When you get angry or upset, do people around you know about it? How do you show it?

12. When you are in your automobile, and there is a car in your lane going far too slowly for you, what do you do about it? Would you mutter and complain to yourself? Would anyone riding with you know that you are annoyed?

14. If you make a date with someone for, oh, two o'clock in the afternoon, for example, would you be there on time?
    a. If you are kept waiting, do you resent it?
    b. Would you say anything about it?

17. Do you eat rapidly? Do you walk rapidly? After you've finished eating, do you like to sit around the table and chat, or do you like to get up and get going?

19. How do you feel waiting in lines: Bank lines, or supermarket lines? Post office lines?

From "The Interview Methods of Assessment of the Coronary-Prone Behavior Pattern," by R.H. Rosenman, pp. 68–69. In T.M. Dembroski, S.M. Weiss, J.L. Shields, S.G. Haynes, and M. Feinleib (Eds.) (1978), *Coronary-prone Behavior*, Springer-Verlag.

Monitoring Your Behaviour

For three days, keep a journal of your reactions to some of the situations in which you find yourself. For example, record your thoughts and actions while working to complete an assignment before the deadline, working on a group assignment with classmates, driving your car, waiting in line at the cafeteria or other location, and engaging in athletic activities. How do you respond to these situations? Do you rush to get things done and feel like you are in a race against time? Are you a work-alcoholic? A perfectionist? Do you get annoyed with classmates who don't do their share of the work? Are you overly competitive in sports or games, to the extent it is no longer fun for you or people playing with you? Do you arrive early for appointments? Do you get annoyed with people who arrive late? Do you take on more responsibility even though you know you are swamped?

Keep track of your emotions and behaviours as honestly as you can. At the conclusion of the week, go back and evaluate how many of those behaviours would be classified as Type-A behaviours.

	Situation	Your response	Type A?
1.			
2.			
3.			
4.			
5.			
6.			
7.			
8.			
9.			
10.			
11.			
12.			

Social Psychology Online Lab
The Barnum Effect

One of the social psychology lab exercises for this chapter, Personality Test, demonstrates the Barnum effect—people's tendency to accept vague and general personality descriptions as uniquely applicable to themselves without realizing that the same description could be applied to just about anyone. It is also known as the Forer effect (after the psychologist who initially reported it), and also, the subjective or personal validation effect. The Barnum Effect is named after circus man P.T. Barnum who had a reputation as a master of psychological manipulation.

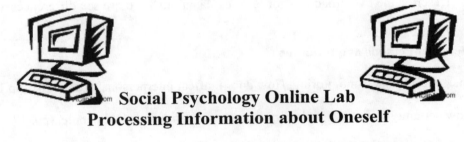

Social Psychology Online Lab
Processing Information about Oneself

Hazel Markus (1977) collected ratings from individuals to determine the dimensions of personal identity that were especially important to the people's self-concepts. Separately, she had participants make quick "me/not me" judgments for a large set of trait adjectives. She found that people were faster at making the judgments when the traits related to important dimensions of self and were positive. You can try a variation of this procedure yourself in the Online Lab, Self-Description.

Learning Objectives

Self-Concept and Identity

1. What is the self-concept? What factors can influence it? (pp. 155–158)

2. How does group membership contribute to identity? (pp. 158–161)

3. Explain how culture can play a role in the establishment of personal identity. (pp.161–163)

4. What are some of the sources of self-esteem? (pp. 163–165)

5. Describe the different effects that self-esteem can have on people's lives. (pp.165–168)

Gender and Social Behaviour

6. What are the traits on which men and women differ more dramatically? What accounts for those differences? Describe the two broad categories of explanations for these sex differences. (pp. 169–174)

Interactions Between Persons and Situations

7. Describe the concept of self-monitoring. How does it affect interpersonal attraction? (pp.175–176)

8. Describe how certainty-oriented people differ from uncertainty-oriented people. (pp. 177–178)

9. Describe the trait of perfectionism. What is the difference between self-oriented and socially prescribed perfectionism? Are these two types of perfectionism associated with other desirable or undesirable characteristics? (pp. 178–180)

Dispositions and Health

10. Can personality traits influence health? How? Provide three examples. (pp. 180–184)

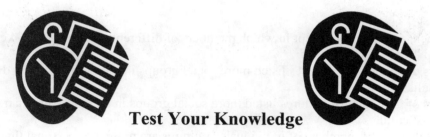

Test Your Knowledge

Multiple Choice Questions

1. Which of the following could best be considered a psychological disposition?
   A. hair colour
   B. handedness
   C. extraversion
   D. eye color

2. Which statement best describes the difference between self-concept and identity?
   A. Identity and self-concept are identical, interchangeable terms.
   B. Self-concept refers to all the information about the self in memory; identity refers to characteristics that make up a person's most important qualities.
   C. Self-concept refers to characteristics that make up a person's most important qualities; identity refers to all the information about the self in memory.
   D. Individuals have only one identity, but multiple self-concepts.

3. One of the earliest researchers on self-concept found that people become aware of a specific characteristic when it makes them distinctive, and that characteristic then becomes more accessible. That researcher was
   A. Henri Tajfel.
   B. Darryl Bem.
   C. Harry Triandis.
   D. William McGuire.

4. Jason and Tom are twins and huge baseball fans. However, Tom roots for the New York Yankees and Jason is a diehard supporter of the rival Toronto Blue Jays. At a Jays/Yankees game at Yankee Stadium, a poor call by the umpire in favour of the Jays leads to fans throwing debris on the field in protest. Jason feels superior to his brother, knowing that Blue Jay fans would never act in such a boorish manner. Jason's feelings are an example of
   A. secure high self-esteem.
   B. self-perception theory.
   C. upward social comparison.
   D. social identity theory.

5. The experiment on the self-concept in which members of different cultures were asked to complete the statement "I am…" found that
   A. members of collectivist cultures listed more social groups in their answers than did members of individualist cultures.
   B. members of individualist cultures listed more social groups in their answers than did members of collectivist cultures.
   C. the self-concepts of members of individualist cultures are more interpersonal than those of members of collectivist cultures.
   D. there was no difference in the responses of members of collectivist cultures and members of individualist cultures.

6. Which of the following is *not* considered a source of self-esteem?
   A. past negative outcomes
   B. past positive outcomes
   C. parental labels
   D. heredity

7. Self-esteem can have wide-ranging consequences. According to most research, people with high self-esteem are more likely than people with low self-esteem to
   A. attribute success to external factors.
   B. attribute failure to external factors.
   C. underestimate their control over situations.
   D. have high rates of depression and anxiety.

8. Stephanie thinks very highly of herself and her abilities. After being cut from her school's orchestra, however, she began sabotaging her fellow musicians by stealing their music and hiding their instruments. Stephanie's behaviour is an example of
   A. threatened egotism.
   B. secure high self-esteem.
   C. implicit self-esteem.
   D. destructive low self-esteem.

9. Which characteristic is most often used to spontaneously categorize people we encounter?
   A. age
   B. race
   C. gender
   D. height

10. Recent research on reactions to threat has proposed that
    A. men and women both respond to threats with a fight-or-flight response.
    B. women are more likely than men to respond to threats with a fight-or-flight response.
    C. women are more likely than men to respond to threats by blending in with their environment.
    D. men are more likely than women to respond to threats by affiliating with others.

11. All of the following areas are ones in which, on average, men and women differ **except**
    A. self-esteem.
    B. romantic attraction.
    C. violent physical aggression.
    D. nurturance.

12. The parental investment hypothesis refers to the tendency of
    A. men and women to have an equal say in how their children are raised.
    B. women to place more emphasis on a man's desire to reproduce when choosing a mate.
    C. men to place more emphasis on a woman's ability to provide a home for children when choosing a mate.
    D. women to place more emphasis on men who can support and protect her children when choosing a mate.

13. Which statement best describes the source of gender differences?
    A. All gender differences can be explained biologically.
    B. All gender differences can be explained socially.
    C. Both biological and social processes contribute to gender differences.
    D. Socialization can never overcome any biological differences.

14. In a study by Snyder, Berscheid, and Glick (1985), participants were given the choice of dating a physically attractive woman with negative personality characteristics, or a physically unattractive woman with positive personality characteristics. What were the results of the study?
    A. High self-monitors chose the physically attractive woman.
    B. High self-monitors chose the physically unattractive woman.
    C. Participants with secure high self-esteem chose the physically attractive woman.
    D. All participants chose the physically attractive woman.

15. Which of the following dispositions has been found to be correlated with depression and anxiety?
    A. Narcisism
    B. High self-monitoring
    C. Self-oriented perfectionism
    D. Socially prescribed perfectionism

16. Which of the following dispositions has been found to be correlated with positive outcomes such as academic achievement?
    A. Narcissism
    B. High self-monitoring
    C. Self-oriented perfectionism
    D. Socially prescribed perfectionism

17. What might explain the positive relationship between dispositional optimism and physical well-being?
    A. Optimists are more likely to engage in healthy behaviours compared to pessimists.
    B. Optimists avoid dwelling on negative affect.
    C. Optimists are more likely to focus on positive ways to deal with real risks to health.
    D. All of the above.

18. Which of the following individual differences has **not** been found to be related to overall well-being?
    A. extraversion
    B. type A personality
    C. intelligence
    D. optimism

Sentence Completion

1. Cody is among a handful of Protestant students who attend a predominantly Jewish school, and Daniel is one of his Jewish classmates. _____ is more likely than _____ to view his religion as part of his self-concept while at school.

2. People in _____ cultures value distinctiveness as a unique pattern of social roles and relationships, whereas people in _____ cultures value distinctiveness as a unique set of traits and characteristics.

3. Compared to people with _____ self-esteem, people with _____ self-esteem are more likely to process information to magnify their own virtues, be happier, and have greater satisfaction in their personal relationships.

4. Well-adjusted individuals are _____ in self-esteem and _____ in narcissism, whereas obnoxious, overly arrogant people are _____ in both self-esteem and narcissism.

5. In choosing a romantic partner, _____ place more weight on the status and material assets of possible mates whereas _____ place more weight on the physical attractiveness of possible mates.

6. _____ explanations for gender differences assume that divergent physical attributes of men and women produce the gender differences, whereas _____ explanations assume that women and men are exposed to different environments that produce the gender differences.

7. The parental investment hypothesis is an _____ explanation for gender differences.

8. Alexis acts very differently depending on whom she is with and what situation she is in. Alexis is probably a _____ self-monitor.

9. People who are _____ - _____ want to learn new things about themselves and are attracted by novelty and predictability.

10. Childhood intelligence is _____ correlated with a person's subsequent health and longevity.

Matching I – Key Terms

_____ 1.	dispositions	A. a hostile, aggressive response to criticism from others, which has been linked to narcissism
_____ 2.	self-esteem	B. all information about the self in memory
_____ 3.	self-concept	C. a disposition that represents the extent to which people have excessive love for themselves
_____ 4.	identity	D. a model hypothesizing that people want to have positive appraisals of groups to which they belong
I 5.	spontaneous self-concept	E. a model hypothesizing that people want to maintain a balance between similarity to other people and individuality from other people
D 6.	social identity theory	F. a disposition that represents people's judgments of their own worthiness
G 7.	minimal group paradigm	G. a procedure in which participants are divided into groups based on trivial features or information
E 8.	optimal distinctiveness theory	H. the characteristics that individuals think define them and make up their most important qualities
_____ 9.	narcissism	I. the aspects of identity that are in conscious awareness at a given point in time
_____ 10.	threatened egotism	J. individuals' consistencies across time and settings in a specific type of feeling, thought, and/or action, which make individuals different from other people

Matching II – Key Terms

_____ 11. secure high self-esteem	A. a disposition that represents the extent to which people rely on external or internal cues to guide their behaviour
_____ 12. defensive high self-esteem	B. a measure of dispositional optimism
_____ 13. parental investment hypothesis	C. a constellation of characteristics, including impatience, anger, and hostility, which has been linked to heart disease
_A_ 14. self-monitoring	D. a positive self-view that is fragile and vulnerable to threat
_J_ 15. uncertainty orientation	E. a disposition that represents the extent to which individuals believe that other people expect exceptional performance from them and will judge them negatively if such standards are not achieved
_____ 16. perfectionism	
_____ 17. self-oriented perfectionism	F. a disposition that represents the extent to which individuals strive for error-free performance
	G. a positive self-view that is confidently held
_____ 18. socially prescribed perfectionism	H. a disposition that represents the extent to which people have positive, confident expectations about their own future outcomes
_H_ 19. dispositional optimism	I. a disposition that represents the extent to which individuals set extremely high standards for themselves and are satisfied only when their performance is flawless
_____ 20. Life Orientation Test (LOT)	J. a disposition that represents the extent to which people want to learn new things about themselves and their environment
_____ 21. "Type A" coronary-prone behaviour pattern	K. the idea that having children is more costly for women than for men, which has led to the evolution of some differences between the sexes in the characteristics they seek in mates

Answers to Test Your Knowledge

Multiple Choice Questions

1. C	6. D	11. A	16. C
2. B	7. B	12. D	17. D
3. D	8. A	13. C	18. A
4. D	9. C	14. A	
5. A	10. C	15. D	

Sentence Completion

1. Cody, Daniel	6. Biological, social
2. collectivist, individualist	7. biological
3. low, high	8. high
4. high, low, high	9. uncertainty-oriented
5. women, men	10. positively

Matching I – Key Terms

1. J	6. D
2. F	7. G
3. B	8. E
4. H	9. C
5. I	10. A

Matching II – Key Terms

11. G	16. F
12. D	17. I
13. K	18. E
14. A	19. H
15. J	20. B
	21. C

Chapter 6
Attitudes and Social Behaviour

Thinking Critically about Social Psychology
Lockhart v. McCree: Social Science Evidence and the Supreme Court

American juries trying capital cases—that is, cases in which the death penalty might be given—must deliberate and answer two questions. The first question is whether the defendant is guilty beyond a reasonable doubt (guilt phase of the trial). If the defendant is convicted of a capital offense, then secondly the jury must also decided whether the defendant should receive the death penalty (penalty phase of the trial). In a capital case, the judge questions potential jurors to identify and exclude from serving on the jury those people whose attitude toward the death penalty are thought to be incompatible with performing these duties. The questioning and exclusion process is called "death qualification."

Until 1968, the judge could exclude a person from a capital jury if the person had *any* problem with imposing the death penalty. However, in *Witherspoon v. Illinois* (1968), the United States Supreme Court held that excluding people with *any* reservations toward the death penalty produced a jury that was biased against the defendant during the **sentencing phase** of the trial. That is, it produced a jury that was more likely to impose the death penalty. The Court ruled that a judge could only exclude from a capital jury those people who:
- would not, because of their views about the death penalty, be fair and impartial in determining the defendant's guilt or innocence, or:
- would never return a verdict of death regardless of the evidence produced at trial.

People who are or could be excluded from serving on capital juries under the *Witherspoon* standard are often referred to as "**Witherspoon excludables**." People who would not be excluded are called "**death qualified**."

The defendants in Witherspoon also argued that "death qualification" produced juries that are biased against the defendant during the **guilt phase** of the trial or in other words, produced juries that were more likely to convict the defendant. They presented 2–3 empirical studies to support this position, but the Supreme Court dismissed the studies as too tentative to justify the Court's reliance on them. However, the Court seemed to encourage social scientists to study this question in a footnote to the court opinion.

In the 1986 case of *Lockhart v. McCree*, the Supreme Court directly considered whether death qualification produced juries that were biased against the defendant during the guilt phase of the trial. In this case, the respondents raised three constitutional challenges against death qualification.

The first constitutional challenge was that <u>death qualification violates the fair-cross-section requirement of the Sixth amendment</u>. Under the sixth amendment, a criminal defendant is entitled to have his or her jury selected from a fair cross-section of the community. More specifically, the respondents argued that excluding "Witherspoon-excludables" (WEs) violated the fair-cross-section requirement because WEs share inter-related ideas about the criminal justice system that are different from those possessed by death qualified jurors. Surveys were introduced to show that the group of WEs was of substantial size both nationally and state-wide, and that WEs share interrelated attitudes toward the criminal justice system that are different from those shared by death qualified jurors. Surveys also showed that a disproportionate number of blacks and women were among the WEs.

The Supreme Court rejected this argument, providing two reasons. First, the Court said that the fair-cross-section requirement only applied to the pool of people from which the jury was to be selected and not the jury itself. The Court also said that groups of people defined solely in terms of shared attitudes were not considered "distinctive" groups for the purposes of applying the fair-cross-section requirement.

The second constitutional challenge was that <u>death qualification may lead to juries that are "less than neutral on the issue of guilt," thus violating the Sixth and Fourteenth amendments.</u> The respondents offered several types of empirical evidence to show that death qualified jurors are more likely to convict than are non-death qualified jurors. The empirical evidence included attitude surveys showing that people who favour the death penalty have "pro-prosecution" attitudes while those who oppose it have "pro-defense" attitudes. For example, people who favour the death penalty tend to believe effective crime control depends on harsh penalties whereas those who oppose it tend to protect procedural protections for defendants. The empirical evidence also included:

- simulation studies revealing that people against the death penalty are less likely to vote guilty in simulated trials than are people in favour of it;
- field studies in which the attitudes of ex-jurors were found to be highly correlated with whether they voted guilty in non-capital cases; and
- a single study that showed that the experience of going through the death-qualification process itself may make jurors more likely to convict the defendant because the process increases their estimates of whether the prosecutor, defense attorney, and judge believe the defendant is guilty.

In response to this challenge, the Supreme Court ruled that death qualification did not produce jurors that were "less than neutral on the issue of guilt" in violation of the sixth and fourteenth amendments.

The third constitutional challenge was that death qualification <u>interferes with the proper functioning of the jury during the guilt phase of capital trials,</u> by decreasing the thoroughness and the accuracy of the jury's deliberation. This challenge derives from the reasoning in *Ballew v. Georgia*, in which the Supreme Court held that criminal convictions rendered by five-person juries violated the Sixth and Fourteenth amendments. Social science studies were introduced to show that death qualified juries were less likely to foster effective group deliberation. For example, one jury simulation study found that the ability to recall evidence by death-qualified jurors was worse than that of other jurors.

The Supreme Court did not directly address this claim, disposing of the case on the other two constitutional grounds.

To recap the Supreme Court's legal rulings, death qualification does not violate a defendant's right to trial by an impartial jury selected from a fair cross-section of the community. Not all of the Supreme Court Justices agreed with the majority ruling and those Justices entered a dissenting opinion in the case.

Of interest to social scientists is the Court's treatment of the social science evidence. As the dissenting opinion in the case noted, the strength of the social evidence was that the results obtained by different researchers using diverse populations of people and a variety of research methods were consistent. The use of different research designs (i.e., attitude surveys, jury simulation studies, field studies) minimizes the shortcomings of the body of research by balancing the strengths and weaknesses of the different methods.

However, instead of considering the evidence in the aggregate, the majority of the Court critiqued and identified what they considered to be serious flaws in individual studies. For example, two simulation studies were criticized because they did not attempt to simulate the process of jury deliberation. Several studies were criticized because the participants were individuals randomly selected from a segment of the population at large and not the population eligible for jury duty. The majority also more generally noted that none of the studies was able to predict the extent to which the presence of one or more "Witherspoon-excludables" on the guilt phase jury would have altered the outcome of the guilty determination. Although it is true that none of the studies compared post-deliberation groups verdicts, evidence concerning statistical evidence projecting the effect of "conviction-prone" jurors was available to the court.

The majority Court opinion concluded that even if it were assumed that the studies were both methodologically valid and adequate to establish that death qualification produces conviction-prone juries, the Constitution does not prohibit the States from death qualifying juries. In contrast, the dissenting opinion considered the majority's disregard of the empirical evidence to flagrantly misconstrue established Sixth and Fourteenth amendment principles. Although judges, not social scientists, determine the nature of the empirical issues that are decisive of the larger constitutional questions, consideration of empirical research when it is relevant is crucial to an informed decision.

Question:

1. Do you think the Supreme Court should have relied on the social science evidence? Why or why not?

Afterword

The American Psychological Association has issued a resolution that calls upon each jurisdiction in the United States that imposes capital punishment not to carry out the death penalty until the jurisdiction implements policies and procedures that can be shown through psychological and other social science research to ameliorate a number of noted deficiencies. One of the deficiencies mentioned in the resolution is that the process of qualifying jurors for service on death penalty cases shows that jurors who survive the qualification process ("death-qualified jurors") are more conviction-prone than jurors who have reservations about the death penalty and are therefore disqualified from service. You can read the entire resolution at http://www.apa.org/pi/deathpenalty.html.

Try It Yourself

Caffeine and Patriotism: Demonstrating the Function of Attitudes

Sharon Shavitt (1990) demonstrated that attitudes toward particular objects often fulfill the same function for most people. Her research suggests, for example, your attitude toward coffee is most likely based on your previous positive or negative experiences with it. If, in the past, you have become too jittery to work after drinking coffee, you may have a negative attitude towards it. However, if it has helped you stay awake to fulfill an important assignment without too many negative side effects, you may have a positive attitude. These types of attitudes fulfill the object appraisal function of attitudes.

Other attitudes you might hold, however, tell other people about what sort of values you have and the identity you wish to project; these are value-expressive attitudes. For example, your attitude toward perfume most likely fulfills the value-expressive function. You may like a particular brand of perfume because you identify with the particular model who endorses it.

Still other attitudes might serve both functions. For example, your attitude towards a particular brand of car is based partially on the transportation it will provide you, but also on what it signifies about your identify. Even coffee might serve both functions. Do you think differently about people who consume Starbuck's versus Maxwell House?

Below we explain how you can conduct a simplified version of Sharon Shavitt's study. Using copies of the following form: First, ask five of your friends to write down their attitudes toward coffee (i.e., is it positive or a negative? Do they like it or not?). Then ask them to write a brief explanation of why they feel that way. Next, ask them to write down their attitude toward the Canadian flag, and again ask them to explain why they feel that way about the flag.

Questions:

1. Look at your friends' responses and see if you can classify their explanations into one of the two attitude function categories. Do you see the same sort of pattern that Sharon Shavitt found in her research? If her theory is correct, you would expect your friends write down positive and negative things about coffee, as well as the rewards (such as feelings of alertness) and punishment (such as a bad case of the jitters) they have experienced after drinking coffee. On the other hand, when your friends are explaining their attitudes towards the Canadian flag, you might expect them to write about how their own values and identity are reflected in what the flag represents.

2. Can you think of any other targets or objects that would illustrate the two functions of attitudes?

3. Can you think of attitude targets that might serve both the object appraisal and value expressive functions?

Attitudes Toward Coffee and the Canadian Flag

What is your attitude toward **coffee**? For example, is positive or negative? Do you like or dislike coffee?

Explain why you feel this way.

What is your attitude toward the **Canadian flag**? For example, is it positive or negative? Do you like or dislike the flag?

Explain why you feel this way.

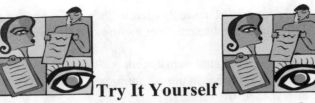# Try It Yourself
Measuring Attitudes Using a Single-Item Scale and a Likert Scale

In this exercise, you will construct two attitude scales—a single-item self-rating scale and a Likert scale—to measure your classmates' attitudes on an important topic.

Below we explain step-by-step how to develop, administer, and score both scales. But first you should select an attitude topic for which you will be developing the scales. Some examples are:

Death penalty
Abortion
Marriage between same-sex couples
Organized religion
Fast food
Seperatist movement in Quebec
Smoking
War on terrorism
Public education
Same-sex secondary schools

Developing your Scales

Single-item self-rating scale. One of the scales you will use should be a **single-item self-rating scale**. An example of such a scale is:

Circle a number between 1 and 7 to indicate whether your attitude toward abortion is negative or positive, or somewhere in between.

Negative	1	2	3	4	5	6	7	Positive

Develop your single-item self-rating scale and record it on the page titled "Attitudes towards _____" that follows.

Likert scale. Developing the Likert scale is much more complex. To develop this scale, follow these steps:[1]

1. First, generate statements each of which expresses a clear (favourable or unfavourable attitude) toward your chosen target. If you were actually constructing a scale to be used in research, you should come up with about 100 statements. For the purposes of this exercise, 20 such statements will suffice. Write them on the Likert Scale Development sheet that follows.

---

[1] This method is fundamentally the same as that described by Trochim, William M. *The Research Methods Knowledge Base,* 2nd Edition. Internet WWW page, at http://www.socialresearchmethods.net/kb/ (version current as of 01/16/2005). However, it has been simplified for the purposes of this exercise.

The statements should be declarative statements (that is, they should not in the form of a question) with which people can either agree or disagree. For example, statements about the death penalty could include:

>The death penalty is cruel and unusual punishment.
>Society should never commit murder to punish murder.
>Murderers deserve to lose their own life.
>The death penalty is necessary to deter dangerous criminals.

The first two statements express an anti-death penalty attitude whereas the second two express a pro-death penalty attitude.

2. The next step is to determine how well the statements you generated actually reflect clear positive and negative attitudes. Make four copies of the Likert Scale Development sheet on which you wrote your 20 statements. Ask four friends to rate each statement according to how negative or positive the statement is toward your chosen target, using the scale on the sheet. At this point, your friends are not reporting their own attitudes toward the death penalty, but are merely saying whether each statement reflects a negative or positive sentiment toward the death penalty.

   If you were actually constructing a scale to be used in research, you would ask many more people (e.g., 50) to complete this step.

3. The third step is to select the statements to include in your final scale. If you were actually constructing a scale to be used in research, this step would involve statistical analyses that are not being taught in social psychology class.

   For the purpose of this exercise, we'll take a simplified approach. For each statement, average the ratings of your four friends from Step 2. For example, suppose your four friends rated the statements about the death penalty as shown in the following table. The average rating is in the last column. The closer the average is to "1", the more the statement indicates a negative attitude toward the death penalty, and the closer the average is to "5" the more the statement indicates a positive attitude toward the death penalty.

	Friend 1	Friend 2	Friend 3	Friend 4	Average
1. The death penalty is cruel and unusual punishment.	1	1	1	1	1
2. Society should never commit murder to punish murder.	1	2	2	3	2
3. Murderers deserve to lose their own life.	5	4	5	3	4.2
4. The death penalty is necessary to deter dangerous criminals.	5	5	5	5	5

For your final scale, select the five statements with averages closest to "1" and the five statements with averages closest to "5." Record these ten statements on the page titled, "Likert Scale to Measure Attitudes Towards _____," intermixing statements that are positive and statements that are negative toward the your chosen target.

Using Your Scales

First, ask three to five friends to complete the **single-item self-rating scale** and the Likert Scale that you have developed. Then, enter their scores on the Summary Results Table below. Their score on the single-item self-rating scale is simply the number they circled.

To calculate their score on the Likert scale, you need to first reverse-score the statements that are negative toward the target. For example, suppose your friends responded to the two negative statements toward the death penalty as follows.

	Friend 1	Friend 2	Friend 3	Friend 4	Average
1. The death penalty is cruel and unusual punishment.	1	1	1	1	1
2. Society should never commit murder to punish murder.	1	2	2	3	2

Their reverse scores for these items would be calculated by subtracting their responses from 6, and would be:

	Friend 1	Friend 2	Friend 3	Friend 4	Average
1. The death penalty is cruel and unusual punishment.	5	5	5	5	5
2. Society should never commit murder to punish murder.	5	4	4	3	4

Once you have reversed scored the negative statements, sum the responses to all statements. The higher the total score, the more positive the attitude.

Summary Results Table

	Score on the Likert Scale	Score on the Single-Item Self-Rating Scale
Friend 1:		
Friend 2:		
Friend 3:		
Friend 4:		
Friend 5:		

Questions:

1. Explain briefly how you went about constructing your attitudes scales.

2. What are the shortcomings of your scales and how might they be improved?

3. Did the scores of your friends on the Likert scale correspond to their scores on the single-item, self-rating scale? Did each of them score either low, high, or in the middle of both scales? If not, what might explain the different results obtained between the two scales?

4. What are the shortcomings of using verbal report scales to measure attitudes?

Attitudes towards _____
Single-Item Self-Rating Scale

Likert Scale Development (Step #1)

Instructions: Circle a number to indicate whether each of the following statements is a negative statement or a positive statement towards _____

Statement	Negative toward the target				Positive toward target
1.	1	2	3	4	5
2.	1	2	3	4	5
3.	1	2	3	4	5
4.	1	2	3	4	5
5.	1	2	3	4	5
6.	1	2	3	4	5
7.	1	2	3	4	5
8.	1	2	3	4	5
9.	1	2	3	4	5
10.	1	2	3	4	5
11.	1	2	3	4	5
12.	1	2	3	4	5
13.	1	2	3	4	5
14.	1	2	3	4	5
15.	1	2	3	4	5
16.	1	2	3	4	5
17.	1	2	3	4	5
18.	1	2	3	4	5
19.	1	2	3	4	5
20.	1	2	3	4	5

Likert Scale to Measure Attitudes
Towards _____ (Step #3)

Instructions: Indicate the extent to which you disagree or agree each of the following statements by circling a number between 1 and 5.

Statement	Strongly Disagree				Strongly agree
1.	1	2	3	4	5
2.	1	2	3	4	5
3.	1	2	3	4	5
4.	1	2	3	4	5
5.	1	2	3	4	5
6.	1	2	3	4	5
7.	1	2	3	4	5
8.	1	2	3	4	5
9.	1	2	3	4	5
10.	1	2	3	4	5

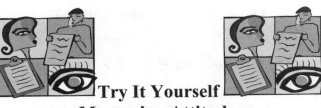

Try It Yourself
Measuring Attitudes
Do Semantic Differentials Measure Affect or Cognition?

Steven Breckler and other social psychologists have identified three elements of attitudes: affect, cognition, and past behaviour. Whether a person evaluates a target positively or negatively depends on (1) how the object makes the person feel (affect), (2) the person's beliefs about the object (cognition), and (3) the person's previous actions toward the object (past behaviour).

For some attitude targets, a person's feelings, beliefs, and past behaviour are consistent with one another—all are either positive or negative. For example, you may believe that a community service project has positive consequences and the project may make you feel good. For other attitude objects, your feelings, beliefs, and past behaviour are in conflict. For example, a person may have positive beliefs about snakes (e.g., they eat insects) but negative affect towards them. These attitudes are called ambivalent attitudes.

Attitudes measured on semantic differential scales have traditionally been interpreted as reflecting the affective component of attitude. It may, however, be just as appropriate to regard these scales as measures of the cognitive or belief component of attitude. This exercise will demonstrate that semantic differential scales can be used to (1) measure either the affective or cognitive component of attitude depending on how you ask the question, (2) help identify which attitudes depend mostly on people's feelings (i.e., affect) and which depend mostly on people's knowledge and beliefs (i.e., cognitions), and (3) identify ambivalent attitudes.

On the following pages, we provide three sets of scales. The first set of scales (Set #1) is made of semantic differential scales intended to measure people's knowledge and beliefs about five targets. Set #2 is also made up of semantic differential scales, but this time, they are intended to measure people's affect about the targets. Notice that the two sets of scales are identical except in the instructions that are provided and the stem to be completed ("Attitude object is" versus "attitude object makes me feel"). Set #3 is intended to measure global attitudes toward the targets.

Directions:

- Ask three to five friends to complete each set of scales.

- Using the Set #1 scales, calculate a score to represent each person's beliefs about each target. To do this, sum the numbers each person circled for the target on the scales in Set #1 and divide by the number of ratings that were made. For example, suppose a person circled the bolded numbers on the scales associated with nuclear weapons. The score for his or her beliefs about nuclear weapons would be: $(2 + 2 + 1 + 3)/4$ or 2. Record these numbers on the Summary Results Table.

Nuclear Weapons are:

Bad	1	2	3	4	5	6	7	Good
Foolish	1	2	3	4	5	6	7	Wise
Useless	1	2	3	4	5	6	7	Useful
Unsafe	1	2	3	4	5	6	7	Safe

- Using the Set #2 scales, calculate a score to represent each person's affect towards each target. This is done as described above using the person's response to the scales in Set 2. Record these numbers on the summary results sheet.

- Using the Set #3 scales, record on the summary results sheet each person's global attitudes toward the targets.

Questions:

Now, examine the summary results sheet and answer the following questions.

1. For any given target, are your friends' belief scores different from their affect scores? If so, you've shown that semantic differential scales can measure beliefs or affect depending on how you ask the question.

2. For which targets, if any, are your friends' belief scores more like their global attitude scores than are their affect scores? Attitude towards these targets may depend mostly on people's knowledge and beliefs. For which targets, if any, are your friends' affect scores more like their global attitude scores than are their belief scores? Attitude towards these targets may depend mostly on people's affect.

3. For which targets do your friends have ambivalent attitudes or in other words, for which targets are their beliefs and affect fairly different? For which targets, if any, are your friends' beliefs and affect relatively the same?

Summary Results Table

	Belief Score Set 1	Affect Score Set 2	Global Attitude Set 3
Blood Donation			
Friend 1:			
Friend 2:			
Friend 3:			
Friend 4:			
Friend 5:			
Legalized Abortion			
Friend 1:			
Friend 2:			
Friend 3:			
Friend 4:			
Friend 5:			
Computers			
Friend 1:			
Friend 2:			
Friend 3:			
Friend 4:			
Friend 5:			
Nuclear Weapons			
Friend 1:			
Friend 2:			
Friend 3:			
Friend 4:			
Friend 5:			
Snakes			
Friend 1:			
Friend 2:			
Friend 3:			
Friend 4:			
Friend 5:			

Set #1
Instructions: Think about the following topics, and then circle a number on each scale to indicate your beliefs about them.

Blood Donation is:

Bad	1	2	3	4	5	6	7	Good
Foolish	1	2	3	4	5	6	7	Wise
Unimportant	1	2	3	4	5	6	7	Important
Selfish	1	2	3	4	5	6	7	Unselfish
Unsafe	1	2	3	4	5	6	7	Safe
Worthless	1	2	3	4	5	6	7	Valuable

Legalized Abortion is:

Bad	1	2	3	4	5	6	7	Good
Foolish	1	2	3	4	5	6	7	Wise
Cruel	1	2	3	4	5	6	7	Kind
Selfish	1	2	3	4	5	6	7	Unselfish

Computers are:

Bad	1	2	3	4	5	6	7	Good
Foolish	1	2	3	4	5	6	7	Wise
Useless	1	2	3	4	5	6	7	Useful
Unimportant	1	2	3	4	5	6	7	Important

Nuclear Weapons are:

Bad	1	2	3	4	5	6	7	Good
Foolish	1	2	3	4	5	6	7	Wise
Useless	1	2	3	4	5	6	7	Useful
Safe	1	2	3	4	5	6	7	Unsafe

Snakes are:

Bad	1	2	3	4	5	6	7	Good
Safe	1	2	3	4	5	6	7	Unsafe

Set #2

Instructions: For each attitude target, circle a number on each of the corresponding scales to indicate how the target makes you feel.

Blood Donation makes me feel:

Bad	1	2	3	4	5	6	7	Good
Foolish	1	2	3	4	5	6	7	Wise
Unimportant	1	2	3	4	5	6	7	Important
Selfish	1	2	3	4	5	6	7	Unselfish
Unsafe	1	2	3	4	5	6	7	Safe
Worthless	1	2	3	4	5	6	7	Valuable

Legalized Abortion makes me feel:

Bad	1	2	3	4	5	6	7	Good
Foolish	1	2	3	4	5	6	7	Wise
Cruel	1	2	3	4	5	6	7	Kind
Selfish	1	2	3	4	5	6	7	Unselfish

Computers make me feel:

Bad	1	2	3	4	5	6	7	Good
Foolish	1	2	3	4	5	6	7	Wise
Useless	1	2	3	4	5	6	7	Useful
Unimportant	1	2	3	4	5	6	7	Important

Nuclear Weapons make me feel:

Bad	1	2	3	4	5	6	7	Good
Foolish	1	2	3	4	5	6	7	Wise
Useless	1	2	3	4	5	6	7	Useful
Safe	1	2	3	4	5	6	7	Unsafe

Snakes make me feel:

Bad	1	2	3	4	5	6	7	Good
Safe	1	2	3	4	5	6	7	Unsafe

Set #3
Instructions. Rate your attitude toward each of the following targets by circling a number on the scale.

My attitude toward **blood donation** is:

Negative	1	2	3	4	5	6	7	Positive

My attitude toward **legalized abortion** is:

Negative	1	2	3	4	5	6	7	Positive

My attitude toward **computers** is:

Negative	1	2	3	4	5	6	7	Positive

My attitude toward **nuclear weapons** is:

Negative	1	2	3	4	5	6	7	Positive

My attitude toward snakes is:

Negative	1	2	3	4	5	6	7	Positive

On the Web
Implicit Intergroup Bias and the Implicit Association Test

A great deal of social psychology research has been devoted to the study of stereotypes, and you learned about some of that research in Chapter 6 of your textbook (Attitudes and Social Behaviour) and will learn more in Chapter 9 (Stereotypes, Prejudice, and Discrimination). This research tells us that it's possible for an individual to act in a biased or prejudiced way without being aware of it. The notion that knowledge of stereotypes can influence judgments without the person's awareness has been termed **implicit intergroup bias**. It is *implicit* because it is outside of conscious awareness and control—it is not deliberate and is unrecognized by the person. It is *intergroup bias* because it reflects distorted judgments about a group. Implicit intergroup bias has been demonstrated for several kinds of stereotypes, including racial, gender, and age stereotypes. Do you think you exhibit implicit intergroup bias?

You can test your implicit biases using a tool called the Implicit Association Test, or IAT. The IAT is based on the assumption that people automatically associate concepts, and that the strength of those associations can be measured. For example, most people are more likely to associate the concept of "flower" with "good" than they would be to associate the concept of "flower" with "bad." On the other hand, most people are more likely to associate the concept of "maggot" with "bad" than they would "maggot" and "good."

The IAT is completed on the computer. You are asked to categorize stimuli (generally words or pictures) using two keys of a computer keyboard. The idea is that when strongly associated concepts are on the same key (such as flower and good), you will respond faster than when weakly associated concepts (such as flower and bad) are paired on the same key. The difference in speed between the two key configurations is a measure of implicit preference.

Think about how this would work. When you see the word "flower" or the word "good" appear on the computer screen, you would press the "a" key; when you see the word "maggot" or the word "bad" appear on the screen, your would press the "5" key. You would be instructed to do this as quickly as possible—as soon as the words appear. It should be pretty easy, because the word pairs seem to go together.

But if you switch the pairings around so that you press the "a" key when you see the word "good" or when you see the word "maggot"; and press the "5" key when you see the word "bad" or the word "flower," it would become much harder. Most people find the second task more difficult because the pairs don't seem to go together. "Maggot" and "good" don't go together as naturally as "maggot" and "bad," so it takes a bit longer to think about which key to press.

The time it takes you to press the computer key after the word appears on the screen can be measured to the millisecond on the computer. As you read in Chapter 2, response time has become an increasingly popular form of measurement in social psychology. The computer records exactly how much time elapsed between when the word appears on the screen and when you press either the "a" or the "5" key. For example, it might take you 50 milliseconds to press the "a" key when you see the word "good" and 40 milliseconds to press the "a" key when you see the word "flower," for an average response time of 45 milliseconds. When the pairs are changed, however, it may take you 100 milliseconds to press the "a" key for the word "good" but 500 milliseconds to press the "a" key for the word "maggot," for an average response time of 300 milliseconds. Because the pairs don't naturally go together in your mind, it will take you longer to make that association, and that hesitation will be reflected in the response time. This hesitation is known as response competition—you naturally want to pair good and flower on one key, and bad and maggot on one key, and having to mix them up produces interference. In other words, the response you are instructed to make (good and maggot) is competing with the response you naturally want to make (good and flower).

Because you are faster at pairing "good" and "flower" than you are at pairing "good" and "maggot," we can conclude that good and flower are concepts that are associated in your mind, whereas good and maggot are not. This is basic idea of the IAT—that we can figure out what things go together (or are associated) in people's minds and what things don't by looking at what pairs of words slow people down in the key-pressing task. Now that you know how it works, you can visit the IAT website at https://implicit.harvard.edu/implicit to try it yourself!

Social Psychology Online Lab
Evaluative Conditioning

The online lab, Word Evaluation, demonstrates how a neutral stimulus (in this case, a nonword) comes to be evaluated positively or negatively by being incidentally associated with positive or negative things. This type of conditioning—evaluative conditioning—is at the basis of many of our attitudes. For example, you may dislike a restaurant not because you dislike its food, but because you had a serious disagreement with a friend there. The disagreement with your friend is responsible for your negative attitude toward the restaurant, even though it is only incidentally associated with it. Try the online lab to get a better understanding of how evaluative conditioning works.

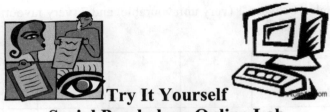

Try It Yourself
Social Psychology Online Lab
What's in a Name? Demonstrate the Mere Exposure Effect

When you were reading about people's tendency to prefer the letters in their own name, did you feel that was true for you? You can test the mere exposure effect on your friends by asking them to rate how favourably they feel about the different letters in the alphabet using the Likert-type scale on the next page. (You may want to reproduce this page to use with several friends.) After your friends have rated every letter of the alphabet, look at their ratings, and answer the following questions.

Questions:

1. Do the letters in their names get higher scores than other letters?

2. Are the first letters of their first and last names more highly ranked than other letters in their names?

The **online lab**, "Shape Judgment," also contains an exercise to demonstrate the mere exposure effect. That exercise uses a set of novel stimuli (i.e., geographical shapes). The stimuli are displayed repeatedly and the participant is asked to judge in which direction the shape is pointed, and at the end of the lab, to rate their liking for each shape.

Instructions: Circle a number between 1 (very unfavourable) and 7 (very favourable) to rate how you feel about each letter in the alphabet.

	1 Very unfavourable	2	3	4	5	6	7 Very favourable
A	1	2	3	4	5	6	7
B	1	2	3	4	5	6	7
C	1	2	3	4	5	6	7
D	1	2	3	4	5	6	7
E	1	2	3	4	5	6	7
F	1	2	3	4	5	6	7
G	1	2	3	4	5	6	7
H	1	2	3	4	5	6	7
I	1	2	3	4	5	6	7
J	1	2	3	4	5	6	7
K	1	2	3	4	5	6	7
L	1	2	3	4	5	6	7
M	1	2	3	4	5	6	7
N	1	2	3	4	5	6	7
O	1	2	3	4	5	6	7
P	1	2	3	4	5	6	7
Q	1	2	3	4	5	6	7
R	1	2	3	4	5	6	7
S	1	2	3	4	5	6	7
T	1	2	3	4	5	6	7
U	1	2	3	4	5	6	7
V	1	2	3	4	5	6	7
W	1	2	3	4	5	6	7
X	1	2	3	4	5	6	7
Y	1	2	3	4	5	6	7
Z	1	2	3	4	5	6	7

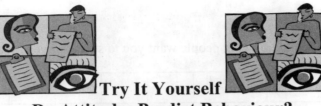

Try It Yourself
Do Attitudes Predict Behaviour?
The Theory of Reasoned Action

The theory of reasoned action is based on the idea that people's behaviour is rational and follows from their intentions. According to the theory, your intention to behave in a certain way depends on your attitudes toward the behaviour (based on your beliefs about the consequences of that behaviour) and on the social norms concerning the behaviour. The textbook gave an example about flossing one's teeth every day: attitudes, beliefs, subjective norms, and behavioural intentions toward daily flossing were measured, and the results supported the theory of reasoned action.

The theory of reasoned action has four basic components: (1) attitudes, (2) beliefs, (3) subjective norms, and (4) behavioural intentions. Below we show you how to measure each component for a different attitude target: studying for your social psychology class.

Once you have read through the following example, think of another attitude target (such as waking up early, drinking less alcohol, exercising more, or becoming a vegetarian), and develop scales to show how you would measure each component.

Theory of Reasoned Action
Studying for Social Psychology

(1) Attitudes
Circle a number of each of the following scales to indicate your attitude toward "studying for social psychology."

Bad	1	2	3	4	5	6	7	Good
Boring	1	2	3	4	5	6	7	Interesting
Useless	1	2	3	4	5	6	7	Useful
Harmful	1	2	3	4	5	6	7	Beneficial
Unpleasant	1	2	3	4	5	6	7	Pleasant
Worthless	1	2	3	4	5	6	7	Valuable

(2) Beliefs
Do you think that studying for your social psychology class will:

	Definitely NO						Definitely YES
Help you do well on upcoming tests	1	2	3	4	5	6	7
Allow you to participate in class more often	1	2	3	4	5	6	7
Prevent you from getting a good night's sleep	1	2	3	4	5	6	7
Boost your overall grade in the class	1	2	3	4	5	6	7
Make you feel good about yourself	1	2	3	4	5	6	7
Interfere with your social life	1	2	3	4	5	6	7
Help you understand difficult concepts	1	2	3	4	5	6	7

(3) Subjective Norms

To what extent do you think the following people want you to study for your social psychology class?

	Not at all						Very Much
Parents	1	2	3	4	5	6	7
Roommate	1	2	3	4	5	6	7
Friends	1	2	3	4	5	6	7
Psychology Professor	1	2	3	4	5	6	7

How motivated are you to do what the following people want you to do?

	Not at all motivated						Very Motivated
Parents	1	2	3	4	5	6	7
Roommate	1	2	3	4	5	6	7
Friends	1	2	3	4	5	6	7
Psychology Professor	1	2	3	4	5	6	7

(4) Behavioural Intentions

How likely is it that you will study for your social psychology at least three times a week over the next 2–4 weeks?

Not at all likely	1	2	3	4	5	6	7	Very likely

Behaviour

Over the next 2–4 weeks, record the amount of time (in hours and minutes) that you spend studying social psychology each day.

Developing Your Own Scales

Now, for the attitude target you have selected, develop scales to measure each component of the Theory of Reasoned Action (i.e., attitudes, beliefs, subjective norms, and behavioural intentions) and behaviour.

Topic: _____

Scale(s) to Measure Attitudes

Scales to Measure Beliefs

Scale(s) to Measure Subjective Norms

Scales to Measure Behavioural Intentions

Method to Measure Behaviour

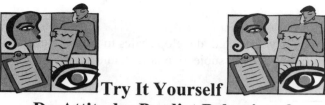

Try It Yourself
Do Attitudes Predict Behaviour?
Demonstrating the Compatibility Principle

Many early studies indicated that attitudes do not accurately predict behaviour. However, some of those findings may be due to the ways in which attitudes were measured—a broad attitude was being used to predict a specific behaviour. As the compatibility principle states, the level of specificity of the attitude and the behaviour must match. In other words, specific attitudes predict specific domains of behaviour, and general attitudes predict general behaviour measures. For example, a person's general attitude towards making donations to charity may not predict whether he or she donates to the United Way, but the person's general attitude may predict whether he or she makes a donation to any charity at all.

You can see the importance of the compatibility principle for yourself with a simple demonstration similar to the one described in the book. First, ask five friends to report their attitudes toward watching televised hockey games on a scale from 1 to 9 (with 1 representing "Extremely Unfavourable" and 10 representing "Extremely Favourable"). Then, ask them to report, on the same scale, their attitudes toward several related targets: professional sports, hockey, watching television, and watching sports on television. You can make copies of the "Rate Your Attitudes" sheet that follows to do this.

Examine their ratings and answer the following questions.

Questions:

1. Do you find that your friends' attitude toward watching hockey on television is more similar to their attitude toward professional sports or toward the more related target, hockey?

2. Do you find that their attitude toward watching hockey on television is more similar to their attitude toward watching television or toward the more related target, watching sports on television?

3. Does the compatibility principle hold true with these attitude targets?

4. Can you think of sets of other attitude targets that might demonstrate the compatibility principle? Post your suggestions on the website, and see what your fellow students have come up with.

Rate Your Attitudes

Rate your attitude toward **watching televised hockey games** by circling a number on the following scale:

Very unfavourable	1	2	3	4	5	6	7	8	9	Very favourable

Now, rate your attitude toward the following other things, again by circling a number on the scale.

Professional sports

Very unfavourable	1	2	3	4	5	6	7	8	9	Very favourable

Hockey

Very unfavourable	1	2	3	4	5	6	7	8	9	Very favourable

Watching television

Very unfavourable	1	2	3	4	5	6	7	8	9	Very favourable

Watching sports on television

Very unfavourable	1	2	3	4	5	6	7	8	9	Very favourable

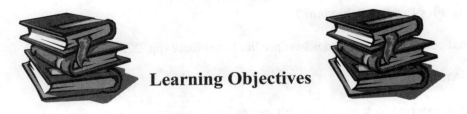

Learning Objectives

What Are Attitudes?

1. How do social psychologists define attitudes? How does that definition differ from the lay definition of an attitude? (p. 191)

2. What are the three components that determine how a person evaluates (either positively or negatively) a target? Describe each in regard to your attitude towards cockroaches? (pp. 191–193)

3. Explain the role of current attitudes with regard to both past and future behaviour. (pp. 192–193)

4. Describe the difference between implicit and explicit attitudes, and give an example of how each type can be measured. (p. 194)

Why Do We Evaluate?

5. Identify the two primary functions that attitudes serve. (pp. 195–198)

Measuring Attitudes

6. Briefly describe four self-report measures used to measure attitudes. What are the benefits and drawbacks of each? (pp. 198–202)

7. Describe three nonverbal methods of measuring attitudes. What are the benefits and drawbacks of each? (pp. 202–204)

How Do Attitudes Form?

8. What are the four potential sources of attitudes? Give an example of each. (pp. 205–211)

9. Briefly explain the roles of evaluative conditioning, mere exposure, alcohol myopia, and heritability in attitude formation and/or expression. (pp. 205–214)

Parents, Peers, and Attitudes

10. Other people can shape our attitudes. What are the means by which your parents can influence your attitudes? The means by which your friends can influence your attitudes? (pp. 214–217)

How Do Attitudes Affect Behaviour?

11. Explain the two principle mechanisms by which attitudes can influence behaviour. In which domains does a rational choice mechanism apply to how attitudes can predict behaviour? In which domains does the selective perception mechanism best apply? (pp. 218–225)

When Do Attitudes Predict Behaviour?

12. Under what conditions do attitudes best predict behaviour? (pp. 225–231)

Culture and Attitudes

13. Explain how external factors such as culture can influence attitude formation. (pp. 231–233)

Test Your Knowledge

Multiple Choice Questions

1. According to social psychologists, what is the best definition of an attitude?
   A. a general approach to life
   B. an individual's evaluation of a target
   C. a system of categorizing objects
   D. a theory of social cognition

2. Which of the following is not a commonly recognized component of an attitude?
   A. affect
   B. cognition
   C. intuition
   D. past behaviour

3. An implicit attitude is one that
   A. can occur without your awareness.
   B. can be consciously reported.
   C. is based on uniformly negative elements.
   D. is based on uniformly positive elements.

4. You've been asked to design an advertising campaign for a brand of coffee using the results of Sharon Shavitt's research on the function of attitudes. How should you structure your ad to be most effective?
   A. focus on glamorous movie stars who drink that coffee brand
   B. focus on the coffee's limited quantity
   C. focus on the coffee's freshness and pleasing aroma
   D. focus on the coffee's elite, sophisticated appeal

5. As a participant in a study about attitudes toward abortion, you are given several dimensions, such as "support-oppose" and "good-bad," and asked to indicate where you fall on each dimension by marking an X on a scale. This method for measuring attitudes is an example of a(n)
   A. Likert-type scale.
   B. opinion survey.
   C. semantic differential scale.
   D. behavioural measure.

6. In a related study about attitudes toward abortion, you are asked to respond either "yes" or "no" to several questions, such as "Do you think that women deserve the right to choose?"and "Do you think that abortion is murder?" You are asked to indicate which statements you agree with. This method for measuring attitudes is an example of a(n)
   A. Likert-type scale.
   B. opinion survey.
   C. semantic differential scale.
   D. behavioural measure.

7. In one final study about attitudes toward abortion, you are asked to indicate how strongly you agree or disagree with a series of statements about abortion by circling "disagree strongly," "disagree," "undecided," "agree," or "agree strongly." This method for measuring attitudes is an example of a(n)
   A. Likert-type scale.
   B. opinion survey.
   C. semantic differential scale.
   D. behavioural measure.

8. Which of the following is *not* a commonly recognized problem with self-report measures of attitudes?
   A. Respondents don't always report their attitudes honestly.
   B. Respondents don't always know what their attitudes are.
   C. They can't easily measure ambivalent attitudes.
   D. They are difficult for researchers to construct.

9. Which of the following methods would be best for providing an accurate picture of a person's attitude towards female leaders?
   A. a self-report measure such as an opinion survey
   B. an implicit measure such as the Implicit Association Test
   C. a nonverbal measure such as behavioural observation
   D. a physiological measure such as facial electromyography

10. Rebecca and her roommate Ava go shopping for posters to decorate their residence room. Ava insists on buying one that Rebecca doesn't like. After weeks of looking at the poster on the wall, however, Rebecca becomes quite attached to it, and even begins to like it. Rebecca's response is an example of
    A. evaluative conditioning.
    B. self-perception.
    C. socialization.
    D. mere exposure.

11. Which of the following most accurately summarizes the results of the MacDonald, Zanna, and Fong studies on alcohol myopia and willingness to engage in unprotected sex?
    A. Intoxicated participants were more willing to engage in unprotected sex than sober participants were.
    B. Sober participants were more willing to engage in unprotected sex than intoxicated participants were.
    C. Both sober and intoxicated participants were unwilling to engage in unprotected sex.
    D. Both sober and intoxicated participants were willing to engage in unprotected sex.

12. Recent research with twins suggests that certain attitudes can be inherited. Which of the following attitudes yield the highest genetic influence?
    A. Attitudes toward capitalism.
    B. Attitudes toward reading.
    C. Attitudes toward alcohol.
    D. Attitudes toward philanthropy.

13. Theodore Newcomb's (1943) study of Bennington College students demonstrates the influence of
    A. restrictive parenting.
    B. rational choice.
    C. ridicule.
    D. reference groups.

14. In Fishbein and Ajzen's theory of reasoned action, behavioural intentions are caused by
    A. behavioural evaluations only.
    B. subjective norms only.
    C. attitudes only.
    D. both subjective norms and attitudes.

15. In the study by Lord, Ross, and Lepper (1979) in which students were given opposing articles about the effectiveness of the death penalty, the researchers found that students who were initially in favour of the death penalty
    A. became more in favour of the death penalty.
    B. became moderately less in favour of the death penalty.
    C. became significantly less in favour of the death penalty.
    D. showed no change in their attitude toward the death penalty.

16. Which of the following attitude qualities is most likely to predict behaviour?
    A. Moderation
    B. Importance
    C. Indirect experience
    D. Low accessibility

17. How do attitudes predict behaviour?
    A. Broad, general attitudes predict specific behaviours.
    B. Specific attitudes predict broad categories of behaviour.
    C. Broad, general attitudes predict broad categories of behaviour.
    D. Specific attitudes predict both broad categories of behaviour and specific behaviours.

18. All of the following have been shown to be related to attitude-inconsistent behaviour except
    A. external threat.
    B. lack of alternatives.
    C. biological needs or addictions.
    D. lack of time.
    E. none of the above

Sentence Completion

1. The three components of attitude are _affect_, _behaviour_ and _cognition_.

2. People are conscious of their _explicit_ attitudes; however, their _implicit_ attitudes are automatic responses that can occur without their awareness.

3. I like coffee because it wakes me up in the morning and keeps me awake while I am studying. The function of my attitude toward coffee is _object_ _appraisal_

4. Advertisements for products are more successful when they are consistent with the _function_ fulfilled by the targeted attitude.

5. Behavioural, physiological, and implicit measures are better than traditional self-report measures in assessing a person's _implicit_ attitudes.

6. Paul dislikes Akbar, a one-time favourite Indian restaurant, because he and his fiancée ended their engagement there. This is an example of _evaluative conditioning_.

7. According to the _mere exposure effect_, the more often a person is exposed to something, the more he or she tends to like it.

8. In the presence of Daniel, Jim ridiculed a fellow student for wearing shorts that were too short. Daniel subsequently made sure he never wore too-short shorts. Daniel was a victim of _jeer pressure_.

9. According to the theory of reasoned action, behavioural intentions depend on _attitudes_ and _subjective norms_.

10. During the last Federal election, the Liberals complained that the popular press was biased against the Liberal candidate and the Conservatives complained that the popular press was against their candidate. This demonstrates the _hostile media phenomenon_.

Matching I – Key Terms

_____ 1.	attitude	A. evaluations of targets that include both positive and negative elements
_____ 2.	ambivalent attitudes	B. a function of attitudes by which attitudes can communicate individuals' identity and beliefs
_____ 3.	explicit attitudes	C. broad, abstract standards or goals that people consider to be important guiding principles in their life
_____ 4.	implicit attitudes	
_____ 5.	object-appraisal function	D. a procedure for measuring muscle contractions in the face that may be sensitive to positive versus negative responses to a stimulus
_____ 6.	values	E. a process by which objects come to evoke positive or negative affect simply by their association with affect-inducing events
_____ 7.	value-expressive function	
_____ 8.	Likert-type scale	F. a reaction time procedure that provides a measure of implicit attitudes. Participants sort targets into a "good" category or a "bad" category, and the speed at which the sorting is completed is taken as a measurement of one's implicit attitude toward the object
_____ 9.	semantic differential scale	
_____ 10.	facial electromyography (facial EMG)	
_____ 11.	Implicit Association Test (IAT)	G. an individual's evaluation of a target along a good-bad dimension
_____ 12.	evaluative conditioning	H. a function of attitudes by which attitudes provide rapid evaluative judgments of targets, which facilitate approach or avoidance
		I. automatic evaluative responses to a target, which may occur without awareness
		J. an attitude measurement technique that requires respondents to indicate the extent of their agreement or disagreement with several statements on an issue
		K. evaluations that people can report consciously
		L. an attitude measurement technique that requires respondents to rate a target on several evaluative dimensions (such as good-bad and favourable-unfavourable)

Matching II – Key Terms

_____	13.	mere exposure effect
_C_	15.	socialization
_____	16.	reference group
_____	17.	jeer pressure
_A_	18.	theory of reasoned action
_E_	19.	behavioural intention
_____	20.	subjective norm
_B_	21.	IMB model of AIDS-preventive behaviour
_____	22.	hostile media phenomenon
_D_	23.	compatibility principle
_____	24.	culture
_____	25.	power distance

A. a model of behaviour that views humans as rational decision-makers who behave on the basis of logical beliefs

B. a theory postulating that information, motivation, and behavioural skills guide individuals' protective actions in the sexual domain

C. the process by which infants are molded into acceptable members of their society

D. a theory stating that a measure of attitudes will correlate highly with a measure of behaviour only when the two measures are matched in terms of being general/broad or specific/narrow

E. an individual's plan to perform or not perform an action

F. the tendency for people who feel strongly about an issue to believe that the media coverage of the issue is biased against their side

G. the set of values, beliefs, and behaviours shared by a group of people and communicated from one generation to the next

H. the tendency for repeated contact with an object, even without reinforcement, to increase liking for the object

I. the extent to which a culture accepts an unequal distribution of influence within the society

J. the tendency for intoxication to reduce cognitive capacity, which results in a narrowing of attention

K. a collection of people that serve as a standard of comparison for an individual, whether in terms of attitudes, values, or behaviour

L. the conformity pressure that is produced by seeing someone ridiculed by another person

M. an individual's feelings of social pressure to perform or not perform an action

Answers to Test Your Knowledge

Multiple Choice Questions

1. B	6. D	11. A	16. B
2. C	7. A	12. B	17. C
3. A	8. D	13. D	18. E
4. C	9. B	14. D	
5. C	10. D	15. A	

Sentence Completion

1. affect (feelings), cognition (beliefs), past behaviour
2. explicit, implicit
3. object appraisal
4. function
5. implicit
6. evaluative conditioning
7. mere exposure effect
8. peer pressure
9. attitudes, subjective norms
10. hostile media phenomenon

Matching I – Key Terms

1. G	7. B
2. A	8. J
3. K	9. L
4. I	10. D
5. H	11. F
6. C	12. E

Matching II – Key Terms

13. H	19. E
14. J	20. M
15. C	21. B
16. K	22. F
17. L	23. D
18. A	24. G
	25. I

Chapter 7
Attitude Change

Thinking Critically about Social Psychology
Does Hazing Enhance the Attractiveness and Worth of
Sports Teams to Their Members?

Reading

In 2005, a story of a "hazing scandal" at McGill University in Montreal made headlines in the national news. The story made headlines, not because of the hazing, but because one of the students involved in the football team hazing was persuing criminal allegations against McGill University as a result of the hazing.

Student quits McGill over hazing

INGRID PERITZ

Montreal — An 18-year-old football player has withdrawn from McGill University and is weighing criminal action after he said teammates put him through a degrading hazing ritual that involved getting down on all fours with a gag in his mouth and being anally prodded with a broom handle.

The promising rookie, who had been recruited by McGill after playing for teams in Ontario and the United States, has returned home to Toronto.

"If these are the types of people at McGill, I will not associate with and be part of McGill," said the rookie, who asked to remain anonymous but wants to make the incident known.

The controversy at one of Canada's top universities has cast a spotlight on the normally hushed-up world of hazing and initiation rituals in college sports. According to the McGill Tribune, the ritual involving "Dr. Broom" is an annual rite at McGill.

In the wake of the scandal, McGill has started an investigation and principal Heather Munroe-Blum has accepted a recommendation to strengthen university anti-hazing policies.

One player with the McGill Redmen has been suspended indefinitely and five others were suspended for one game last Saturday.

"Hazing is inconsistent with the university's values and it will not be tolerated," the university said in a statement.

Two suspended players, reached by phone yesterday, said they had retained lawyers and had been advised by the university not to comment.

The football recruit, whose father is a former CFL player, said he began to hear ominous warnings from team veterans about "Dr. Broom" on the second day of training camp in August. He eventually asked veterans what the taunts meant. "They said, 'It's really bad; you go through a horrible thing,'" he said in an interview yesterday from Toronto.

On Aug. 27, the last day of training camp, he said all the newcomers were told they had to go to the campus dining hall. Veterans announced they'd be subjected to their "examination" that night.

Toward the end of the meal, he said, one of the veterans entered the room clutching a broom. "The veterans were shouting 'broom, broom, broom,'" he recalled. Meanwhile, two rookies were singled out to simulate oral sex on one another in their boxer shorts, he said.

After being ordered to take off their shirts, he said, everyone was ordered outside, told to hold hands, and sing as they skipped down to the gym.

"They [the veterans] were taunting us, saying, 'Look at the fairies. Look at the gays,'" the rookie recalled.

He added that all the rookies were ordered toward the campus's darkened squash courts and told to hold a penny on the wall with their nose.

"They said, 'Drop the penny, and it's another inch with Dr. Broom,'" the teenager recalled. "Then one by one, they took us out of the room. I was taken out to another room."

In the second squash court, six football veterans were present while another group was in the stands, pelting him with large exercise balls and jeering. The rookie was told to take off his pants. Three times, he said he refused. Finally, he was threatened.

"One of them said, 'Do it or we'll do it for you.' I said 'No, I wasn't raised that way.' They said it doesn't matter."

The rookie said he relented, dropping his pants but keeping on his boxer shorts. He said he was put on his hands and knees and told to bite down on a dog chew toy made of rope. Then they began counting down as they held a broom handle.

"They were poking me on either side of my buttocks cheeks," he said. "Then, they made contact with my rectum with it. They were kind of pushing back and forth and applying pressure."

He was not penetrated with the broomstick, but it did hurt, he said.

He said he got up and left, still in shock.

"I felt completely betrayed by the people I'd just spent 10 days with, and furious that McGill would let people like this into their university and put them in positions of leadership. They're veterans. They should know better."

The rookie's parents are angry that the university athletics department made no effort to reach out to their son, apologize, or deal with his experience.

The rookie's father said he never experienced anything like the McGill ritual during all his years in the Canadian Football League or playing on college teams.

"This is not how you build a strong team," he said from Toronto.

Earl Zukerman, a spokesman for the McGill athletics department, said some rookies refused to take part in the initiation rite and were kept on the team. Although students are told not to take initiations too far, "you can't follow them around with handcuffs, watching what they're doing every minute." *With a report from Caroline Alphonso in Toronto*

Source: Reprinted with permission from The Montreal Gazette.

McGill Hazing Scandal Has Taken a Toll on the Team

Sep 24, 2005 _Football (M)_

By John Meagher, The Montreal Gazette

McGill hazing scandal has taken a toll on the team, says QB

by John Meagher
Montreal Gazette (website edition)

MONTREAL - The McGill Redmen (0-3) will be fighting for more than their first win of the season today when they play host to the St. Francis Xavier X-Men (2-0) at Molson Stadium.

Members of Canada's oldest university football team, rocked by a hazing scandal that has made national headlines, are also battling for their pride.

"We're more pumped than we have been all year," McGill quarterback Matt Connell said Friday. "We have to be even closer as a team now, because we feel we're out on our own now."

He said the football team has been unfairly maligned by the media, which has carried stories about an Aug. 27 hazing incident involving an 18-year-old freshman no longer with the team.

Six McGill players, including Connell, 21, were suspended for last week's game, a 46-5 loss to the Universite de Montreal Carabins. One player is still suspended for today's game.

The players held a closed-door meeting Friday and debated forfeiting today's university football game if all suspensions were not lifted. They backed off, but Connell said it's unfair to scapegoat one player.

"(The initiation) was a team event; 98 per cent of the team were there, and everyone was partaking. What we've been reading in the media has been one-sided, allegations from one individual; guarantee we've learned a hard lesson and have paid a big enough price already."

Connell, a third-year education student, is confident the football program's reputation will be vindicated once all the facts are revealed.

"We feel as though we've been wronged and this has been blown out of proportion. There was no physical harm or anything done to (the hazed rookie), like he's been saying. The facts are going to come out. We all know that, but it's frustrating because it's going to take a while."

Connell now regrets the initiation party.

"What happened is that we had misjudgment, obviously. It was initiation E but we didn't do anything wrong at all. Every other of the 27 rookies are with us and agree nothing was wrongfully done and it brought the team closer together."

"Obviously something went wrong with this one individual. He took something the wrong way and, to this day, we don't know why or what. Something obviously is wrong if he's the only person who's ever had a problem. I went through initiation .... it was along the same lines."

Connell said the hazing scandal has taken a toll on the team.

"It's real tough because we're trying to go school. School and football has just been killing us. Personally, I've been one of the people targeted, and I haven't been able to make one class this week. I've been dealing with the press non-stop. It's been difficult. But at least with football, it's a few hours to clear our minds."

Connell added he has learned a lesson from the ordeal.

"Obviously, something like this will never happen again because this has just been crazy."

McGill head coach Chuck McMann is hoping to get his team some positive ink with a win today, but it won't be easy against the undefeated X-Men, who are ranked ninth in the country.

The X-men have outscored their opponents 91-13 in two games, while the Redmen, who've scored only four touchdowns this season, have been trounced 136-37 in three outings.

jmeagher@thegazette.canwest.com

Source: Reprinted with permission from The Montreal Gazette.

Questions:

1. Consider the statement: "'Dr. Broom' is an annual rite at McGill."

   Give a social psychological explanation why students would voluntarily agree to subject themselves to this treatment.

2. Consider the following quote from one student allegedly involved in the incident: "Obviously something went wrong with this one individual. He took something the wrong way and, to this day, we don't know why or what. Something obviously is wrong if he's the only person who's ever had a problem. I went through initiation .... it was along the same lines."

   Discuss what you think a social psychologist would have to say about this statement in terms of cognitive dissonance and attitude change.

3. Consider the following quote from a student allegedly involved in the incident: "Every other of the 27 rookies are with us and agree nothing was wrongfully done and it brought the team closer together." Give a possible explanation for this statement and particularly why this student would claim that the incident "brought the team closer together."

4. Have you ever undergone hazing rituals to become part of a group? How did it make you feel about the group once you "passed" the initiation?

5. Is all hazing bad? Can mild hazing (or other initiation rites) serve to bring a group closer together and increase loyalty? Where is the line drawn been bonding activities and intentional violence? How can schools and other institutions ensure that line is not crossed?

6. Are there cultural ramifications to hazing? For example, do you think that hazing also occurs in collectivist societies, or is it predominantly a way of breaking down our individualistic impulses to create a more coherent group?

7. Do you think cognitive dissonance theory provides an adequate explanation of the psychological effects of hazing? Do some of the alternative explanations of dissonance findings provide a better explanation?

Commentary:

Inappropriate initiation rites have often been discussed in relation to university sports teams and fraternities and sororities (in the United States). Prospective members (or pledges) have been forced to undergo sometimes embarrassing and occasionally dangerous activities to prove their worth before they become full-fledged members of the team, fraternity, or sorority.

Hazing, and people's responses to hazing, can be viewed in the context of cognitive dissonance. Like the participants in Aronson and Mills' (1959) study who underwent an embarrassing screening test before joining a sexual discussion group, people who undergo rigorous initiation rituals often feel more positively towards the group in the end. To justify the effort and suffering required, the group is seen as attractive and worthwhile. Otherwise, why would one go through such agony?

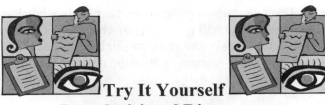

Try It Yourself
Post-decisional Dissonance
How to Make a Candy Bar Taste Better

Making decisions between two equally attractive alternatives can be difficult and can lead to feelings of dissonance. To reduce this dissonance and make ourselves feel better about the choice, we often extol the virtues of the chosen option and disparage the rejected one. Jack Brehm was the first researcher to study this phenomenon in the laboratory, and you can easily do a modified version of his experiment with your friends by asking them to rate different brands of an item (e.g., different brands of pop).

This exercise requires the participation of up to ten other people. Therefore, we suggest that you work on it in groups of two to four classmates so that you can recruit the necessary volunteers. If you are working on it alone, you can limit the number of volunteers to between four and six. However, it will be more difficult to obtain the predicted pattern of results with this number of participants.

Before you begin, you will need to decide on the items you will ask your friends to rate. For the sake of your wallet, we recommend choosing items that are relatively inexpensive, since you will be giving them away at the end of the exercise! You could, for example, use different brands of candy, different brands of soda, different brands or kinds of soup, or different kinds of ice cream bars. You need to have at least 10 different brands of the item. In describing the exercise, we will use candy bars, but you can adapt the rating scales to fit whatever item you choose to use.

First, if you are working in a group, ask eight to ten of your friends if they will help you determine which candy bars are the most popular on campus. If you are working alone, ask four to six friends. Then ask them to indicate, on a 1 to 10 scale (1 = "I hate it" and 10 = "I love it"), how much they like each of the following candy bars. Make copies of the table on the next page and record their responses.

Item 1: Snickers
Item 2: Mars
Item 3: Three Musketeers
Item 4: Reese's Peanut Butter Cups
Item 5: Mr. Big
Item 6: Kit Kat
Item 7: Coffee Crisp
Item 8: Twix
Item 9: Skor
Item 10: Rolo

After they have rated the items, thank them for their participation and offer them a choice of candy bar as a reward. For half of your friends, give them a choice between an item they rated 8 or higher and an item they rated 3 or lower. These friends are in the low dissonance condition. Give the other half of your friends a choice between two items they rated similarly in the middle of the scale (two 5s, for example). These friends are in the high dissonance condition. Give them the item they choose, and then ask them to rate the items again (without letting them see their previous responses).

According to Brehm's theory of post-decisional dissonance, the people who chose between a favourable and an unfavourable item (low dissonance) will not show any changes in their second set of ratings. However, the people who chose between two similar items (high dissonance) should alter their ratings the second time to make the chosen item more favourable than the non-chosen item.

Question:

1. Did you get these results? Share your results with your classmates and see what results they obtained.

Candy Bar First Ratings

Friend # _____   Dissonance Group: Low   High

	First Rating
Item 1: Snickers	
Item 2: Mars	
Item 3: Three Musketeers	
Item 4: Reese's Peanut Butter Cups	
Item 5: Mr. Big	
Item 6: Kit Kat	
Item 7: Coffee Crisp	
Item 8: Twix	
Item 9: Skor	
Item 10: Rolo	

Candy Bar Second Ratings

Friend # _____   Dissonance Group: Low   High

	Second Rating
Item 1: Snickers	
Item 2: Mars	
Item 3: Three Musketeers	
Item 4: Reese's Peanut Butter Cups	
Item 5: Mr. Big	
Item 6: Kit Kat	
Item 7: Coffee Crisp	
Item 8: Twix	
Item 9: Skor	
Item 10: Rolo	

Social Psychology Online Lab
Travel Planner

The purpose of this online lab is to demonstrate the same phenomena as the Candy Bar Experiment. That is, post-decisional dissonance can result in a chosen item being rated higher than a non-chosen item, even when the two items were rated similarly before the choice was made. This time, however, you will be the participant, and will answer questions about preferred travel destinations and the usefulness of various pieces of advice on travelling.

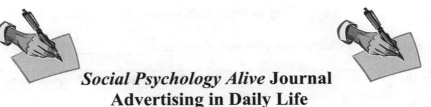

Social Psychology Alive Journal
Advertising in Daily Life

Anthony Pratkanis and Eliot Aronson (2000) estimated that the average American is exposed to more than 200 advertisements per day, or more than 73,000 per year. Do you think your daily ad exposure in Canada is higher or lower than the average 200 in America? To find out, track the number of advertisements—either written, televised, or on the radio—that you are exposed to during the course of one day.

Try to find and briefly describe examples of advertisements that rely on the different types of persuasive techniques listed in the Advertising in Daily Life Summary Sheet that follows. Afterwards, answer the following questions.

1. Which advertisements encourage people to thoughtfully analyze the information presented, and thus, rely on the central route to persuasion?

2. Which advertisements encourage people to rely on cues to make judgments about the message, without thinking carefully about the arguments that are presented, and thus rely on the peripheral route to persuasion?

3. Does the advertisement strategy depend on the type of product or message being marketed? On the targeted population? On whether the advertisement is written, televised, or on the radio?

4. Sang-pil Han and Sharon Shavitt (1994) compared advertisements in United States and Korean magazines and found that, overall, the ads in both countries were rated as more individualistic than collectivistic, which probably reflects that everyone buys products for personal benefits, at least in part. However, American ads were rated as more individualistic than Korean ads, whereas Korean ads were rated as more collectivistic than American ads. Thus, the nature of the advertisements in each country reflected, to some extent, the individualism-collectivism of the culture. Canadian culture also reflects more of an individualism than collectivism. Do any of the advertisements that you have recorded in your *Social Psychology Alive* Journal exploit the individualist nature of Canadians?

Advertising in Daily Life—Summary Sheet

Number of advertisements to which I was exposed in one day: _____

Advertisements that:	Brief Description of Advertisement
Rely on the strength of the arguments presented	
Rely on the credibility, expertise, likeability, or fame of the source of the message	
Rely on the length of the message	
Rely on message repetition	
Rely on arousing positive mood, without providing much information	
Rely on linking a product with success, attractiveness, or high status without providing much information	

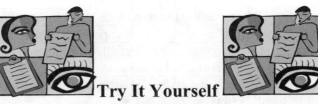

Try It Yourself
Need for Cognition and Persuasive Communications

Cacioppo, Petty, and Kao (1984) developed a scale for measuring individual differences in the motivation to think, called the "need for cognition." People with a high need for cognition tend to enjoy cognitive tasks and effortful thinking more than do people with a low need for cognition. The extent to which people score high or low on the need for cognition scale has been shown to predict the extent to which they are susceptible to different types of persuasive communication. People with a high need for cognition are more affected by the strength of the arguments in a message, whereas people with a low need for cognition are more affected by heuristic cues such as whether the source of the message is likeable, credible, or famous.

The Need for Cognition Scale[1] is reproduced below. You can complete the scale and follow the instructions for scoring to see where you fall along the "need for cognition" spectrum.

Directions: For each of the following statements, please indicate whether or not the statement is characteristic of you. If the statement is extremely uncharacteristic of you (not at all like you), place a "1" next to the statement. If the statement is extremely characteristic of you (very much like you), place a "5" next to the statement. Use the following scale as you rate each of the statements.

1	2	3	4	5
Extremely Uncharacteristic	Somewhat Uncharacteristic	Uncertain	Somewhat Characteristic	Extremely Characteristic

Your rating	Statement
	1. I prefer complex to simple problems.
	2. I like to have the responsibility of handling a situation that requires a lot of thinking.
	3. Thinking is not my idea of fun.
	4. I would rather do something that requires little thought than something that is sure to challenge my thinking abilities.
	5. I try to anticipate and avoid situations where there is a likely chance I will have to think in depth about something.
	6. I find satisfaction in deliberating hard for long hours.
	7. I only think as hard as I have to.
	8. I prefer to think about small daily projects to long-term ones.
	9. I like tasks that require little thought once I've learned them.
	10. The idea of relying on thought to make my way to the top appeals to me.
	11. I really enjoy a task that involves coming up with new solutions to problems.
	12. Learning new ways to think doesn't excite me much.

[1] Cacioppo, Petty, and Kao (1984). The efficient assessment of need for cognition, *Journal of Personality Assessment* 48: 306–307. Reprinted by permission of Lawrence Erlbaum Associates, Inc.

	13. I prefer my life to be filled with puzzles that I must solve.
	14. The notion of thinking abstractly is appealing to me.
	15. I would prefer a task that is intellectual, difficult, and important to one that is somewhat important but does not require much thought.
	16. I feel relief rather than satisfaction after completing a task that required a lot of mental effort.
	17. It's enough for me that something gets the job done; I don't care how or why it works.
	18. I usually end up deliberating about issues even when they do not affect me personally.

Scoring: First you will need to adjust the scores of the reverse-coded items (i.e., items for which a high score indicates low need for cognition instead of high need for cognition). For questions 3, 4, 5, 7, 8, 9, 12, 16 and 17, subtract the answer you provided from 6. Thus, if you answered Question 3 with a response of 2 (somewhat uncharacteristic), subtract 2 from 6 to get 4. Once you have done that for all 9 of the reverse-coded items, you are ready to begin scoring. Sum your responses to all the statements, and then divide that sum by 18, to get your mean response for the scale. If you have a mean response close to 5, you have a high need for cognition. If you have a mean response close to 1, you have a low need for cognition.

Questions:

1. Are you high or low in the need for cognition?

2. What does that tell you about how you respond to different types of persuasive messages? Which types of messages are you most susceptible to? Which types of persuasive messages have less of an effect on you?

On the Web
How to Persuade People Not to Smoke

The website www.joechemo.org is dedicated to persuading people not to smoke. It includes a "Tobacco IQ" test, information about smoking and the cigarette industry (including its advertising strategy), and a "Smoke-o-Scope," which tailors a non-smoking message to individuals based on their demographic information.

Questions:

1. In terms of a persuasion campaign, what are the website's strengths and weaknesses?

2. To what extent do you think smokers will be motivated to process the information presented?

3. By personalizing the message, does the website enhance this motivation?

4. In what ways does the site rely on the peripheral route to persuasion to encourage smokers to consider its substantive anti-smoking messages?

The site has links to "tobacco ads and counter-ads." Peruse the links and consider whether cigarette advertisements and counter-advertisements (as seen on http://www.badvertising.org/) rely on the central or peripheral route to persuasion.

Questions:

1. Do the advertisements generally rely on the strength of the arguments presented? Or do they rely on such things as arousing positive mood and linking cigarette smoking with success, attractiveness, or high status, without providing much information?

2. Given the thrust of cigarette ads, do you think an anti-smoking campaign will have to rely on both hard-sell and soft-sell techniques to be successful? Why or why not?

3. What techniques of persuasion are used in the "counter-ads"?

Try It Yourself
What Is a Cult?

A rigidly structured group ... under a charismatic leader, which isolates itself from established societal traditions, values, and norms, recruits members deceptively without informed consent, and retains them by .... manipulative techniques which deny freedom of choice. (F. MacHovec, 1989. p. 10)

The definition of a destructive cult is a seemingly straightforward one. However, determining whether a particular group is a destructive cult is more difficult. The same group, for example, may be considered a cult by some people or in one culture but a legitimate organization by other people or in other culture. For example, the Hare Krishnas are an integral part of a mainstream religious movement in India, but in the United States, they are viewed as a cult. Also, the determination becomes even more difficult for a person who is being actively recruited by a destructive cult because the person is being subjected to a powerful persuasion campaign. As described in your textbook, cults tend to use many of the same persuasive techniques as salespersons, advertisers, and religious and nonreligious groups that we would not consider cults. But they use the techniques simultaneously, deliberately, and forcefully, which can be very powerful.

In determining whether a group is a destructive cult, it is useful to go beyond the simple definition and examine whether the group has many or all of the following characteristics.

- A cult has a living, self-appointed leader who claims to have authority from a source greater than himself.
- There is an authoritarian system of governance in which leaders exert almost military control over the lives of their followers.
- Cults possess a double set of ethics that enable members to be honest with each other but to deceive outsiders for the protection or benefit of the group.
- The control function of cults is to recruit new members and to raise money for their cause.
- Cults tend to stress feelings at the expense of critical faculties [that is, critical thinking and reasoning]. (As Joseph Fletcher put it: "Brains are bad, guts are good.")
- Cults offer a simple, no option world. They appeal to a person's need to be taken care of . . .
- Cults offer members a sense of being elite, God's elect. They divide the world into the saved (members of the cult) and the unsaved (everyone else).

(quoted from Reed and Hoertdoerfer, 1997, p. 205)

This exercise involves researching one of the following three groups and determining for yourself whether the group has the above characteristics. (If you like, you may choose another group that at least some people define as a cult.)

- The International Church of Christ (this group is different from the Church of Christ)
- Hare Krishnas
- The Branch Davidians

Information about all three groups is found at www.cultsoncampus.com. For the latter two groups, select "News on Specific Groups" to find the information.

Questions:

1. Which of the characteristics of destructive cults does the group have?

2. Which of the persuasive techniques described in your textbook does the group use?

3. Do you think the group is a destructive cult? Why or why not? Was the determination an easy or a hard one for you to make?

To Learn More

If you are interested in learning more about cults, the Cult Information Centre in the UK at http://www.cultinformation.org.uk/home.html includes general information about cults, characteristics of a cult, and how to help cult members. The site contains a list of international links to follow for more information on cults (http://www.cultinformation.org.uk/help.html) including the Canadian Resource Centre on Cultic Thinking at http://www.infocult.org.

As you browse the site and learn more about cults, see if you can identify some of the persuasive techniques described in your textbook.

Learning Objectives

Rationalizing Our Own Behaviour: Cognitive Dissonance Theory

1. Explain cognitive dissonance, and give an example of a situation that might cause someone to experience dissonance. (pp. 239–242)

2. Describe three research paradigms that were first used to study cognitive dissonance. What are the primary differences between them? (pp. 242–247)

3. Describe the three theories that were developed as alternative interpretations of dissonance findings. (pp. 247–251)

4. Describe three areas of recent research on cognitive dissonance theory. (pp. 251–255)

Information-Based Persuasion: Cognitive Response Theory

5. How does cognitive response theory propose that persuasive messages cause attitude change? (p. 256)

6. Can weak arguments be persuasive? If so, under what conditions? (pp. 257–258)

If You Say So: Heuristic Persuasion

7. Explain the difference between a hard sell and a soft sell in terms of an advertising campaign. What types of products are best advertised using a hard sell? A soft sell? (pp. 259–263)

Two Models of Persuasive Messages

8. Describe the two theories that have been proposed to explain the two ways that persuasive communication can produce agreement. What are the primary differences between the two theories? (pp. 262–265)

9. What are two factors that may affect people's motivation or their ability to process a persuasive communication? (pp. 265–268)

Cultural Differences in Attitude Change

10. Do all cultures respond to cognitive dissonance in the same way? If not, how do various types of cultures differ? (pp. 268–271)

Persuasion in the Health Domain: Fear Appeals

11. Describe the four characteristics that must be present before a threatening message can influence attitudes and behaviours. (pp. 272–274)

Propaganda

12. Give three examples of propaganda, and briefly describe how each fits the definition of propaganda. (pp. 275–280)

13. How do cults use persuasive techniques to recruit new members? (pp. 276–279)

14. Explain how you can protect yourself against unwanted persuasive influence. (p. 281)

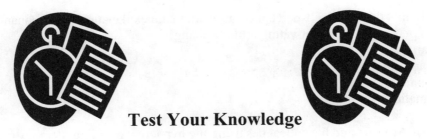

Test Your Knowledge

Multiple Choice Questions

1. The statements "I eat chocolate cake for breakfast" and "Too much sugar is bad for you" are examples of
    A. attitudes.
    B. consonant cognitions.
    C. dissonant cognitions.
    D. stereotypes.

2. For social psychologists, dissonance is best defined as the state of
    A. feeling bad about one's own irrational behaviour.
    B. feeling good about one's own rational behaviour.
    C. feeling good about one's own irrational behaviour.
    D. listening to disjointed and atonal music.

3. Which of the following is *not* a way to reduce dissonance, according to Festinger's dissonance theory?
    A. adding consonant cognitions
    B. changing one of the dissonant cognitions
    C. increasing the importance of a dissonant cognition
    D. increasing the importance of a consonant cognition

4. Your roommate asks if you will help him with his debate project. He asks if you would mind writing an essay supporting something in which you do not believe. You agree to help him, and, as a result you find that your attitude toward the essay topic has altered to be more favourable than it was before you wrote the essay. Your roommate has used a form of which experimental paradigm to create dissonance?
    A. effort justification paradigm
    B. free choice paradigm
    C. hypocrisy paradigm
    D. induced compliance paradigm

5. James is a first year university student on the basketball team. In the weeks preceding the season, he and his fellow first year students are hazed mercilessly by their teammates. After the hazing period, James is accepted as a teammate, but finds he spends all his time on the bench and discovers that his teammates aren't really very interesting. He remains on the team, however, arguing that he expended a great deal of effort to get to that point. This is a real-world example of which experimental paradigm to create dissonance?
    A. effort justification paradigm
    B. free choice paradigm
    C. hypocrisy paradigm
    D. induced compliance paradigm

6. Research on Bem's theory of self-perception as an alternate explanation for dissonance confirmed the importance of _____ in motivating attitude change.
   A. positive arousal
   B. aversive arousal
   C. self-presentation
   D. self-affirmation

7. The research of Aronson and his colleagues using the hypocrisy paradigm demonstrated that dissonance can
   A. only occur when the behaviour results in negative consequences.
   B. only occur when the behaviour results in positive consequences.
   C. occur when behaviour results in negative or positive consequences.
   D. only occur if there are no consequences.

8. Which of the following is most accurate with regard to recent research in dissonance?
   A. Dissonance has been shown to change implicit attitudes.
   B. Dissonance is more pronounced with individuals who have a high preference for consistency.
   C. Dissonance is more pronounced with individuals who have a low preference for consistency.
   D. Dissonance findings can be completely explained by self-perception theory.

9. Petty et al.'s study, in which students listened to either strong or weak tuition-reduction arguments while being distracted, demonstrated that weak
   A. arguments were less persuasive when participants were distracted than when they were not distracted.
   B. arguments were more persuasive when participants were distracted than when they were not distracted.
   C. arguments were more persuasive than strong arguments when participants were distracted.
   D. and strong arguments were equally persuasive when participants were not distracted.

10. As an intern at an advertising agency, you are asked to find the right spokesperson for an advertisement for a new MP3 player aimed at college and university students. Your boss doesn't want to spend the time researching the positive aspects of the device, so your spokesperson will have to rely on the soft sell approach. According to social psychological research, which of following people would you suggest?
    A. a university professor
    B. a TV news anchorman or woman
    C. a classical violinist
    D. the lead singer of a popular group

11. Which of the following is *not* one of the factors which effects persuasion, according to the systematic-heuristic and elaboration-likelihood models?
    A. impression management
    B. motivation
    C. personal relevance
    D. message complexity

12. The researchers most closely associated with the elaboration-likelihood model of persuasion are
    A. Aronson and Mills.
    B. Festinger and Carlsmith.
    C. Petty and Cacioppo.
    D. Visser and Krosnick.

13. The research of Hoshino-Brown and her colleagues in which European-Canadians and Asian-Canadians were asked to rate various Chinese restaurant dishes demonstrated that members of
    A. individualist and collectivist cultures experience equal dissonance when making a choice for themselves.
    B. individualist and collectivist cultures experience equal dissonance when making a choice for a friend.
    C. collectivist cultures are more likely to experience dissonance when making a choice for themselves.
    (D.) collectivist cultures are more likely to experience dissonance when making a choice for a friend.

14. According to the protection-motivation theory, which of the following factors must be present for fear to influence attitudes and behaviour?
    (A.) The problem is severe.
    B. The problem is uncommon.
    C. The problem is remedied by difficult action.
    D. The problem may or may not be avoided by taking action.

15. Which of the following is *not* a technique used by destructive cults to recruit and retain members?
    A. fear mongering
    (B.) isolation within the cult
    C. love-bombing
    D. foot-in-the-door technique

16. Which of the following is *not* a source of everyday propaganda?
    A. educational systems
    B. religious institutions
    C. advertising
    (D.) genetic predisposition

Sentence Completion

1. "Regular exercise is good for you" and "I exercise regularly" are _consonant_ cognitions whereas "I dislike cats" and "I own two cats" are _dissonant_ cognitions.

2. _Dissonance_ is the state of feeling bad or conflicted about one's own irrational behaviour.

3. The induced compliance paradigm investigates dissonance that results from _counterattitudinal behaviour._

4. The _effort justification_ paradigm investigates dissonance that results from wasted effort.

5. The _free choice_ paradigm is used to study postdecisional dissonance.

6. Dissonance theorists predict that aversive _arousal_ motivates attitude change whereas self-perception theorist predict that there is no _arousal_ at all, and that people infer their attitudes from their behaviour and the situation in which the behaviour occurs.

7. _Impression management_ theory proposes that people in dissonance studies do not want to appear inconsistent to the experimenter and therefore falsely report attitudes that are consistent with their counterattitudinal behaviour.

8. Cognitive response theory assumes that the effectiveness of a message in causing attitude change is determined by the thoughts evoked by the message; these thoughts can be about the _communicator_, the _issue_, or the _message_.

9. _strong_ messages are less persuasive when a person is distracted, whereas _weak_ messages are more persuasive when a person is distracted.

10. Jayne is persuaded that cell phones should be banned when driving as she quickly skims a long and detailed magazine article written by a policy analyst from a well-respected university. This is an example of _heuristic_ persuasion.

11. Both _motivation_ and _ability_ to process a message are necessary for systemic processing to occur.

12. The warning, "Smoking Causes Cancer," on a cigarette package is an example of a _fear_ appeal.

13. Suppose the parents of a high school student tell him that he can't go to a party. _reactance_ theory predicts that he will now want to go to the party more than ever; this theory predicts that people will resist overt pressure to adopt a certain view because their perceived _freedom_ to hold a different view is threatened.

Matching I – Key Terms

_____ 1. **cognitive dissonance theory**

_____ 2. **consonant cognitions**

_____ 3. **dissonant cognitions**

_____ 4. **induced compliance paradigm**

_____ 5. **effort justification paradigm**

_____ 6. **free choice paradigm**

_____ 7. **impression management theory**

_____ 8. **self-affirmation theory**

_____ 9. **hypocrisy paradigm**

_____ 10. **preference for consistency (PFC)**

A. a disposition that represents the extent to which people desire predictability and compatibility within their own responses and within others' responses

B. an alternative to dissonance theory that argues that participants in dissonance experiments want to appear consistent to the experimenter and therefore lie about their attitudes

C. a research methodology used to test dissonance theory that arouses dissonance by getting people to engage in counterattitudinal behaviour. Participants are induced to comply with an experimenter's request that they behave in a way that is inconsistent with their attitudes.

D. a model proposed by Leon Festinger that states that awareness of consonant cognitions makes us feel good, whereas awareness of dissonant cognitions makes us feel bad. Further, the unpleasant feelings produced by dissonant cognitions motivate us to do something to change our state

E. a research methodology used to test dissonance theory that arouses dissonance by getting people to choose between two or more alternatives

F. beliefs that are inconsistent or logically discrepant with one another

G. a research methodology used to test dissonance theory that arouses dissonance by having people publicly promote a socially desirable behaviour and then be made aware that they have not always exhibited the behaviour themselves in the past

H. an alternative to dissonance theory that argues that people are threatened by behaviour that challenges their self-worth and can deal with this threat by reaffirming an important value

I. beliefs that are consistent or compatible with one another

J. a research methodology used to test dissonance theory that arouses dissonance by getting people to invest time or energy to achieve a goal that may not be worthwhile

Matching II – Key Terms

_____ 11. cognitive response theory

_____ 12. hard sell

_____ 13. heuristic persuasion

_____ 14. soft sell

_____ 15. systematic-heuristic model

_____ 16. elaboration likelihood model

_____ 17. systematic processing

_____ 18. heuristic processing

_____ 19. central route to persuasion

_____ 20. peripheral route to persuasion

A. a theory of attitude change that specifies the conditions under which people will think carefully about the content of a persuasive message. It distinguishes between two types of processing—the central route to persuasion and the peripheral route to persuasion

B. attitude change resulting from cues indicating that the position advocated in a message is valid

C. a theory of attitude change that distinguishes between two types of processing that can occur in response to a persuasive message—systematic processing and heuristic processing

D. superficial analysis of a message that focuses on cues indicating the validity or invalidity of the advocated positions

E. persuasion that occurs when attitude change results from non-cognitive factors; it encompasses evaluative conditioning and mere exposure

F. a model of persuasion that assumes that the impact of a message on attitudes depends on the thoughts evoked by the message

G. persuasion that occurs when attitude change results from a careful analysis of the information in a persuasive communication

H. careful, deliberative analysis of the arguments in a message

I. an advertising strategy that relies on presenting information about the positive features of a product

J. an advertising strategy that relies on the use of images, emotions, symbols, or values to promote a product

Matching III – Key Terms

_____ 21. **peripheral cues**	A. a rigidly structured group, led by a charismatic leader, that recruits and retains members using manipulative, deceptive techniques
_____ 22. **protection motivation theory**	B. a persuasive attempt that is motivated by an ideology, or set of values, and that is deliberately biased in its presentation of information
_____ 23. **propaganda**	C. a model that articulates how threatening messages can influence attitudes and behaviour
_____ 24. **destructive cult**	D. simple features or heuristics that are assumed to show that a message is valid

Answers to Test Your Knowledge

Multiple Choice Questions

1. C	6. B	11. A	16. D
2. A	7. C	12. C	
3. C	8. B	13. D	
4. D	9. B	14. A	
5. A	10. D	15. B	

Sentence Completion

1. consonant, dissonant
2. dissonance
3. counterattitudinal behaviour
4. effort justification
5. free choice
6. arousal, arousal
7. impression management
8. communicator, issue, message
9. strong, weak
10. heuristic
11. motivation, ability
12. fear
13. reactance, freedom

Matching I – Key Terms

1. D	6. E
2. I	7. B
3. F	8. H
4. C	9. G
5. J	10. A

Matching II – Key Terms

11. F	16. A
12. I	17. H
13. B	18. D
14. J	19. G
15. C	20. E

Matching III – Key Terms

21. D
22. C
23. B
24. A

Chapter 8
Conformity, Compliance, and Obedience

Thinking Critically about Social Psychology
Can a Strategy Based on Social Norms Reduce Student Drinking?

Canadian study reveals major misperceptions about student drinking patterns

August 30, 2004
A press release issued by The Student Life Education Company, Toronto

The Student Life Education Company today released a groundbreaking Canadian study into post-secondary student drinking that shows a significant difference between actual and perceived behaviour in four primary areas.

The study findings will be used to develop targeted social norms marketing campaigns that provide students with an accurate picture of drinking behaviour and encourages them to drink responsibly.

Leading the study and present for the launch was Dr. Wesley Perkins, researcher with the Canadian Centre for Social Norms and Research, a branch of the Student Life Education Company.

First, the survey found that the majority of students (63%) drink twice per month or less. However, 80% of students believe that their peers typically drink once per week or more often. One-third believe that their fellow students drink at least three times per week.

Second, most students (64%) consume 1 to 4 drinks at parties or bars. The survey found that 67% believe students consume 5 or more drinks per occasion at parties or bars. One-quarter of students believe that average consumption is 7 or more drinks. These first two results indicate that most students overestimate both the quantity other students drink as well as the frequency with which they drink.

Next, 93% of students stated that one should not drink to levels that interfere with academics or other responsibilities. In contrast, the survey found that 32% of students believe that the majority of their peers consider such behaviour acceptable.

Lastly, 80% of students reported that they always or usually have a designated driver when they know they will be travelling by car. The survey found that students believe only 59% of their peers always or usually used a designated driver. More then one-third of students believe that less than half of their peers used a designated driver with such regularity.

"By correcting misperceptions and demonstrating positive peer trends in student drinking patterns, our goal is to bring more students in line with the norms expressed by their peers, and ultimately, to eliminate unsafe drinking behaviour," said Dr. Perkins. "Similar social norm campaigns have led to significant reductions in student drinking at a number of colleges and universities in the United States."

Promoting these findings in a fall marketing campaign is the first stage in an effort to educate students about drinking patterns and to ultimately lead them to make safer and more responsible choices about alcohol consumption.

"The Brewers of Canada are pleased to provide a one-million-dollar grant to the Student Life Education Company to carry out such an innovative student education program on responsible drinking. This initiative is a valuable contribution to a very important issue in Canadian society—the health and safety of our young people—and is an important plank in our industry's effort to promote responsible drinking amongst Canadian youth," said Jeff Newton, President and CEO of the Brewers of Canada. "Canadian brewers view the promotion of responsible drinking not only as an important corporate social responsibility but also as a key business priority. Ensuring that people drink responsibly is integral to the future health and image of our business and this project is a meaningful investment against that objective."

To gauge the success of the marketing campaign, the Student Life Education Company will retest in October 2004. A second marketing campaign will follow in January, and another retest will occur in October 2005.

The study on student drinking patterns was conducted by the Canadian Centre for Social Norms Research. Over 5000 students from 10 colleges and universities in 7 provinces took part in the study. The survey was conducted in October 2003.

Social norms research is based on the premise that people's behaviour is influenced by the perception of how other members of their social group behave. Social norms theory dictates that when students misperceive the amount of alcohol consumed by their peers, they are at greater risk of increasing their own alcohol intake. Conversely, by promoting the truth about student drinking patterns, those students who do engage in unsafe or irresponsible drinking will see that their behaviour is outside the norm.

Source: Reprinted by permission of The Student Life Education Company

About The Student Life Education Company Inc.

The Student Life Education Company (SLEC) is a not-for-profit organization established in 1986. SLEC is dedicated to enhancing the quality of student life in Canada by working with students and schools nationwide to encourage healthy decision-making about alcohol use. The Student Life Education Centre is comprised of three divisions including BACCHUS Canada, Student Life NOW and The Canadian Centre for Social Norms Research.

About The Canadian Centre for Social Norms Research

The Canadian Centre for Social Norms was launched in 2001 with the aim of decreasing at-risk drinking behaviour on Canadian post-secondary campuses. The only centre of its kind in Canada, the Centre for Social Norms Research researches and develops targeted responsible-use education campaigns directed at students. The Centre is financially supported by an operating grant from the Brewers Association of Canada.

About the Brewers of Canada

The Brewers of Canada represent brewing companies operating in Canada. BOC members account for 98% of the jobs and economic activity in Canada's brewing sector. The Brewers of Canada promotes the interests of Canadian Brewers through the pro-active management of key regulatory, taxation, trade, and social policy issues. Canadian brewers pride themselves on many things—from brewing the best beer in the world to being a leader in educating consumers about responsible drinking. The Brewers of Canada, in operation since 1943, has offices in Ottawa, Toronto, and Vancouver.

FACT SHEET

What is social norms theory?

- Social norms theory is based on a scientific, environmental model used in most developed countries

- It states that much of people's behaviour is influenced by their perception of how other members of their social group behave.

- It advocates communicating an accurate picture of peer behaviour, so that individual behaviour can be positively impacted

How does social norms theory apply to student drinking?

- By studying campus drinking habits and providing students with accurate information, social norms theory contends that students will become aware of positive peer trends. This in turn will contribute to a reduction of unsafe or high-risk drinking behaviour

How is social norms research conducted?

- Post-secondary students are surveyed about how much they are drinking and how much they think others are drinking

- Surveys also ask about the consequences of alcohol consumption and collect information about student demographics

How is social norms data used?

- Survey data is used as the basis for the development of educational campaigns directed towards its subjects (i.e., students)

- The campaigns will inform students about actual patterns of behaviour and encourage safe and responsible consumption of alcohol

What Canadian schools are participating in the social norms research project?

- Participating universities are the University of Toronto, Victoria College (Toronto, ON), Simon Fraser University (Burnaby, BC), University of Alberta (Edmonton, AB), University of New Brunswick (Fredericton, NB), University of Manitoba (Winnipeg, MB), University of Saskatchewan (Saskatoon, SK), and Saint Mary's University (Halifax, NS)

- Participating colleges are Humber College (Toronto, ON), Lakeland College (Lloydminster, AB), Sault College (Sault Ste. Marie, ON)

Questions:

1. An increasingly popular strategy of reducing student drinking in Canada and the United States is based on principles of social norms. Is the theory of social norms and how they influence the behaviour upon which this strategy is based an accurate theory? Does it reflect the theories of social norms that you read about in the text?

2. Many of the results cited in the text rely on students' self-reports of how much they drink. What are the problems with this type of measurement? Can you think of other dependant variables that may more accurately reflect changing drinking patterns on campus? How would you design a study to test the theory that changing the social norm can reduce drinking?

3. Traditional campaigns aimed at reducing drinking have included graphic depictions of the negative consequences of binge drinking (e.g., wrecked cars, hospitalized students). These campaigns have reportedly had very little effect on the percentage of students who categorize themselves as binge drinkers. Can you think of other explanations for why such campaigns seem to have little effect? For example, is it possible that the old tactics have no effect because students are so used to seeing them that their message doesn't register? Could the decrease in self-reported drinking be a result of the novelty of the new social norms campaign? Is it possible that binge drinking will increase again when students get used to seeing the social norms plastered everywhere?

Further Reading on Social Norms:

Visit the website for the National Social Norms Resource Center at http://www.socialnorms.org/index.php to find more information on the social norms approach to various issues in society (e.g., health, alcohol-related, tobacco, etc.). Follow the link to "Research" to find a list of recently published articles, including articles on the reduction of alcohol consumption based on the social norms approach (http://www.socialnorms.org/Research/RecentArticles.php).

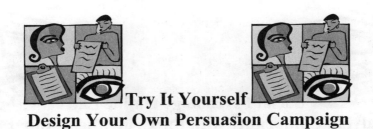

Try It Yourself
Design Your Own Persuasion Campaign

Imagine that you work for your school's administration and you have been asked to develop a campaign to meet one of the following goals, or a goal of your own choosing.

- Encourage college and university students to exercise regularly
- Encourage sexually active people to practice "safe sex"
- Encourage designated drivers not to drink and to otherwise meet the responsibilities they have promised to undertake
- Encourage people to donate blood
- Encourage people to attend women's sporting events at your school
- Encourage people to vote in campus elections

Using the conformity, compliance, and obedience principles that you read about in the chapter, how would you go about structuring such a persuasion campaign?

1. What topic would you choose?

2. Who would you choose to be the spokesperson(s) for your campaign, and why? For example, the liking principle suggests that college and university students might be more persuaded by people who are similar to them, such as other college and university students. On the other hand, authority figures, as illustrated so vividly by the Milgram experiments, are also likely to induce compliance.

3. What messages could you incorporate into your campaign to induce compliance, and what persuasive techniques might you use? For example, having the spokesperson say the desired behaviour is socially validated is one way to induce compliance. Or perhaps you could plan a campaign of serial advertisements and use the foot-in-the-door or door-in-the-face technique.

Social Psychology Online Lab
Studying Conformity with the Crutchfield Apparatus
A Computerized Demonstration

Most research on the conformity effect uses the Asch-type procedure involving face-to-face interaction between the "critical subject," or actual participant and confederates of the experimenter. This procedure creates a powerful social situation. But it also involves elaborate stage-setting, and allows many factors to go uncontrolled. The confederates need to be carefully trained and rehearsed. Like any theater production, their acting will differ from session to session and day to day. And there is the possibility that the confederates will act differently depending on how the critical subject responds.

To gain more control, Richard Crutchfield (1955) developed a new procedure for studying conformity. Rather than using confederates, the Crutchfield apparatus simulates the responses of other people. For example, when participants arrive for the experiment (usually in groups of five), they are seated in separate cubicles. Each cubicle contains an electrical panel with five rows of 11 lights and one row of 11 switches. The experimenter explains that each of the five participants controls one row of lights. Participants are told that they will answer questions projected on the wall facing the cubicles, so everyone can see the question at the same time. They are also told that, as each person indicates his or her response (by throwing one of the 11 switches), a corresponding light will be illuminated on the panel in all cubicles. Thus, each participant believes that he or she will learn about the responses of others and that his or her own responses will be publicly known. In reality, the experimenter controls all of the lights.

The Social Psychology Lab, "Judging Groups," includes a computerized version of the Crutchfield apparatus. Try it yourself and view the results of other students in your class.

Question:

1. Were the results of your class consistent with those found in the Asch experiments? If not, what do you think explains the conflicting results?

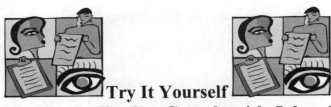

Try It Yourself
Are You Inclined to Comply with Others?
Test Your Need for Consistency

Some compliance techniques are effective because they rely on people's motivation to achieve and maintain personal consistency in their thoughts, feelings, and actions. For example, the foot-in-the-door technique is effective because it would seem inconsistent to turn down a request after agreeing to a slightly smaller, but similar, one. A person who has agreed to donate $5 for a disaster relief fund, for instance, might have a hard time turning down a request to donate $5 to the fund each month for the next year.

This desire for consistency varies from person to person; some people have a higher preference for consistency than others. The scale that begins on the next page measures people's preference for consistency.

Step 1: Complete the scale to get a sense of how susceptible you may be to certain types of compliance techniques.

Step 2: To obtain your score on the Preference for Consistency scale:
a. Adjust your response to Question 18, by subtracting your response from 10. For example, if you circled 2, your adjusted response to Question 18 is 10 - 2, or 8.
b. Sum up your responses to all the questions, making sure to use the adjusted response for Question 18.
c. Divide the sum of your response by 18 to get your overall personal consistency score.

Your Score: _____

Step 3: Interpret your score.

A score of 7 or higher indicates a high preference for personal consistency. If you scored in this range, you are a more likely target for compliance techniques that exploit a person's desire for personal consistency, such as the foot-in-the-door and the low-ball techniques. If you scored 3 or lower, you are less likely to fall victim to compliance techniques that exploit a person's desire for personal consistency. This does not mean, however, that you are immune to other methods of social influence, such as the door-in-the-face technique that does not exploit a person's need for personal consistency. For instance, you might turn down a request to make a $5 donation to a disaster relief fund every month for a year, but comply when asked to make a one-time donation of $5 to the fund.

Preference for Consistency Scale[1]

Indicate how you feel about the following statements.

1. I prefer to be around people whose reactions I can anticipate.

1	2	3	4	5	6	7	8	9
Strongly Disagree				Neither agree nor disagree				Strongly Agree

2. It is important to me that my actions are consistent with my beliefs.

1	2	3	4	5	6	7	8	9
Strongly Disagree				Neither agree nor disagree				Strongly Agree

3. Even if my attitudes and actions seemed consistent with one another to me, it would bother me if they did not seem consistent in the eyes of others.

1	2	3	4	5	6	7	8	9
Strongly Disagree				Neither agree nor disagree				Strongly Agree

4. It is important to me that those who know me can predict what I will do.

1	2	3	4	5	6	7	8	9
Strongly Disagree				Neither agree nor disagree				Strongly Agree

5. I want to be described by others as a stable, predictable person.

1	2	3	4	5	6	7	8	9
Strongly Disagree				Neither agree nor disagree				Strongly Agree

---

[1] Cialdini, Trost, and Newsom (1995). Preference for consistency: The development of a valid measure and the discovery of surprising behavioral implications, *Journal of Personality and Social Psychology* 69(2): 318–328. Copyright © 1995 by the American Psychological Association. Reprinted by permission.

6. Admirable people are consistent and predictable.

1	2	3	4	5	6	7	8	9
Strongly Disagree				Neither agree nor disagree				Strongly Agree

7. The appearance of consistency is an important part of the image I present to the world.

1	2	3	4	5	6	7	8	9
Strongly Disagree				Neither agree nor disagree				Strongly Agree

8. It bothers me when someone I depend upon is unpredictable.

1	2	3	4	5	6	7	8	9
Strongly Disagree				Neither agree nor disagree				Strongly Agree

9. I don't like to appear as if I am inconsistent.

1	2	3	4	5	6	7	8	9
Strongly Disagree				Neither agree nor disagree				Strongly Agree

10. I get uncomfortable when I find my behaviour contradicts my beliefs.

1	2	3	4	5	6	7	8	9
Strongly Disagree				Neither agree nor disagree				Strongly Agree

11. An important requirement for any friend of mine is personal consistency.

1	2	3	4	5	6	7	8	9
Strongly Disagree				Neither agree nor disagree				Strongly Agree

12. I typically like to do things the same way.

1	2	3	4	5	6	7	8	9
Strongly Disagree				Neither agree nor disagree				Strongly Agree

13. I dislike people who are constantly changing their opinions.

1	2	3	4	5	6	7	8	9
Strongly Disagree				Neither agree nor disagree				Strongly Agree

14. I want my close friends to be predictable.

1	2	3	4	5	6	7	8	9
Strongly Disagree				Neither agree nor disagree				Strongly Agree

15. It is important to me that others view me as a stable person.

1	2	3	4	5	6	7	8	9
Strongly Disagree				Neither agree nor disagree				Strongly Agree

16. I make an effort to appear consistent to others.

1	2	3	4	5	6	7	8	9
Strongly Disagree				Neither agree nor disagree				Strongly Agree

17. I'm uncomfortable holding two beliefs that are inconsistent.

1	2	3	4	5	6	7	8	9
Strongly Disagree				Neither agree nor disagree				Strongly Agree

18. It doesn't bother me much if my actions are inconsistent.

1	2	3	4	5	6	7	8	9
Strongly Disagree				Neither agree nor disagree				Strongly Agree

Thinking Critically about Social Psychology
Social Norms and Suicide Bombings

In a July 2004 poll of Palestinians in the West Bank and Gaza Strip, 62% said they supported suicide-bombing operations against Israeli civilians. In a poll taken a few years earlier in May 1997, the level of support was much lower. At that time, just 24% of Palestinians supported suicide bombings. [The polls were conducted by Jerusalem Media & Communication Centre, which was established by a group of Palestinian journalists and researchers to provide information on events in the West Bank and the Gaza Strip.] These polls suggest that public opinion toward suicide bombing changed dramatically among Palestinian people over the course of a few years.

Source: The reported results appeared in Volume 5, Number 14 of the *Palestinian Opinion Pulse* (July 2004), and are reproduced below with permission from Jerusalem Media and Communicate Centre. See www.JMCC.org.

Support for Suicide Operations

Respondents were asked whether they supported or opposed suicide-bombing operations against Israeli civilians. Sixty-two percent of Palestinians supported suicide operations. This figure is similar to the figure obtained in the latest JMCC poll conducted in October 2003.

As Figure 7 shows, the level of support for suicide bombing operations has increased dramatically after the onset of the current Intifada to reach a high of 76% in April 2001. It should be noted that only 24% of Palestinians supported suicide operations in May 1997.

Figure 7:

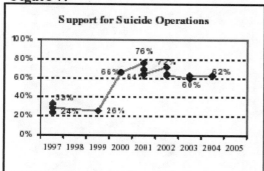

Support for suicide operations varied by several personal characteristics, including area of residence (71% among Gaza Strip residents versus 57% among both West Bank and East Jerusalem residents), type of locality (70% among refugee camp residents versus 61% among both city and village residents), refugee status (69% among refugees versus 56% among nonrefugees), political party supported (62% among Fateh supporters, 83% among supporters of Islamic parties, 55% among supporters of other parties, and 46% among respondents who did not support any Palestinian party), and level of education (66% among respondents with high school or higher education versus 52% of those with less than high school education).

Additionally, support for suicide bombing was highest among the younger age group and decreased with increasing age (see Figure 8).

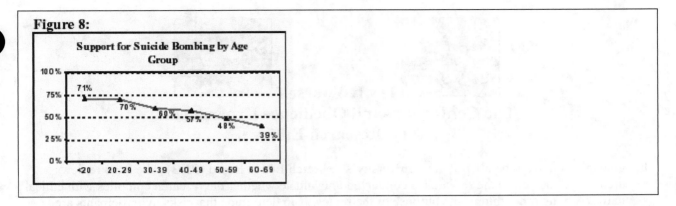

Figure 8:

Support for Suicide Bombing by Age Group

Questions:

1. What do you think accounts for the change in reported public opinion? Do you think it reflects a deep adjustment in the social norms of the Palestinian people? Or, could it be just a temporary spike in response to events that are taking place in the country?

2. How might the change be explained by the operation of social norms, conformity, and compliance?

3. What other questions would you like to ask the Palestinian people who were polled to help make these determinations?

Additional Sources

Sources that you may find helpful in exploring this area are:

Atran, S. (2002). *In Gods we trust: The evolutionary landscape of religion.* Oxford University Press. ISBN 0-19-514930-0.

Atran, S. (2003). Genesis of suicide terrorism. *Science*, 299, 1534–1539.

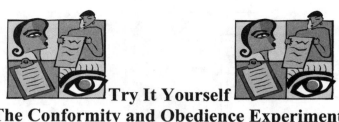

Try It Yourself
The Conformity and Obedience Experiments
and Research Ethics

Imagine that you are a member of your university's Research Ethics Board (REB). The REB reviews research proposals before the research is conducted to evaluate whether the research complies with ethical standards. Among other things, the purpose of the review is to determine that risks to participants are minimized and are reasonable in relation to the anticipated benefits of the study, and to determine whether the procedure for obtaining participants' consent is adequate. (See Chapter 2 of the workbook for more information about the review process.)

Below are some hypothetical cases for you to consider in your new role:

Case 1

You are transported back to 1960 before Stanley Milgram has conducted his obedience experiments. Professor Milgram submits to the REB a proposal that describes the methods of his first obedience experiment (see pages 307-308 of the textbook) and states that the experimenter will present the study to participants as an investigation of memory and learning and will tell them nothing about the true purpose of the study until its conclusion. Professor Milgram also gives the REB the following statement concerning how participants are likely to perform in the study. The statement indicates that everyone thinks they would defy the experimenter at some point and not administer the strongest shocks.

> **Statement of anticipated results**. Three groups of people—psychiatrists, university students, and middle-class adults of various occupations—were asked how they would perform in the experiment. They were shown a schematic diagram of the shock generator that showed shock levels of 1 to 30, with both numeric and verbal labels of the associated voltage, and were asked to indicate where they would stop shocking the "learner" if they were the "teacher" in the experiment.
>
> The following table (adapted from Milgram [1974], p. 28) shows the stopping points reported by the three groups. The average break-off point for the psychiatrists was in the moderate shock range and that for the students and middle-class adults was at the low end of the strong shock range. Everyone thought that they would defy the experimenter at some point and not administer the strongest shocks. A similar pattern of results was found when the three groups were asked how they thought other people would perform in the experiment.
>
> We thus anticipate that most, if not all, participants will defy the experimenter at some point and not administer the strongest shocks.

Shock Level	Verbal Labels and Voltage	Psychiatrists (n=39)[*]	University Students (n=31)	Middle-class Adults (n=40)
	Slight Shock	2[**]		3[**]
1	15	1		
2	30			
3	45			1
4	60	1		1
	Moderate Shock			
5	75	6	4	7
6	90	1	3	1
7	105	4		1
8	120	4	1	3
	Strong Shock			
9	135	1	3	2
10	150	14	12	9
11	165		1	2
12	180	2	6	3
	Very Strong Shock			
13	195	2		1
14	210		1	
15	225			1
16	240			1
	Intense Shock			
17	255			1
18	270			
19	285			
20	300	1		3
	Extreme Intensity Shock			
21	315			
22	330			
23	345			
24	360			
	Danger: Severe Shock			
25	375			
26	390			
27	405			
28	420			
	XXX[***]			
29	435			
30	450			
Mean Maximum Shock Level		8.20	9.35	9.15

* "n" refers to the number of people in each group. Entries in Columns 3, 4, and 4 indicate the number of people providing the particular response.

** These people said they would not have administer even the lowest shock.

*** "XXX" near the bottom of the second row is the label used in the study to indicate the most severe grouping of shocks.

In thinking about whether you would approve his proposal, assume you do not know the experiment's results and consider the following questions.

1. Does the deception about the purpose of the study allow the investigators to obtain information that would otherwise be unobtainable? Does the importance of the information justify the deception and override the potential harm to the participants? Why or why not?

2. Can debriefing participants about the true purpose of the experiment and its results restore them to a state of emotional well-being? Would, for example, the following procedures work? Why or why not?

    > During debriefing, each participant will be told that the victim had not received any dangerous shocks and will meet the unharmed victim. The experimenter will explain the experiment to participants in a way that supports their decision to obey or disobey and that assures the participant that their behaviour, thoughts, and feelings are "normal." All participants will have the opportunity to discuss their participation with the experimenter to the extent he or she desires. At the end of the study, all participants will be sent a written report explaining the experimental procedures and the results in depth. All participants will also be sent a follow-up questionnaire concerning their feelings and thoughts about their participation in the study. [Adapted from the description of the debriefing procedure used by Milgram (1974), p. 24.]

3. Would you approve Professor Milgram's proposal? Why or why not?

4. Assume now that Milgram's survey findings indicated that psychiatrists, university students, and middle-class adults all predicted that the participants would obey the experimenter and administer very strong shocks. Does this change your answers to the above questions, and your opinion about whether the REB should approve the proposal? Why or why not?

5. To what extent do you think present-day evaluations of the ethics of the Milgram study are coloured by knowledge of the study's results? In other words, do people evaluate the study's ethics based on its outcome rather than its basic methods?

For more information about Stanley Milgram, his work, and its implications, go to www.stanleymilgram.com. The website is maintained by Professor Thomas Blass, University of Maryland, Baltimore County, who has written a biography of Milgram[2].

Case 2

The next proposal comes in from Professor Solomon Asch. He plans to study conformity by telling research participants that they are participating in a perception experiment and leading them to believe that the experiment's "confederates" are also participants in the study. The participant's task is to publicly state which of three comparison lines match a standard line in length. The participant will do this for a number of trials, with all the judgments being objectively easy. Before the participant states his or her judgment, the seven confederates of the experimenter will state their judgments, and they will be wrong on designated trials. (See pages 291-293 in the textbook for a more complete description of the study's methods.)

1. Does the deception about the purpose of this study allow us to obtain information that would otherwise be unobtainable?

2. Does the importance of the information justify the deception and override the potential harm to the participants?

3. Can debriefing participants about the true purpose of the experiment and its results restore them to a state of emotional well-being?

---

[2] Blass, T. (2004). *The man who shocked the world: The life and legacy of Stanley Milgram.* New York, NY: Basic Books.

4. Would you approve Professor Asch's proposal? Why or why not?

5. Do your answers differ from the ones in relation to the Milgram experiment? Why or why not?

Case 3

The final proposal comes in from Professor Phillip Zimbardo. He plans to recruit male volunteers for a study of the psychological effects of prison life. Volunteers for the study will be given diagnostic interviews and personality tests to eliminate volunteers with psychological problems or a criminal background. The volunteers chosen to participate in the study will be randomly assigned to be a prisoner or a guard, and placed in a prison-like environment. Professor Zimbardo will act as the prison superintendent and he and his colleagues will observe and record the interactions between the "prisoners" and "guards."

1. Does the importance of the information to be obtained in the study justify the potential harm to the participants?

2. Would debriefing participants about the experiment after its completion rectify any emotional distress experienced by them?

3. What other questions would you like to ask Professor Zimbardo before making a decision about his proposal?

4. Now go to this website (www.prisonexp.org) and view a slide show of the procedures and results of Zimbardo's prison experiment. Does this change your assessment of the study's ethics? Why or why not?

Summary

All of the above studies were conducted in the pursuit of important research goals, goals that continue today. For example, two professors in the United Kingdom—Professor Alex Haslam of Exeter University and Professor Steve Reicher of St. Andrews University—have challenged the conclusions of Zimbardo's study because they believed the study to be methodologically flawed. They believe it is important to revisit the issue because Zimbardo's conclusions "allow tyrants everywhere to avoid responsibility for their acts. They legitimate the defense 'I couldn't help it, it was the uniform that made me do it.' The message also demotivates the struggle against tyranny by representing it as futile" (Haslam and Reicher, 2002). So recognizing the ethical issues involved, they embarked on a conceptually similar study, one that featured improved procedures for safeguarding the well-being of the participants. For more information about their study, go to www.ex.ac.uk/psychology/seorg/exp.

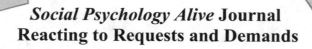

Social Psychology Alive Journal
Reacting to Requests and Demands

Our day-to-day lives are bombarded with requests—some direct and some more subtle—from our family, friends, teachers, co-workers, supervisors, acquaintances, strangers, and the mass media. We comply with some requests and reject others, sometimes with much thought and sometimes mindlessly. Track these requests for a few days, and for at least some of the requests, identify the underlying conformity, compliance, and obedience principles. Also state whether or not you conformed, complied, or obeyed, and why.

What request or demand was made of you?	What psychological principle underlies the request or demand?	How did you react to the request or demand?	Why did you react the way you did?

Learning Objectives

Defining Conformity, Compliance, and Obedience

1. Briefly explain the concepts of conformity, compliance, and obedience, and how they are similar and different from one another. (pp. 287–288)

Conformity: Doing As Others Do

2. What are social or group norms and what are the consequences of complying with and rejecting such norms? (pp. 289–290)

3. Be able to describe the method of the following experiments conducted by Muzafer Sherif, and the implications of their results for the establishment of group norms. (pp. 290–291)
    - The experiment with 2–3 naïve participants who either first made their judgments alone or in a group setting;
    - The experiment in which a confederate varied his or her judgments around an arbitrary standard in the presence of a naïve participant;
    - The experiment in which an arbitrary group norm was shown to persist as membership of the group of participants changed.

4. Describe the Asch conformity situation. In what significant way does the judgment task differ from that in the experiments using the autokinetic effect? Explain the procedure and findings of the basic Asch experiments. (pp. 291–293)

5. How is the Crutchfield apparatus used to study conformity? What is the advantage of this procedure over the traditional Asch procedure? Crutchfield replicated the findings of Asch using a variety of tasks but found no conformity due to group pressure on one task. What was that task and why do you think people behaved independently when doing it? (p. 293)

6. How do the ambiguity and difficulty of the judgment task affect the extent to which people conform? How do non-conformers differ in character from people who consistently conform? How does the propensity to conform vary according to a person's age? (pp. 293–295)

7. Describe the relationship between the size of the majority and the likelihood that an individual will conform. (p. 295)

8. Describe two methods for reducing or completely eliminating conformity. (pp. 295–296)

9. How do people in individualist versus collectivist cultures differ in their tendency to conform? How do people with independent versus interdependent self-concepts differ in their tendency to conform? How do women versus men differ in their tendency to conform? (pp. 296–299)

Compliance: Doing As Others Want

10. Describe the following six compliance techniques and explain why each tends to elicit compliance: foot-in-the door, door-in-the-face, free gift, low-ball, what-is-scarce-is-valuable, and like-me-then-help-me. (pp. 299–305)

Obedience: Doing As Others Command

11. Describe the basic procedures used in the Milgram experiments. (pp. 307–308)

12. What did Milgram's colleagues and students predict the performance of the "teachers" to be? In other words, were they expected to defy the experimenter early on or to administer very strong shocks? (pp. 308–309)

13. Explain the results of the first Milgram experiment. Explain variations of the original study: How was the "teacher's" willingness to deliver shocks affected by: 1) the teacher receiving more extensive vocal feedback from the learner? 2) the teacher moving closer to the learner? 3) the presence of a "peer" teacher who actually issued the shocks? 4) allowing the teachers to select their own shock level? 5) the presence of two experimenters-in-charge who issued contradictory orders? (pp. 309–310)

14. Do you think the results of the Milgram's work can be generalized to the real-world? Why or why not? (pp. 311–312)

15. Why did ethicists criticize Milgram's experiments? (p. 312)

General Mechanisms Underlying Conformity, Compliance, and Obedience

16. How do accuracy and social motivation help explain a person's acceptance or rejection of social influence? (pp. 312–314)

17. How does terror management theory help explain a person's acceptance or rejection of social influence? (pp. 314–317)

18. Describe social impact theory and its predictions about the strength, immediacy, and number of social forces and overall social influence. (pp. 317–318)

Test Your Knowledge

Multiple Choice Questions

1. According to social psychologists, what is the difference between compliance and obedience?
   A. Compliance is a change in behaviour that is ordered by another person, whereas obedience is a change of behaviour that is requested by another person.
   B. Compliance is a change in behaviour that is requested by another person, whereas obedience is a change of behaviour that is ordered by another person.
   C. Compliance is a change in attitude that is ordered by another person, whereas obedience is a change of behaviour that is requested by another person.
   D. Compliance is a change in attitude that is requested by another person, whereas obedience is a change of behaviour that is ordered by another person.

2. Alison is spending her first Christmas with her boyfriend's family. Her boyfriend is Catholic; Alison is not. As part of the holiday tradition, the entire family attends Midnight Mass, and Alison joins them. Having never been to a Catholic ceremony, she is unsure of the proper behaviour, and looks to her boyfriend's family for cues about when to sit, stand, and kneel. Alison's behaviour is an example of
   A. informational influence.
   B. normative influence.
   C. rational influence.
   D. prosocial influence.

3. Muzafer Sherif's research in which participants judged the distance a point of light appeared to move was designed to study the development and impact of
   A. the autokinetic effect.
   B. the Crutchfield apparatus.
   C. social norms.
   D. gender norms.

4. The researcher most closely associated with using the line judgment task to induce conformity is
   A. Muzafer Sherif.
   B. Solomon Asch.
   C. Jim Jones.
   D. Robert Cialdini.

5. Which of the following characteristics does *not* influence the amount of conformity displayed in tasks like the line judgment task?
   A. difficulty of task
   B. ambiguity of task
   C. age of participants
   D. intelligence of participants

6. In traditional conformity experiments like the line judgment task, which strategies have been shown to reduce conformity?
   A. providing the critical participant with an ally who also gave the correct answer
   B. increasing the group size from 5 to 6 people
   C. using participants from collectivist cultures
   D. allowing the experimenter to be in the room with the critical participant

7. The norm of reciprocity is responsible for the success of which compliance technique?
   A. low-ball technique
   B. foot-in-door technique
   C. door-in-face technique
   D. what-is-scarce-is-valuable technique

8. As a part of your social psychology requirement, you have to recruit participants for an experimental session. According to the compliance techniques described in your text, what strategy should you follow to most successfully obtain the cooperation of your peers in the study?
   A. Tell the prospective participant that the experiment will take several hours.
   B. Persuade someone the prospective participant does not know to ask for you.
   C. Buy the prospective participant a cup of coffee before you ask.
   D. Play up how different the prospective participant is from you before asking.

9. In Milgram's series of experiments in which increasingly intense shocks are delivered to the "learner" by a "teacher," which of the following increased obedience to authority?
   A. increasing the vocal feedback from the learner
   B. bringing the learner into the same room as the teacher
   C. requiring the teacher to hold the learner's hand on the shock plate
   D. giving the teacher an assistant to deliver the shocks

10. The historical event that led Milgram to study obedience to authority was the
    A. My Lai massacre.
    B. Holocaust.
    C. Jonestown massacre.
    D. Watergate scandal.

11. Milgram's obedience to authority experiments led to
    A. federal regulations governing the treatment of human participants in research.
    B. federal regulations governing the treatment of animals in research.
    C. federal regulations requiring a one-year follow-up interview for all participants in research.
    D. revised military regulations governing the treatment of prisoners of war.

12. Bassili's study in which surveys of attitudes about social issues were conducted over the telephone found that in general, participants who held
    A. less common views answered more quickly than participants who held more common views.
    B. more common views answered more quickly than participants who held less common views.
    C. less common views answered more questions than participants who held more common views.
    D. more common views answered more questions than participants who held less common views.

13. One theory of understanding conformity hypothesizes that conformity to social values can protect people from anxiety about death. This theory is called the
    A. terror management theory.
    B. mortality protection theory.
    C. fear validation theory.
    D. cultural worldview theory.

14. Which of the following is *not* a component of the social forces that result in social influence, according to the social influence theory?
    A. immediacy
    B. number
    C. strength
    D. accuracy

15. According to the psychosocial law, how will overall social influence change as the number of social forces changes?
    A. Decreasing the number of social forces will increase the overall social influence, but at a declining rate.
    B. Decreasing the number of social forces will increase the overall social influence, but at an exponential rate.
    C. Increasing the number of social forces will increase the overall social influence, but at a declining rate.
    D. Increasing the number of social forces will increase the overall social influence, but at an exponential rate.

Sentence Completion

1. After they arrived at university for their freshman year, Stan, Steve, and Scott all changed their style of dress. Stan spontaneously changed his style to match those of his new friends; he _conformed_ his behaviour to theirs. Steve changed the way he dressed because his new girlfriend asked him to do so; he _complied_ with her request. Scott changed his style because his new fraternity brothers emphatically told their pledges to dress in a certain way; he _obeyed_ their command.

2. Conformity is more likely when a task is _ambiguous_ and _difficult_ because on these tasks, other people's responses exert both _informational_ and _normative_ influence.

3. Melissa is a born leader; she has high self-esteem and prides herself on her honesty and generosity. Daphne is somewhat low in self-esteem, but is conscientious and concerned with obtaining and maintaining the approval of others. Compared to Melissa, Daphne would be _more_ likely to conform in an Asch experiment.

4. Women are _slightly more_ likely to conform than men, but only in _public_.

5. Self-perception and consistency processes help explain the effectiveness of the _foot in the door_ technique. The norm of reciprocity helps explain the effectiveness of the _door in the face_ technique and the _free gift_ technique. Both consistency processes and post-decisional dissonance help explain the _low ball_ technique.

6. *Hurry, only 5 cars will be sold at this price!* is an example of the _scarcity_ technique.

7. It is harder to say *no* when a friend asks a favour or when a friendly and attractive salesperson makes a pitch, than when a stranger asks a favour or when an unfriendly, dislikeable salesperson makes a pitch. This illustrates the ___likeability___ technique.

8. The predictions of Milgram's students as to how the teachers would administer shocks were ___inconsistent___ with the actual results of the study.

9. ___Terror Management___ theory hypothesizes that conformity to social values and cultural worldviews can serve to protect people from death anxiety.

10. Social Impact Theory predicts that the ___strength___, ___immediacy___, and ___number___ of social forces are related to overall social influence.

Matching I – Key Terms

_____	1.	conformity	A. a change in behaviour that is requested by another person or group
_____	2.	compliance	B. a change in behaviour that is ordered by another person or group
_____	3.	obedience	C. any change in behaviour caused by another person or group
_____	4.	informational influence	D. in a darkened room, a stationary point of light will appear to move periodically
_____	5.	normative influence	E. influence from other people that is motivated by a desire to gain rewards or avoid punishment
_____	6.	social norm	F. a machine that consists of an electrical panel with several rows of lights; it allows the efficient study of conformity by simulating the responses of numerous hypothetical participants
_____	7.	autokinetic effect	G. a strategy to increase compliance, based on the fact that agreement with a small request increases the likelihood of agreement with a subsequent larger request
_____	8.	Crutchfield apparatus	H. a strategy to increase compliance, based on the fact that refusal of a large request increases the likelihood of agreement with a subsequent smaller request
_____	9.	foot-in-the-door technique	I. a rule or guideline in a group or culture about what behaviours are proper and improper
_____	10.	door-in-the-face technique	J. influence from other people that is motivated by a desire to be correct and to obtain accurate information

Matching II – Key Terms

_____ 11. **norm of reciprocity**	A. a strategy to increase the attractiveness of a product by making it appear rare or temporary
_____ 12. **free-gift technique**	B. a strategy to increase compliance, in which something is offered at a given price, but then, after agreement, the price is increased
_____ 13. **low-ball technique**	C. a model hypothesizing that recognition of their own mortality raises anxiety in humans, which they can reduce by affirming and conforming to their cultural worldview
_____ 14. **what-is-scarce-is-valuable technique**	D. the principle that we should give back in return any favours that are done for us
_____ 15. **like-me-then-help-me technique**	E. a strategy to increase compliance, based on the fact that giving someone a small gift increases the likelihood of agreement with a subsequent request
_____ 16. **norm of obedience**	F. a model that conceives of influence from other people as being the result of social forces acting on individuals, much like physical forces can affect an object
_____ 17. **terror management theory**	G. a principle in social impact theory which specifies the nature of the relation between the size of a group and its social influence; the principle predicts that as the number of social forces increases, overall social influence also increases, but at a declining rate
_____ 18. **social impact theory**	H. a strategy to increase compliance, based on the fact that people are more likely to assist others they find appealing than others they do not find appealing
_____ 19. **psychosocial law**	I. the principle that we should obey legitimate authorities

Test Your Knowledge

Multiple Choice Questions

1. B	6. A	11. A
2. A	7. C	12. B
3. C	8. C	13. A
4. B	9. D	14. D
5. D	10. B	15. C

Sentence Completion

1. conformed, complied, obeyed
2. ambiguous, difficult, informational, normative
3. more
4. slightly more, public
5. foot-in-the-door, door-in-the face, free gift, low-ball
6. what-is-scarce-is-valuable
7. like-me-then-help-me
8. inconsistent
9. terror management
10. strength, immediacy, number

Matching I – Key Terms

1. C	6. I
2. A	7. D
3. B	8. F
4. J	9. G
5. E	10. H

Matching II – Key Terms

11. D	16. I
12. E	17. C
13. B	18. F
14. A	19. G
15. H	

Chapter 9
Stereotypes, Prejudice, and Discrimination

Thinking Critically about Social Psychology
The Death Penalty and Aversive Racism

In the 1972 decision of *Furman v. Georgia*, a United States Supreme Court declared that the death penalty violated the U.S. Constitution because of the arbitrary way in which it was administered. After a temporary moratorium, the Court approved revised capital sentencing laws in 1976, and the states resumed their task of executing criminals. Despite new rules designed to eliminate discrimination in the capital sentencing process, the administration of the death penalty arguably remains biased in a number of crucial ways.

Race remains a powerful determinant of who will be executed and who will not. Even correcting for the circumstances of the cases, defendants accused of killing a White victim are more likely to be sentenced to death than are defendants accused of killing a Black victim.

Studies have demonstrated that the race of the victim is most likely to play a role in cases in which the crime was only moderately aggressive. David Baldus and his colleagues (1990) undertook one of the most extensive analyses of capital sentencing. They examined more than two thousand murder cases and concluded that the race-of-victim effect was most prominent in mid-level aggression cases. In cases in which multiple victims are cruelly tortured and killed, all defendants are likely to be sentenced to death, regardless of the race of the victim or defendant. Similarly, in cases in which the victim is killed as a result of a drunken brawl, no defendant receives the death penalty, again regardless of race. It is in the middle range of aggression—the range into which the majority of capital cases fall—in which racial disparities are particularly salient. For example, a defendant may be treated more harshly when a White person is murdered during a robbery than when a Black person is murdered. Other researchers have replicated these findings over the years.

Social psychology offers one explanation for the "race of victim" effect in capital sentencing—the theory of aversive racism, as formulated by Dovidio and Gaertner (1986, 1991). According to this theory, many White Americans have ambivalent feelings toward racial minorities. They often support equal opportunities for racial minorities and regard themselves as unprejudiced and nondiscriminatory. However, they simultaneously harbor some negative beliefs and hostile feelings toward minorities and exhibit discrimination when their discriminatory behaviour can be justified on nonracial grounds.

In an employment context, for example, an aversive racist manager might assess White and Black job applicants similarly except when their qualifications are ambiguous (i.e., not clearly qualified or nonqualified for the job). In that case, the manager would assess White applicants more favourably than the Black applicants because their discriminatory behaviour towards Black applicants could be justified by the Blacks' lack of clear qualifications.

By similar reasoning, juries treat murder defendants similarly when the defendant's level of aggression clearly supports a particular outcome (e.g., the death penalty), but when their level of aggression would support either the death penalty or a prison sentence, they treat defendants whose victims are White more harshly. In effect, they are discriminating against the Black victims, but their discriminatory behaviour can be explained away by the circumstances of the crime.

Questions:

1. Can you explain the trend in capital sentencing with the theory of aversive racism? Would an aversive racism explanation be more or less likely if the race of victim effect was found in every case, regardless of level of aggression?

2. What are some other plausible explanations for the "race of victim" effect?

3. Based on the theory of aversive racism, would you expect Black defendants to be convicted more or less often than White defendants when the evidence supporting their guilt was clear-cut? How about when the evidence supporting their guilt was ambiguous?

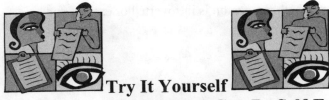

Try It Yourself
Understanding How Stereotypes Can Be Self-Fulfilling
The Use of a Positive Test Strategy

Self-fulfilling prophecies often result from the way in which we gather information about other people. We may ask questions and look for information that confirms our expectations, and disregard information that would disconfirm our expectations. For example, if you think a friend is shy, you probably attend to information that confirms your view such as noting that she did not attend a recent party. That is certainly consistent with shyness. But suppose you also know your friend recently volunteered to chair a student body committee. That fact is inconsistent with shyness, so you may discount or disregard that information because it fails to confirm your preconceived notion of her shyness.

This strategy is known as the positive test strategy, and it is commonly used in daily social interactions. You can see for yourself how frequently people use this strategy by asking two friends to come up with questions that determine whether a person is extraverted and two other friends to come up with questions that determine whether a person is introverted. If your friends use the positive test strategy, then they will probably ask questions to confirm what they are looking for. For example, a confirming question for whether a person is extraverted would be: "Do you like to go to parties? And a confirming question for whether a person is introverted would be: "Do you like to spend quiet time alone?" The problem with these questions is that most people would answer "yes" to both of them, and so they provide little distinguishing information.

One way to encourage friends not to use a positive test strategy is to ask them to come up with questions that determine whether a person is either introverted or extraverted. Try this with another two friends. An example of the type of question these friends might come up with is: "If you have nothing to do on Saturday night, would you rather read a book or go to a party?" An answer to this question provides valuable information about whether a person is introverted or extraverted.

You can try this with other traits too—for example, optimistic versus pessimistic, studious versus non-studious, or sociable versus non-sociable.

1. Questions to determine whether a person is extraverted:

2. Questions to determine whether a person is introverted:

3. Questions to determine whether a person is introverted or extraverted:

Question:

1. Do the questions your friends proposed reflect a positive test strategy? That is, in the first two instances, do they primarily ask questions that will support the answer they are trying to receive, or do they ask disconfirming questions as well? Are their questions more balanced in the third instance, that is, when the questions are to make an "either or" determination?

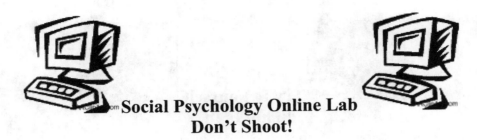

Social Psychology Online Lab
Don't Shoot!

The computerized laboratory for this chapter, Fast Responses, is based on a study by Correll, Park, Judd, and Wittenbrink (2002), which required participants to decide as quickly as possible whether a male target person was armed or unarmed. Sometimes the target person is White and sometimes the target person is Black. Try it yourself and then answer the following questions.

Questions:

1. Were you *faster* to judge correctly that Black targets were armed than to judge correctly that White targets were armed?   Yes _____No_____

2. Were you *slower* to judge correctly that Black targets were unarmed than to judge correctly that White targets were unarmed?   Yes _____No_____

3. When confronted with an unarmed target, were you more likely to erroneously identify a Black target as armed than a White target?   Yes _____No_____

4. When confronted with an armed target, were you more likely to erroneously identify a White target as unarmed than a Black target?   Yes _____No_____

5. Did your performance mirror that found in the study?   Why do you think it did or did not?

6. The results of this study lead to the prediction that unarmed Black men are more likely to be shot in error by police officers than are unarmed White men.   What suggestions do you have for law enforcement training to reduce this bias?

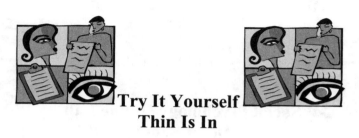

Try It Yourself
Thin Is In

The health risks associated with obesity have been well documented: obese and overweight individuals are at greater risk of diabetes, heart disease, and other illnesses. In addition, obesity is associated with negative social consequences, ranging from ridicule to denial of employment. Obese people are viewed as less intelligent, less popular, less athletic, and less successful. The impact of being overweight is greater on women because our society more highly values physical appearance for women than for men.

It is therefore not surprising that even normal weight women tend to be concerned about their weight. Patricia Pliner and her colleagues (1990) found that on average women are less satisfied with their appearance than are men, no matter what their age. Other researchers have found that exposure to thin media images can have negative effects on women's self-concepts and eating patterns (e.g., Mills, Polivy, Herman, & Tiggemann, 2002; Stice & Shaw, 1994).

Do you see this trend among your own friends? Ask five of your female friends and five of your male friends to complete Patricia Pliner's appearance self-esteem scale that appears on page 244.

Scores on the scale can range from 6 to 30, with higher scores representing higher self-esteem. To obtain the score for each of your friends:

1. For items, 1, 3, 5, and 6, subtract the number your friend circled from 6. For example, if your friend answered item 1 by circling 4, his or her adjusted answer would be 6 minus 4, or 2.

2. Sum the adjusted answers to items 1, 3, 5, and 6 and the original answers to items 2 and 4.

Record the Scores

Record your friends' scores in the table below and then complete the questions that follow.

Scores of male friends	Scores of female friends
1.	1.
2.	2.
3.	3.
4.	4.
5.	5.

Questions:

1. What is the average score of your male friends? What is the average score of your female friends? (To calculate the average, sum the scores for the five friends and then divide by five.)

    Male average: _____

    Female average: _____

2. Did you find the same trends as Patricia Pliner and her colleagues? Were women more likely than men to express dissatisfaction with their physical appearance? Looking just at item 6, were they more anxious about their weight?

3. The media plays an important role in setting unrealistic standards for female body weight. Magazines, television shows, commercials, and movies constantly bombard us with images of extremely thin women, and those images can have negative effects on women's self-concepts and eating patterns. During the week, pay attention to how the media portrays women.

    a. Why do you think the media is so focused on portraying women as unrealistically thin and attractive?

    b. Are there contexts in which more healthy body images of women are promoted? For example, are images of female athletes more realistic?

Please answer each of the following questions by circling a number between 1 and 5, with 1 meaning "never" and 5 meaning "always."[1]

	Never				Always
1. How often do you have the feeling you are unattractive?	1	2	3	4	5
2. After you have dressed for the day, how pleased are you with your appearance?	1	2	3	4	5
3. How often are you dissatisfied with the way you look?	1	2	3	4	5
4. How often do you feel as attractive as most of the people you know?	1	2	3	4	5
5. How much do you worry about your appearance?	1	2	3	4	5
6. How often do you worry about your weight?	1	2	3	4	5

---

[1] Pliner, P., Chaiken, S., & Flett, G. (1990). Gender differences in concern with body weight and physical appearance over the lifespan. *Personality and Social Psychology Bulletin, 16,* 263–273.

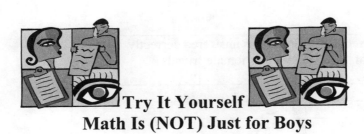

Try It Yourself
Math Is (NOT) Just for Boys

The performance difference between men and women in math and science has been well-documented by the media—men are more likely than women to follow career paths dominated by the hard sciences, such as math, engineering, and physics. One explanation for this difference is stereotype threat: the very existence of a social stereotype that women are less able than men in certain fields may actually create the performance difference. Claude Steele and his colleagues have studied the concept of stereotype threat, and you can replicate the basic experiment with your friends.

Method

Recruit about ten female friends, telling them that you are interested in seeing how many algebra problems they can solve in 15 minutes.

Provide each friend with a copy of the algebra test that appears on page 247.[2] Tell them they have 15 minutes to solve the problems. Tell half of them that the problems are part of a test that has revealed sex differences in the past. Do not make any reference to sex differences to the other half—simply ask them to solve the problems. After the allotted time, collect the test and note how many problems your friend solved correctly.

The answers to the algebra test are:

1. 400
2. $19y^3$
3. $4s^2 - 1.3s - 1$
4. $-14a^8$
5. $p^2 - 2p$
6. 107.1

7. \$41,440
8. 3,200 lb.
9. 115,200 min.
10. $x = -3$
11. 14 hr., 6 hr.
12. 356 23/30

Record the scores

Record how many problems your friends answered correctly in the table below and answer the questions that follow.

---

[2] The problems on the test were drawn from A. S. Tussy and R. D. Gustafson (2002), *Prealgebra*, 2nd ed. (Pacific Grove, CA: Brooks/Cole).

Problems answered correctly by female friends told of "sex difference"	Problems answered correctly by other female friends
1.	1.
2.	2.
3.	3.
4.	4.
5.	5.

Questions:

1. How many problems did your female friends who were alerted to the sex difference answer correctly on average? How many problems did your other female friends score on average? (To calculate the average for each group, sum the scores for the five friends in the group and then divide by five.)

   Average for female friends told of sex difference: _____

   Average for other female friends: _____

2. Did you find any evidence of stereotype threat? Did women who were told of the sex differences solve fewer problems than women who were not told of sex differences? (If you did not see evidence of the effect, it is probably because the effect is small and you need more people to demonstrate it.)

3. The concept of stereotype threat is one that can apply to many areas, not just women and math. How could you alter the basic methodology to study how stereotype threat can influence performance in other domains? For example, consider the stereotype that White men can't play basketball. How would you design a study to examine the role of stereotype threat in athletic performance?

1. BROADWAY MUSICAL. A theater usher at a Broadway musical finds that seventh-eighths of the patrons attending a performance are in their seats by show time. The remaining 50 people are seated after the opening number. If the show is always a complete sellout, how many seats does the theater have?

2. Add: $7y^3 + 12y^3$

3. Add: $(s^2 + 1.2s - 5) + (3s_2 - 2.5s + 4)$.

4. Multiply: $-7a^3 \cdot 2a^5$

5. Subtract: $(5p^2 - p + 7.1) - (4p^2 + p + 7.1)$

6. Find the product: $(-2x^2)(3x^3)$

7. 102% of 105 is what number?

8. COST-OF-LIVING INCREASE. A teacher earning $40,000 just received a cost-of-living increase of 3.6%. What is the teacher's new salary?

9. A car weighs 1.6 tons. Find its weight in tons.

10. LITERATURE. An excellent work of early science fiction is the book *Around the World in 80 Days* by Jules Verne (1828-1905). Convert 80 days to minutes.

11. Solve $4x = -13 - (3x + 8)$

12. MOVER'S PAY SCALE. A part-time mover's regular pay rate is $6 an hour. If the work involves going up and down stairs, his rate increases to $9 an hour. In one week, he earned $138 and worked 20 hours. How many hours did he work at each rate?

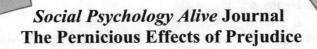

Social Psychology Alive Journal
The Pernicious Effects of Prejudice

Sometimes social prejudice has rather subtle effects, but prejudice can also have a profound effect on targeted persons' very identity. The article, reproduced below, about Jamaican youth who apply dangerous skin lightening cream to achieve a more socially desirable appearance, brings home this point. During the week, keep your eyes and ears out for other such examples in the media and in your day-to-day life. Record your findings below and share them with your classmates.

Our example:

A Section

In Jamaica, Shades of an Identity Crisis; Ignoring Health Risk, Blacks Increase Use of Skin Lighteners

Serge F. Kovaleski

Washington Post Foreign Service

Despite youthful good looks, Latoya Reid was bothered by her dark skin. The 17-year-old felt it was a hindrance to attracting boyfriends and finding opportunities for a better life away from the poor Torrington Park section of Kingston.

So Reid recently set her mind on becoming a "brownin'," a term used on this Caribbean island to refer to blacks who have light skin. She took up "bleaching," coating her face with layers of illegally imported skin cream containing steroids or using less expensive homemade concoctions that produce the desired whitening effect.

Regardless of warnings that the practice could damage her skin, rarely a day goes by when Reid does not bleach--and she is pleased with the results. "When I walk on the streets you can hear people say, 'Hey, check out the brownin'.' It is cool. It looks pretty," she said. "When you are lighter, people pay more attention to you. It makes you more important."

Throughout Jamaica's vast underclass, and sometimes in upper classes as well, women and an emerging segment of men are ignoring public health warnings and resorting to skin bleaching in what government officials and doctors describe as unprecedented numbers.

The controversial phenomenon, which has been on the rise for three years, is largely rooted in a belief among Jamaica's poor that a lighter complexion may be a ticket to upward mobility, socially and professionally, as well as to greater sex appeal.

A number of social commentators and other intellectuals here have decried skin bleaching as an affront to black dignity. Observers said it was for that reason during the 1920s in the United States that Marcus Garvey refused to carry advertisements in his publications for skin lighteners, whose origins date to before the turn of the century.

More recently, bleaching became a particularly poignant topic here in the weeks leading up to Monday's 161st anniversary of Jamaicans' emancipation from slavery.

"Shouldn't we think of emancipation as that glorious opportunity to open our minds, freeing ourselves not just from physical servitude but also from the deep self-contempt that has for too long enslaved us," attorney Audley Foster wrote in an op-ed piece about skin bleaching in the Weekend Observer newspaper last month.

"All this sounds like an identity crisis of major proportions. The only thing any face needs to be pretty . . . is regular soap and water," columnist Dawn Ritch recently wrote in the Gleaner newspaper.

Bleaching has long been popular in such predominantly black nations as the Bahamas and South Africa, where lighter skin has historically been a symbol of privilege, as it has been in Jamaica and throughout the Caribbean since colonial days. It also has been practiced for decades in the United States. Today in many of Kingston's hard-bitten communities, it is not unusual to see women passing time on the streets or doing chores with their faces covered in cream.

"Skin bleaching has just become too popular. There have been days when the creams would go like hot bread," said Kathryn Fischer, a sales clerk at a Kingston beauty shop that has carried the illegal steroid products, occasionally selling up to 60 tubes a day. "One girl would come in here and buy three or four every other day because she used it all over her body."

Doctors, however, have recently reported an alarming increase in patients seeking treatment for skin disorders, some of them irreversible, caused by excessive use of the steroid products or abrasive homemade applications that usually contain toothpaste mixed with a facial cream.

The skin creams typically contain hydroquinone, a chemical used in the rubber industry that was found to lighten skin color. They also usually contain steroids, which are hormones that can suppress certain bodily functions. Both substances seem to work by stopping the formation of pigment, according to J. Fletcher Robinson, a Washington dermatologist.

Numerous dermatologists here said people suffering the ill effects of bleaching—which include severe acne, stretch marks, increased risk of skin cancer and even darkening of the skin—now account for up to 20 percent of their patients. When used in high concentrations or for long periods, steroids can produce adverse side effects by interfering with the growth of skin cells, Robinson said.

Over the last several months, bleaching has sparked an intense public debate about black identity and self-respect in this nation of 2.6 million people, about 90 percent of whom are black, as well as the influence of American and European models of success and glamour.

"With Jamaica so close to North America, we are bombarded with images of a white culture. People have come to feel that lighter skin is a passport to better relationships and making it in this world," said Kingston dermatologist Clive Anderson. "The use of skin bleaching is spreading rapidly, and unfortunately men are starting to use it as well."

A number of women also have started taking what has been nicknamed the "fowl pill," an anti-infection drug approved only for veterinary use here. It is given to chickens and other fowl to, among other things, enhance their appetites. Although its label reads, "Poison . . . not for human use," women have been using the pill to develop larger breasts and buttocks, which they say Jamaican men prefer, along with whiter skin.

"This is a particularly unique phenomenon," said Grace Allen-Young, director of the Pharmaceutical Services Division of the Ministry of Health. "There seems to be an emerging need to change body features for whatever reason. It has become part of the grass-roots culture."

Alarmed by the surge in medical cases stemming from bleaching, Allen-Young's office last month launched a crackdown on sales of the nine or so brands of steroid creams that are not licensed for use in Jamaica. In one case, investigators seized more than 200 tubes from a Kingston wholesaler.

Efforts are also underway by customs officials to curb the smuggling of the products onto the island. Most are made in Europe, where they are used legally to treat a variety of skin conditions.

Nonetheless, the creams remain widely available—and in demand—in this capital. "I know they can do bad to your skin, but I have nothing to lose in wanting to be a brownin'. I am poor and bored, and being whiter would make me happier," said Sheri Roth, 22, who had just bought a tube of cream that promised "a brighter, cleaner, smoother complexion."

She added, "I want people to think I am more than a ghetto girl. . . . I want to walk into dance halls and feel like a movie star, a white one."

Staff writer Rob Stein in Washington contributed to this report.

Record your examples of the effects of prejudice below:

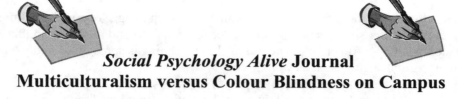

Social Psychology Alive Journal
Multiculturalism versus Colour Blindness on Campus

College or University is often the first time young adults encounter people of many different races, ethnicities, sexual orientations, and ideologies. Ideally, these interactions will result in all groups living in harmony. However, since that is not often the case, colleges and universities use the approaches described in your text to try to make the experience positive for everyone involved. Multiculturalism involves each group maintaining its own identity while simultaneously respecting other groups, whereas color blindness involves recognizing that everyone is equal. Both approaches are common on campuses, both formally in school policies and organized events, and informally in student-driven activities.

Each approach has advantages and disadvantages. Multiculturalism embraces diversity, celebrating each group's unique history and qualities, which may increase people's willingness to stereotype (both positively and negatively). Colour blindness, on the other hand, promotes overlooking or ignoring group differences so that all individuals are treated equally. While that approach may reduce stereotypes, it can also be detrimental to a group member's self-esteem if her cultural or ethnic identity is neglected.

Question:

1. Is multiculturalism or colour blindness more prevalent on your campus? Does the administration have a stated policy endorsing one over the other? Is there separate housing for certain special interests? What about student activities? Is there a thriving multicultural centre, or are students encouraged to look beyond race and ethnicity to the individual?

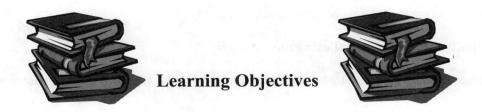

Learning Objectives

1. Define and differentiate the concepts of prejudice, discrimination, and stereotypes. (pp. 324–325)

Prejudice and Discrimination Today

2. What is aversive racism? How did John Dovidio and Samuel Gaertner's (2000) study illustrate aversice racism? (pp. 326–328)

Stereotypes: Cognitive Sources of Prejudice and Discrimination

3. Stereotypes efficiently provide us with information about target persons that helps us make rapid inferences and guides our behaviour, but this comes at a cost. What are two costs of stereotypes, and in what two ways do stereotypes distort information processing? (pp. 328–332)

4. Describe the study by Joshua Correll and his colleagues (2002). How do the findings regarding reaction time and error rate demonstrate the way stereotypes distort information processing? Are personal or cultural stereotypes at work? (pp. 330–332)

5. What is a self-fulfilling prophecy? Explain how the studies by Carl Word and his colleagues (1974) illustrate this concept. (pp. 334–336)

6. Explain how Patricia Devine (1990) used a subliminal priming procedure to demonstrate that even stereotypes with which we disagree can influence our perceptions. (pp. 336–337)

7. What is implicit intergroup bias? How might it be reduced? (pp. 337–338)

8. What are meta-stereotypes? Give and example of a meta-stereotype found by Vorauer and her colleagues (1998). (p. 338)

Emotional Sources of Prejudice and Discrimination

9. Describe the scapegoat theory of prejudice and the support for it generated by Carl Hovland and Robert Sears (1940). (pp. 339–340)

10. Describe the realistic group conflict of prejudice. What support does Victoria Esses's attitude study and Muzafer Sherif's Robber's Case experiment provide for it? Explain another type of competition studied by Mohipp and Morry (2004). (p. 340)

11. Explain the social identity theory of prejudice. (p. 341–342)

12. Explain the integrated threat theory of prejudice. (pp. 342–343)

Sexism: Prejudice and Discrimination against Women

13. Define neosexism and explain how Tougas and her colleagues (1995) measure this form of sexism. (p. 344)

14. Provide several examples of beliefs or behaviours that reflect benevolent sexism and hostile sexism, as defined by Peter Glick and Susan Fiske (1996). (pp. 346–347)

15. Name three factors that contribute to gender stereotypes. To what extent are gender stereotypes accurate portrayals of the differences between women and men? (pp. 346–349)

16. Describe research that demonstrates the prejudice our culture generally holds against overweight women and the effect this prejudice has on women's self-esteem and eating behaviours. (pp. 349–351)

The Victim's Perspective: Prejudice and Discrimination from the Inside

17. Describe the phenomenon labeled the personal-group discrimination discrepancy. Why might people be motivated to understate discrimination against themselves personally and to exaggerate discrimination at the group level? (pp. 352–354)

18. What is stereotype threat and how have Claude Steele and Joshua Aronson empirically demonstrated it with respect to African-Americans? For what other groups of people has it been empirically demonstrated? What mechanisms explain stereotype threat and how might its impact be reduced? (pp. 354–357)

Genocide

19. What five factors may contribute to genocide? (pp. 357–359)

Reducing Prejudice and Discrimination

20. How might dissonance be used to reduce prejudice and discrimination? (pp. 360–361)

21. According to the contact hypothesis, how would one reduce prejudice? What prerequisites must be met for contact to have a positive effect on inter-group attitudes? (pp. 361–363)

22. Differentiate the color-blind and the multiculturalism approaches to prejudice reduction. (pp. 363–365)

23. Why might anti-discrimination legislation reduce prejudice over time? (pp. 365–366)

Test Your Knowledge

Multiple Choice Questions

1. Negative behaviour toward a person based on that person's group membership is known as
   A. stereotyping.
   B. prejudice.
   C. discrimination.
   D. outgroup homogeneity effect.

2. According to Dovidio and Gaertner, an aversive racist is a person who would discriminate against a member of a racial minority
   A. only when an ambiguous situation can be used as an excuse.
   B. in all situations.
   C. only when the situation is clear-cut.
   D. under no circumstances.

3. If a White Canadian believes that Aboriginal Canadians hold a negative stereotype of his or her group, they can be said to have a(n)
   A. stereotype.
   B. implicit intergroup bias.
   C. meta-stereotype.
   D. integrated threat

4. Identify the statement that most accurately describes stereotypes about groups of people.
   A. Stereotypes are always unfavourable.
   B. Stereotype interpretation can be influenced by the perceiver's mood.
   C. Stereotypes are the result of critical thinking.
   D. Stereotypes have no basis in truth.

5. How do stereotypes distort information processing?
   A. Actions consistent with the stereotype are disregarded.
   B. Only actions inconsistent with the stereotype are noticed.
   C. Ambiguous actions are interpreted as disconfirming the stereotype.
   D. Ambiguous actions are interpreted as consistent with stereotype.

6. Which statement best describes the results of the Correll, Park, Judd and Wittenbrink studies using the shoot/don't shoot paradigm to study racial stereotyping?
   A. White participants took less time to judge whether Blacks were unarmed than whether Whites were.
   B. Black participants were equally likely to inaccurately judge Blacks as armed as White participants were.
   C. Black participants took less time to judge whether Blacks were unarmed than whether Whites were.

D. White participants were more likely to inaccurately judge Blacks as armed than Black participants were.

7. Emily is asked to interview her school's star quarterback for a journalism assignment. Expecting the athlete to be aloof and conceited, she is very shy and nervous during the interview, rarely making eye contact. As a result, the quarterback gives monosyllabic responses and doesn't look at Emily during the interview. Emily's behaviour is an example of
A. self-fulfilling prophecy.
B. self-handicapping.
C. stereotype threat.
D. scapegoat theory.

8. The researcher most associated with using the subliminal priming procedure to activate stereotypes of African-Americans is
A. John Dovidio.
B. Carl Hovland.
C. Janet Swim.
D. Patricia Devine.

9. Which of the following statements is *not* true about implicit intergroup bias?
A. It can be reduced by attempts to be open-minded.
B. It is less likely to occur in non-prejudiced people than in prejudiced people.
C. It occurs only in people who agree with a particular stereotype.
D. It does not dictate discriminatory behaviour toward a member of the stereotyped group.

10. The Robber's Cave Experiment, in which competing teams of boys at summer camp expressed hostility and discriminatory behaviour toward each other, is an example of which theoretical model of prejudice?
A. integrated threat theory
B. realistic group conflict theory
C. scapegoat theory
D. social identity theory

11. The 1971 blue-eye/brown-eye classroom experience, in which third graders were told that children with a particular eye color were superior to those with other eye colors, is an example of what theoretical model of prejudice?
A. integrated threat theory
B. realistic group conflict theory
C. scapegoat theory
D. social identity theory

12. According to integrated threat theory, which of the following is *not* a type of threat that can result in negative attitudes toward an outgroup?
A. symbolic threat
B. threats arising from intergroup anxiety
C. realistic threat
D. stereotype threat

13. As defined by Glick and Fiske, benevolent sexism and hostile sexism are
A. two dimensions of sexism, measured by the ambivalent sexism inventory.
B. two dimensions of neosexism, measured by the neosexism scale

256

C. biological bases for gender discrimination.
D. the response of men with unambiguous responses to women.

14. According to the personal group discrimination discrepancy, members of disadvantaged groups report
    A. personally experiencing less discrimination than the average group member.
    B. personally experiencing more discrimination than the average group member.
    C. personally engaging in less discrimination than the average group member.
    D. personally engaging in more discrimination than the average group member.

15. Under which of the following conditions are individuals susceptible to stereotype threat?
    A. when the domain is not important to them
    B. when they are not aware of the stereotype
    C. when they identify strongly with their group
    D. when they identify weakly with their group

16. Which of the following was not studied in the context of investigating the negative effects of stereotype threat?
    A. women and math
    B. Blacks and academic performance
    C. Asians and athletic ability
    D. low socioeconomic status individuals and academic performance

17. Imagine you have been asked to design a program aimed at improving race relations between Black and White students at a largely white suburban high school. Using the principles of the contact hypothesis, what would be the best way to structure your program?
    A. Bus in minority students from the inner city in the morning, and bus them back out right after classes end.
    B. Include group projects in all classes to ensure students of both races share a common goal.
    C. Create an integration program even though parents and teachers are against the idea.
    D. Show black-themed movies to white students.

18. Which statement best describes the difference between multiculturalism and the color-blind approach to prejudice reduction?
    A. The color-blind approach involves perceiving people as individuals rather than group members, whereas multiculturalism involves celebrating the diversity of groups.
    B. Multiculturalism involves perceiving people as individuals rather than group members, whereas the color-blind approach involves celebrating the diversity of groups.
    C. The color-blind approach involves emphasizing shared memberships and common identities, whereas multiculturalism involves celebrating the diversity of groups.
    D. There is no difference between the two approaches.

Sentence Completion

1. The manager of a local grocery store has negative attitudes toward people who live in a particular neighborhood; this is _prejudice_. He will never consider hiring people from that neighborhood in his store; this is _discrimination_.

2. In judging the qualifications of potential employees, a manager assessed White and Black applicants similarly except when their qualifications were ambiguous (i.e., not clearly qualified or nonqualified). In that case, the manager assessed the White applicants more favourably than the Black applicants. This is an example of _aversive_ racism.

3. Stereotypes can guide _attention_ and _interpretation._ ; that is, they can affect what people notice about members of a stereotyped group and they can affect how people construe that behaviour.

4. Bill expected members of a rival fraternity to be unfriendly towards him and they were. This might be an example of a _self_ - _fulfilling prophecy_ .

5. Hovland and Sears (1940) found that between 1882 and 1930, more Black people were lynched in the Southern United States when the price of cotton was lower. This finding demonstrates the _scapegoat_ theory.

6. According to the integrated threat theory of prejudice, _realistic_ threats are those related to competition for jobs, political power, and other scarce resources; _symbolic_ threats are threats to the ingroup's important attitudes, beliefs, and values; threats from _intergroup anxiety_ arise when people feel uncertain about interacting with members of the outgroup; and threats from _negative stereotypes_ occur when people believe members of the outgroup possess undesirable characteristics which may lead to detrimental actions toward the ingroup.

7. Nick thinks women should be cherished and protected by men whereas Mike thinks feminists are making entirely unreasonable demands of men. Nick is more likely to demonstrate _benovalent_ sexism and Mike is more likely to demonstrate _hostile_ sexism.

8. Measures of _appearance_ self-esteem show woman are _less_ satisfied with how they look than men.

9. Emmett, a young Black man reports that he has experienced less personal discrimination compared to most young Black men. This demonstrates _personal_ - _group discrimination discrepency_ .

10. According to the contact hypothesis, people who have more experiences of a positive nature with gay men should exhibit more _positive_ attitudes toward gay men.

Matching I – Key Terms

_____ 1. prejudice

_____ 2. discrimination

_____ 3. genocide

_____ 4. aversive racism

_____ 5. meta-stereotype

_____ 6. self-fulfilling prophecy

_____ 7. subliminal priming procedure

_____ 8. implicit intergroup bias

_____ 9. scapegoat theory

_____ 10. realistic group conflict theory

A. a theory proposing that when groups in society are perceived to be competing with one another for resources, intergroup hostility can be aroused, which leads to prejudice

B. a person's beliefs about the stereotype that outgroup members hold concerning his or her own group

C. a theory proposing that prejudice occurs because members of dominant groups use discrimination against members of weak target groups to vent their frustration and disappointment

D. a method of activating a schema or stereotype by flashing words or pictures very briefly on a computer screen in front of a participant

E. distorted judgments about members of a group based on a stereotype, which can occur without the person's awareness

F. negative, harmful behaviour toward people based on their group membership

G. a negative attitude toward members of a group, which is often very strongly held

H. an attempt to systematically eliminate an ethnic group through banishment or murder

I. a "modern" kind of prejudice held by people who do not consider themselves prejudiced and who would find any accusation of being prejudiced aversive, but who nevertheless harbor some negative beliefs and hostile feelings toward members of minority groups

J. a process in which a perceiver's expectancy about a target person influences the perceiver's behaviour toward the target person in such a way as to elicit the expected actions from the target person

Matching II – Key Terms

_____ 11. **integrated threat theory**

_____ 12. **sexism**

_____ 13. **neosexism**

_____ 14. **ambivalent sexism inventory**

_____ 15. **benevolent sexism**

_____ 16. **hostile sexism**

_____ 17. **appearance self-esteem**

_____ 18. **personal-group discrimination discrepancy**

_____ 19. **stereotype threat**

_____ 20. **contact hypothesis**

_____ 21. **jigsaw classroom**

_____ 22. **color-blind approach**

_____ 23. **multiculturalism**

A. the idea that exposure to members of an outgroup will produce more favourable attitudes toward that group

B. an individual's satisfaction with his or her physical looks

C. the hypothesis that to reduce prejudice, different cultural groups within a society should each maintain their own identity while simultaneously respecting all other groups

D. negative attitudes toward women who violate the traditional stereotype of women

E. the pressure experienced by individuals who fear that if they perform poorly on a task, their performance will appear to confirm an unfavourable belief about their group

F. a measure of stereotyped attitudes toward women, which is composed of two dimensions, one positive and one negative: benevolent sexism and hostile sexism

G. the hypothesis that to reduce prejudice, people should be encouraged to categorize other people as individual persons rather than as members of groups

H. the tendency for people to report that they as individuals have experienced less negative treatment based on their group membership than the average member of their group

I. positive but paternalistic attitudes toward women

J. a theory proposing that prejudice results from four types of threats: realistic threats, symbolic threats, threats stemming from intergroup anxiety, and threats arising from negative stereotypes

K. a method of teaching designed to foster positive interracial contact, which involves forming small, culturally diverse groups of students who are each given one part of the material to be learned

L. prejudice and discrimination directed against women because of their gender

M. a subtle form of sexism, which includes beliefs that women are no longer disadvantaged and antagonism toward women's demands for better treatment

Answers to Test Your Knowledge

Multiple Choice Questions

1. C	6. B	11. D	16. C
2. A	7. A	12. D	17. B
3. C	8. D	13. A	18. A
4. B	9. C	14. A	
5. D	10. B	15. C	

Sentence Completion

1. prejudice, discrimination
2. aversive
3. attention, interpretation
4. self-fulfilling prophecy
5. scapegoat
6. realistic, symbolic, intergroup anxiety, negative stereotypes
7. benevolent, hostile
8. appearance, less
9. personal-group discrimination discrepancy
10. positive

Matching I – Key Terms

1. G	6. J
2. F	7. D
3. H	8. E
4. I	9. C
5. B	10. A

Matching II – Key Terms

11. J	18. H
12. L	19. E
13. M	20. A
14. F	21. K
15. I	22. G
16. D	23. C
17. B	

Chapter 10
Group Dynamics and Intergroup Relations

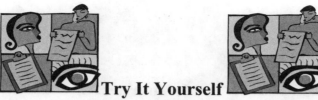

Try It Yourself
How Do You Define a Group and Its Leader?

Think about all the groups to which you belong, ranging from broadly defined collections of people (e.g., people of a certain gender, people from a certain part of a province or country) to those that are more specifically defined (e.g., your family, psychology majors at a certain university, members of a university social or scholastic club).

1. In the following chart, list five collections of people to which you belong. Which of them meet the psychological definition of a group, that is, two or more persons who are interacting with one another and/or influencing one another? Why do certain collections of people not qualify as a group?

2. For two of the groups, identify the leader of the group, and with reference to Table 10.2 in the text, describe what functions each leader fulfills. From your own experience, do you see that leaders can be defined in many ways and can fulfill various functions?

Group to which you belong	Does the group meet the psychological definition of a group?	Who is the group leader?	What function(s) does the group leader fulfill?
1.			
2.			
3.			
4.			
5.			

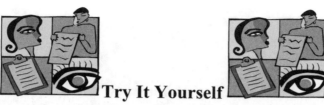

Try It Yourself
Can You Demonstrate These Trademarks of Group Behaviour?

Experiment A
Social Facilitation: Will They Excel or Choke?

This exercise requires the participation of up to thirteen other people. Therefore, we suggest that you work on it in groups of two to four classmates so that you can recruit the necessary volunteers. If you are working on it alone, you can limit the number of participants as noted below. However, the fewer number of participants, the more difficult it will be to obtain the predicted pattern of results.

When other people are present, most people will usually perform better on simple tasks, but not as well on more complex tasks. To demonstrate this effect yourself, recruit ten friends to solve the math problems (provided in Chapter 9 on page 247) and to run a 50-yard sprint. Have five of your friends complete these tasks alone, just in your presence. And have the other five friends complete them in front of a small audience (that is, about three of your other friends who aren't otherwise participating in the experiment). [If you are working alone rather than in a group, have 2–3 friends complete the tasks alone, 2–3 complete the tasks in front of a small audience, and have 2 people participate as the audience.]

For the math problems, record how many problems each friend answered correctly. After 10 minutes, tell your friend that time is up. For the sprint, record how many seconds it took your friend to run 50 yards.

	Number of Math Problems Solved Correctly	Time on 50-yard run
Performed Alone		
Friend 1		
Friend 2		
Friend 3		
Friend 4		
Friend 5		
Performed in Front of Audience		
Friend 6		
Friend 7		
Friend 8		
Friend 9		
Friend 10		

Questions:

1. On average, did the friends performing alone solve fewer or more of the math problems than the friends performing in front of an audience? Did they run the 50-yard dash slower or faster? What pattern of results would Robert Zajonc's dominant response theory of social facilitation predict?

2. Think of other situations in which the differential effects of social facilitation might be seen. For starters, how would you expect it to affect contestants on game shows that require knowledge and intellectual competence versus games shows that require quick performance of routine physical tasks?

Experiment B
Groupthink: Let's All Follow the Leader

Groupthink refers to a way of thinking that can occur in decision-making groups, where pressure to agree leads to inadequate appraisal of options and poor decisions. Research shows that groups with directive leaders used less information and produced fewer possible solutions than did groups with nondirective leaders. Thus, groups with directive leaders are more susceptible to groupthink.

To examine the restrictive effects of directive leadership, ask two groups of three friends (six friends in all) to help you make a decision (e.g., whether you should take a summer course). For one group of three friends, state your preference upfront but for the other group, say nothing about your preference.

Questions:

1. Which group more quickly converges on your preference?

2. Which group discusses all of your options (i.e., taking the summer class and not taking the summer class) more fully?

3. Describe the process that each group used to reach a decision. How did the groups differ in the processes they used?

4. Many different factors contribute to groupthink in addition to directive leadership. How can your two groups be structured differently to make groupthink more likely to occur?

Thinking Critically about Social Psychology
Decisions About the War in Iraq and Groupthink

In 2004, an American Senate Intelligence Committee, chaired by Republican Sen. Pat Roberts of Kansas, concluded that American intelligence agencies gave policy-makers and Congress inaccurate or exaggerated information about Iraq's banned weapons and dismissed contrary viewpoints, and concluded, in effect, that the agencies had fallen victim to groupthink. The following newspaper article provides more detail about the report and the context in which it was released. Read the article and then answer the questions that follow it.

Reading

Information provided prewar was inaccurate, overblown, report says.
By Mark Matthews and Laura Sullivan
Sun National Staff July 9, 2004.
Copyright © 2004 The Baltimore Sun. Used by permission.

WASHINGTON -- Falling victim to "group think," American intelligence agencies gave top policy-makers and Congress inaccurate or overblown information about Iraq's banned weapons and repeatedly dismissed contrary viewpoints, the Senate Intelligence Committee said in a report released Friday. The long-awaited report concluded that the key intelligence judgments used by the Bush administration to justify invading Iraq last year were incorrect or exaggerated. It attributed the failures to reliance on unproven assumptions, inadequate or misleading sources and bad management.

"Before the war, the U.S. intelligence community told the president as well as the Congress and the public that Saddam Hussein had stockpiles of chemical and biological weapons, and if left unchecked, would probably have a nuclear weapon during this decade," said the committee's Republican chairman, Sen. Pat Roberts of Kansas. "Well, today we know these assessments were wrong."

The senior Democrat, Sen. John D. Rockefeller IV of West Virginia, said that if Congress had not been misinformed, "We in Congress would not have authorized that war." The unanimous committee report, 521 pages with all its attachments, found "no evidence" that intelligence agencies exaggerated the Iraqi threat because of political pressure. But in comments appended to the report, Democrats insisted that pressure from an administration bent on war was inescapable. Rockefeller and Sen. Carl Levin of Michigan wrote that intelligence estimates were produced "in a highly-pressurized climate wherein senior administration officials were making the case for military action against Iraq." The scathing report, particularly its statement that the intelligence agencies' corporate culture and management are "broken," seemed sure to increase pressure on President Bush to nominate quickly a replacement for CIA Director George J. Tenet, whose retirement takes effect tomorrow. That could set the stage for an election-year confirmation battle. The committee said the intelligence community had been afflicted with "group think," describing it as "examining few alternatives, selective gathering of information, pressure to conform or withhold criticism, and collective rationalization." The panel found that the CIA "abused its unique position" as the foremost of the nation's 15 intelligence agencies by with holding information from other agencies and at times ignoring or dismissing conflicting views. John E. McLaughlin, the deputy CIA director, who becomes acting director next week, said the findings should not be taken as a broad indictment of all the agencies' vast efforts, but acknowledged, "We get it." "Although we think the judgments were not unreasonable when they were made nearly two years ago, we understand with all that we have learned since then that we could have done better," he said. Bush called the report a useful accounting of the agencies' shortcomings, but defended his decision to go to war and his assertions about Hussein.

"We haven't found the stockpiles, but we knew he could make them," Bush said at a campaign stop in Kutztown, Pa. "The world is better off without Saddam Hussein in power." His presumed Democratic challenger in November, Sen. John Kerry, sought to pin responsibility for the failures on Bush, saying, "The fact is that when it comes to national security, the buck stops at the White House, not anywhere else." Examples of stretching the truth about Iraq's purported arsenal of weapons of mass destruction abound in the report. It describes how a questionable assertion that Iraq was trying to acquire nuclear-weapons fuel found its way into the president's 2003 State of the Union address and how misstatements or exaggerations were used by Secretary of State Colin L. Powell in his Feb. 5, 2003, speech to the U.N. Security Council. On Iraq's biological weapons, the report found intelligence officials based most of their conclusions on a handful of Iraqi defectors with whom they had little direct access and who had been deemed unreliable by lower-level intelligence officers. One dubious source, code-named Curve Ball, was used to bolster the idea that Hussein had mobile biological weapons facilities, despite warnings from the only U.S. intelligence agent to have contact with him that he was an unreliable alcoholic. The agent sent an urgent e-mail to higher-ups expressing his concerns after he read a draft of Powell's speech, saying the one time he was allowed to meet directly with Curve Ball, who was being "handled" by a foreign intelligence agency, Curve Ball showed up almost incapacitated by a hangover. According to the report, the CIA official who received the agent's e-mail, the deputy chief of the CIA's Iraqi Task Force, told staff investigators he didn't forward the e-mail because he didn't believe it "contained any new information." "Let's keep in mind the fact that this war's going to happen regardless of what Curve Ball said or didn't say," the deputy responded in an e-mail to the agent. "The Powers That Be probably aren't terribly interested in whether Curve Ball knows what he's talking about." Despite Powell's demand that all the intelligence provided for his speech be solid and multisourced, his address included exaggerations about magnets and aluminum tubes supposedly intended to make nuclear weapons and possibly misinterpreted satellite imagery. "Much of the information provided or cleared by the Central Intelligence Agency for inclusion in Secretary Powell's speech was overstated, misleading or incorrect," the report said, referring to Powell's assertions on Iraqi weapons of mass destruction. Top intelligence officials also altered the classified October 2002 National Intelligence Estimate, which detailed possible Iraqi weapons programs, when a nonclassified version of it was released to the public. The nonclassified version took out qualifying phrases such as "We believe," or "We assess," stating information as fact. The panel criticized Tenet for not reading the 2003 State of the Union speech, which contained 16 words describing purported Iraqi attempts to acquire the nuclear-weapons fuel in Africa. The CIA and the Defense Intelligence Agency kept issuing reports, noting information that Iraq was trying to procure enriched uranium—a nuclear-weapons fuel—even after the information was discounted. The report is likely to spur efforts to reform and restructure the intelligence community. One failing that needs to be corrected is the apparent absence of a team that can question the assumptions held by top intelligence officials, said committee member Sen. Barbara A. Mikulski, a Maryland Democrat.

"Structural, organizational and jurisdictional reforms must be made and will be made," Mikulski said. "But, the goal ultimately is to create an environment and a culture where truth to power is spoken from the bottom to the top."

Question:

1. The symptoms of groupthink are summarized in the following table and more fully in Table 10.1 in the text. Based on the above article, which symptoms of groupthink, if any, seemed to exist in the prewar intelligence assessment? What changes could be made to reduce the likelihood of groupthink?

Symptoms of Groupthink

Adapted from Janis, 1972 (pp. 197–198).

1. An illusion of invulnerability—nothing can go wrong; we cannot lose.

2. Rationalization of warnings—we can ignore the warning signs because they do not mean anything.

3. An unquestioned belief in the inherent morality of the group—we are good, moral people.

4. Stereotyped views of enemy leaders—they are evil, weak, stupid.

5. Pressure on group members who challenge the consensus—loyal members do not make waves.

6. Self-censorship of misgivings, questions, counterarguments.

7. An illusion of unanimity—everyone agrees with this decision.

8. Emergence of self-appointed mindguards, who protect the leader and the group from information that might threaten the consensus.

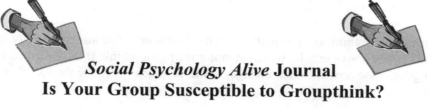

Social Psychology Alive **Journal**
Is Your Group Susceptible to Groupthink?

In our day-to-day lives, we all belong to many cohesive groups— social and special interest clubs, athletic teams, study groups, and school and community committees. Think of one of the groups to which you belong and using the checklist, consider whether it is susceptible to groupthink.

Questions:

1. What is your group?

2. Based on the following checklist and what you have learned in the textbook, is your group susceptible to groupthink? Why or why not?

3. If your group is susceptible to groupthink, what changes could be made to reduce the likelihood of groupthink?

Is your group susceptible to groupthink?[1]

Check all the statements that apply to your group. The more statements you check, the more susceptible to groupthink your group is.

	1. The leader of the group makes his or her views clearly known before the group has a chance to deliberate.
	2. The group quickly seizes on an option offered by a high-status member and does not consider other alternatives.
	3. Members are highly motivated to agree with one another in order to maintain good relationships with one another.
	4. The group is relatively new, and members are uncomfortable challenging one another.
	5. The group is not in the habit of consulting knowledgeable people outside the group.
	6. Decisions are made without listing the pros and cons of the different alternatives and what would happen if each were to be chosen.
	7. The leader is powerful and members do not wish to disagree with him or her.
	8. The group avoids information that might lead them to question their chosen route.
	9. The group feels as though they are under attack and must make a decision quickly.
	10. The group believes in its moral or intellectual superiority and minimizes its opponents or challenges.

[1] This checklist was adapted from: Burn, S. M. (2004). *Groups: Theory and Practice*. Belmont, CA: Thomson/Wadsworth (p. 354). Copyright © 2004. Reprinted with permission of Wadsworth, a division of Thomson Learning: www.thomsonrights.com. Fax 800-730-2215.

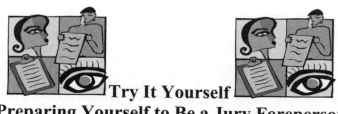

Try It Yourself
Preparing Yourself to Be a Jury Foreperson

Imagine you are on a jury. It's a murder case in which the circumstantial evidence suggests that a woman was brutally killed by her estranged boyfriend. The judge has instructed you and the jurors on the law you are to apply in reaching a decision and has sent you to the deliberation room. Now the other jurors elect you as jury foreperson.

Questions:

1. Keeping the concept of group polarization in mind, how will you direct your fellow jurors during deliberation? Will they take a vote immediately, or after discussion? Will voting be anonymous or not?

2. Keeping in mind what you have learned about minority influences, how will you help ensure all views are heard and given appropriate consideration?

3. If after taking an initial vote, you find yourself in the majority, what measures might you take to ensure all points of view are fully heard and given appropriate consideration? How would this differ if you found yourself in the minority?

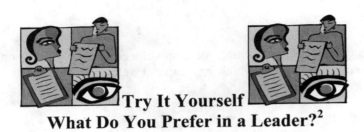

Try It Yourself
What Do You Prefer in a Leader?[2]

Contingency theories of leadership, such as that of Fred Fiedler, suggest that that to be effective, a person's leadership style should be based in part on the characteristics of the people he or she is leading and the characteristics of the situation, including the task. Put yourself in the situations described below and decide what kind of leader you would prefer and why: (a) a highly directive, low socio-emotional leader; (b) a highly directive, highly socio-emotional leader; (c) a low directive, highly socio-emotional leader; or (d) a low directive, low socio-emotional leader. Then answer the other questions about your general leadership preferences.

Scenario One
You are one of five new interns at a prestigious organization and you are all a bit intimidated by the expertise and achievements of the employees there. You are not really sure you can contribute to this impressive organization, and you are really looking forward to the training you will receive.

What type of leader would you prefer? Why?

Scenario Two
You have a master's degree from the same program that your boss does. Although he graduated a year before you did, you had experience in the field prior to entering the program, whereas he did not. You have been on the job for eighteen months now and are comfortable with your job duties and are confident in your ability to perform at a high level on new tasks.

What type of leader would you prefer? Why?

[2] This exercise was adapted from: Burn, S. M. (2004). Groups: Theory and Practice. Belmont, CA: Thomson/Wadsworth (pp. 319, 332). Copyright ©2004. Reprinted with permission of Wadsworth, a division of Thomson Learning: www.thomsonrights.com. Fax 800-730-2215.

Questions:

1. Are there certain leadership styles to which you respond well or poorly based on your personality? Are there certain leadership styles to which you respond well or poorly based on the situation in which you find yourself?

2. Are there certain styles you would have an easier or harder time displaying as a leader? To what extent does this depend on your personality and to what extent does it depend on the situation in which you find yourself?

3. Think about your boss, or if you are not currently employed, a past boss or teacher. Did this person provide the appropriate level of task and socio-emotional leadership, given whom he or she was leading, the task, and the situation? Why or why not?

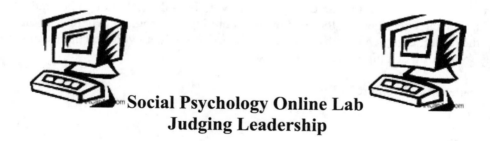

Social Psychology Online Lab
Judging Leadership

The purpose of this online lab is to explore what factors influence a person's perception of the leadership potential of other people. You will see a transcript of a problem-solving session from several different groups. Each group was given a set of line drawings and asked to choose among several alternatives to identify the next picture in the series of drawings. The transcripts provide you with the conversation among group members while solving the problem. Your task will be to read transcripts and evaluate the leadership potential of the members of the groups.

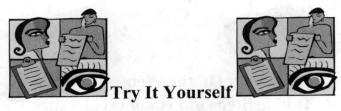

Try It Yourself
So You Want to Be a Diplomat
Preparing for Your Foreign Affairs Job

Imagine that you have just taken a job as a social psychologist with Foreign Affairs Canada to develop strategies for alleviating the Israeli/Palestinian conflict. Your first assignment is to give a talk to senior officials about the relevant research. How would explain each of the concepts to them and what general recommendation or recommendations based on each would you offer? Use the following table to record your answers. Share your suggestions with your classmates and see what recommendations they come up with.

	Explanation	Recommendation
Conflict Escalation: Threats and Self-Presentation Goals		
Conflict Escalation: Dehumanizing the Enemy		
Conflict Escalation: Cultural Differences		
Conflict Reduction: Communication		
Conflict Reduction: Trust		
Conflict Reduction: Initiatives		

On the Web
Taking Steps to Promote Tolerance

A poll conducted by the Evironics Research Groups/Focus Canada on behalf of the Association for Canadian Studies (ACS) surveyed Canadians about tolerance in Canada. The poll identified groups about which intolerance was seen as a problem. People's beliefs about the extent of the problem in society of anti-Native, anti-immigrant, anti-gay, anti-black, and anti-semitic attitudes were measured. The survey also measured which groups projected a negative image in society.

Visit the website: http://www.acs-aec.ca/Polls/Poll27.pdf and read the report based on the survey.

Question:

1. How do the results of the survey, with regard to the way Canadians think about the multicultural groups in society, relate to the concept of integration and assimilation?

2. How could attitudes and beliefs, such as those presented in the report, play a role in the escalation and de-escalation of inter-group conflict?

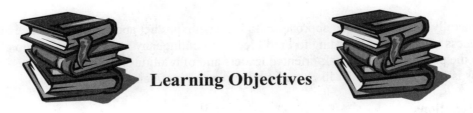

Learning Objectives

Individual Performance and Behaviour in Group Settings

1. How do social psychologists define a "group" and how do the methods for studying small versus large groups differ? (pp. 373–374)

2. How does the presence of other people affect an individual's performance on simple, well-learned tasks and on complex, novel tasks? Why do audiences have these effects? (pp. 374–376)

3. Describe the "social loafing" effect. How does each of the following affect the degree of social loafing: the size of the group, the importance of the task, cohesiveness or attractiveness of the group, gender, and culture? (pp. 376–377)

4. Describe the psychological state termed "deindividuation" and three alternative explanations for its development. (pp. 377–380)

Decision Making in Groups

5. What generally is groupthink and in what types of groups is it most likely to occur? What are its defining symptoms? What strategies can be implemented to reduce the likelihood of it? Does research on group cohesiveness, leadership style, and group norms support Janis's reasoning about groupthink? (pp. 380–385)

6. Define group polarization and describe how it might contribute to the polarization of stereotypes. What are two explanations for this effect? (pp. 385–387)

7. What conditions promote the influence of a minority view in a group? According to Moscovici and other researchers, how are the effects of minorities different from the effects of majorities in terms of divergent versus convergent thinking and willingness to conform? How does social impact theory explain the differential effects of minority views? (pp. 388–390)

Leadership

8. What are three ways of defining a group leader? Into what two major categories do the functions fulfilled by group leaders fall? What are four ways to define or measure the effectiveness of leaders? (pp.390–393)

9. How do the following personal traits predict leader emergence and effectiveness: height, intelligence, gender, achievement and affiliation motivation, and quality versus quantity of group contributions? (pp. 393–399)

10. What are some of the situational factors that may affect leadership emergence? Why might the rule of seniority make sense? (pp. 400–401)

11. What generally do interactionist approaches to leadership predict about the emergence and effectiveness of leaders? According to Fred Fiedler's contingency model of leadership effectiveness, what are the primary goals of task-oriented leaders and of relationship-oriented leaders? Under what situations is each type of leader likely to be effective and ineffective? (pp. 401–402)

Intergroup Relations

12. Define acculturation. Describe the four different goals that can be pursued by cultural groups who are in contact with one another. Distinguish between integration and assimilation goals. (pp. 403–404)

13. Explain why the following three factors might escalate a minor intergroup conflict into a major one: use of threats, certain self-presentation goals, and dehumanization. How do cultural differences affect the likelihood that a conflict will escalate? (pp. 404–409)

14. What type of communication increases the likelihood that intergroup conflict will be reduced and why does it have this effect? (pp. 409–410)

15. How might a conflictive ethos be transformed into an ethos of peace? (p. 411)

16. What are unilateral conciliatory initiatives and why might they reduce intergroup conflict? (pp. 411–412)

Test Your Knowledge

Multiple Choice Questions

1. According to social psychologists, which of the following would be considered the best definition of a group?
   A. three people waiting in line at an ATM
   B. sixty people on board a subway car
   C. seven people in a dentist's waiting room
   D. five students in a discussion class

2. Zajonc's studies of social facilitation demonstrated that the presence of other people makes it
   A. more likely that we will perform a familiar task well.
   B. less likely that we will perform a familiar task well.
   C. more likely that we will perform an unfamiliar task well.
   D. likely that we will perform an unfamiliar task and a familiar task equally well.

3. Chris has been asked to serve on a committee advocating arts education in the local community. He agrees to serve in order to bolster his resume, and is one of nine members. However, at committee meetings, he is content to sit silently unless asked a direct question, and does as little work as possible, allowing his fellow committee members to do most of the work. Chris's behaviour is an example of social
   A. facilitation.
   B. loafing.
   C. perception.
   D. distortion.

4. In which situation is social loafing most likely to occur?
   A. a group of four roommates planning a graduation party
   B. a mother and daughter planning a baby shower
   C. ten male students doing a group project for a pass/fail class
   D. two lawyers preparing for oral arguments in front of the Supreme Court

5. Which of the following is *not* one of the theoretical processes through which deindividuation affects behaviour?
   A. Deindividuation weakens inhibitions about performing a harmful act.
   B. Deindividuation decreases responsiveness to external cues.
   C. Deindividuation heightens responsiveness to external cues.
   D. Deindividuation increases adherence to group norms.

6. The researcher most associated with the Stanford prison study is
   A. Norman Triplett.
   B. Irving Janis.
   C. Robert Zajonc.
   D. Philip Zimbardo.

7. Research has shown that the type of task affects group productivity. Which type of task is a group least likely to perform better than an individual?
   A. additive tasks
   B. conjunctive tasks
   C. disjunctive tasks
   D. facilitative tasks

8. According to Janis's theory, groupthink is most likely to occur in groups that have which of the following characteristics?
   A. high cohesiveness, directive leader, and high stress
   B. low cohesiveness, directive leader, and high stress
   C. high cohesiveness, nondirective leader, and high stress
   D. low cohesiveness, directive leader, and low stress

9. According to its original formulation, how can groupthink be avoided?
   A. Have the group leader speak first.
   B. Limit the number of questions raised.
   C. Discourage outsiders from contributing.
   D. Designate a devil's advocate.

10. You've been selected to serve on a jury deciding an embezzlement case. Entering deliberations, you suspect that you are the only one in favour of a "not guilty" verdict. Using your social psychological training, how can you persuade others to vote with you?
    A. Encourage the foreperson to take an immediate guilty/not guilty poll.
    B. State that it just feels like the defendant is not guilty.
    C. Agree with the majority on other issues, such as the arrogance of the defense attorney.
    D. Be unwilling to compromise on any aspect of deliberation.

11. A leader who serves the "group maintenance" function is known as the
    A. task leader.
    B. maintenance leader.
    C. socio-emotional leader.
    D. virtual leader.

12. Which of the following characteristics has *not* been shown to be a predictor of perceived leadership effectiveness?
    A. age
    B. height
    C. gender
    D. intelligence

13. In Sorrentino and Boutillier's study in which the quality and quantity of a confederate's contributions to group discussions were manipulated, the results indicated that the
    A. number of comments and the quality of the comments had equal impact on the ratings of leadership skills.
    B. number of comments had more impact on ratings of leadership skills than did the quality of comments.
    C. quality of comments had more impact on ratings of leadership skills than did the number of comments.
    D. number of comments only impacted ratings of leadership skills when the comments were of high quality.

14. You are a member of your school's outdoor club, which is looking for a new treasurer, the least popular position. You arrive late to the nominating meeting and walk in just as the group was searching for a volunteer, and you become the new treasurer. This is an example of which approach to leadership?
    A. contingency approach
    B. interactionist approach
    C. situational approach
    D. trait approach

15. Deutsch and Krauss's experiment with threats using a game involving competing trucking companies demonstrated that
    A. companies that used no threats were the most profitable.
    B. companies that used unilateral threats were the most profitable.
    C. companies that used bilateral threats were the most profitable.
    D. threats had no effect on profitability.

16. Which of the following is *not* one of the ways in which communication can serve to reduce conflict, according to Pruitt?
    A. It makes similarities between groups more apparent.
    B. It helps increase trust between parties.
    C. It decreases the chance of reneging on a public statement.
    D. It helps most parties generate personally advantageous strategies.

Sentence Completion

1. Performance on simple and well-learned tasks typically __improves__ in front of an audience, whereas performance on complex, novel tasks typically __worsens__ in front of an audience.

2. The study of children at Halloween (Diener et al., 1976) showed that __anonymity__ could result in deindividuation.

3. The study involving women dressed in Ku Klux Klan attire or in nursing uniforms, either anonymously or identified (Gergen, Gergen, & Barton, 1973), supported the theory that deindividuation increases people's responses to __external cues__.

4. On _additive_ tasks, groups will usually outperform individuals, but will be less efficient than individuals. On _conjunctive_ tasks, where the group's performance depends on its least talented member, groups will usually perform more poorly than individuals. On _disjunctive_ tasks, where the group's performance depends on its most talented member, groups will usually perform better than individuals.

5. Groupthink is more likely to occur in a _higly cohesive_ group with a _directive_ leader.

6. According to the concept of _group polarization_, the position preferred by the majority of group members before discussion will tend to become even more widely preferred after group discussion.

7. Minorities are more influential if they are _confident_ and _persistent_ in their position, but are also reasonable and logical.

8. Leader effectiveness can be measured in several ways: one way is based on the group's _productivity_, a second way is based on the group's _satisfaction_, a third way is based on the leader's _impact_ on the group, and a fourth way is based on group members' ratings of the leader.

9. When the group situation is *favourable* for the leader (e.g., the leader has a lot of power and group members like the leader), Fred Fielder predicted that _T_ - oriented leaders are more effective because they continue to push group members even when things are going well. When the group situation is *mixed* for the leader (e.g., the leader has little power but group members like the leader), _R_ - oriented leaders are more effective because they are more skillful at maintaining the morale and motivation of group members in this mixed situation. Finally, when the group situation is *unfavourable* for the leader (e.g., the leader has little power and group members dislike the leader), _T_ - oriented leaders are once again more effective because they keep trying to push group members even under terrible circumstances, whereas _R_ - oriented tend to withdraw or give up when they are disliked and have no power.

10. A _conflictive ethos_, which is an atmosphere of distrust and hatred, might be transformed into _ethos_ of _peace_, which is an atmosphere of acceptance and cooperation, with strategies that make groups more willing to cooperate in the absence of trust.

Matching I – Key Terms

_____ 1. **group dynamics**	A. the action that is most likely to occur in a situation or on a task when the individual is alone
_____ 2. **group**	B. a psychological state in which people lose their sense of personal identity and feel immersed in a group
_____ 3. **social facilitation**	C. the social psychological study of groups and group processes
_____ 4. **dominant response**	D. two or more persons who are interacting with one another and/or influencing one another
_____ 5. **social loafing**	E. the reduction of effort that people often exhibit when working in a group where individual contributions are unidentifiable
_____ 6. **deindividuation**	F. the effects of the presence of other people on individual performance, which will usually be improved performance on simple tasks and impaired performance on complex tasks

Matching II – Key Terms

_____ 7.	**groupthink**	A. individuals who produce fundamental changes in how members of a group view themselves and the group
_____ 8.	**group cohesiveness**	B. aspects of leadership that relate to group productivity
_____ 9.	**group polarization**	C. a way of thinking that can occur in decision-making groups when pressure to agree leads to inadequate appraisal of options and poor decisions
_____ 10.	**transformational leaders**	D. the tendency for group discussion to strengthen the initial leanings of the members in a group
_____ 11.	**task achievement function**	E. an individual who takes charge of issues related to morale in a group
_____ 12.	**group maintenance function**	F. aspects of leadership that relate to morale in the group
_____ 13.	**task leader**	G. the combined strength of all forces acting on members of a group to remain in the group
_____ 14.	**socioemotional leader**	H. an individual who takes charge of issues related to productivity in a group
_____ 15.	**trait approach to leadership**	I. the perspective that people become leaders, or perform well as leaders, because of their individual characteristics, such as intelligence and charisma

284

Matching III – Key Term

_____ 16. **Great Person theory**

_____ 17. **situational approach to leadership**

_____ 18. **interactionist approach to leadership**

_____ 19. **contingency model of leadership effectiveness**

_____ 20. **acculturation**

_____ 21. **dehumanization**

_____ 22. **terrorism**

_____ 23. **conflictive ethos**

_____ 24. **ethos of peace**

_____ 25. **unilateral conciliatory initiatives**

A. a theory that predicts that task-oriented leaders will be more successful than relationship-oriented leaders in groups where the situation is either very favourable or very unfavourable for the leader, whereas relationship-oriented leaders will be more successful than task-oriented leaders in groups where the situation is mixed for the leader

B. actual or threatened violence against civilians for alleged political purposes

C. the hypothesis that exceptional leaders possess extraordinary qualities and skills—consistent with the trait approach to leadership

D. the perspective that external, situational factors can influence who will become leader of a group, such as seating arrangements

E. an atmosphere of acceptance and cooperation, which can facilitate the resolution of disputes

F. the process of perceiving members of a group as subhuman or inferior to members of one's own group; it allows people to inflict pain and suffering on the group without worrying about the morality of their behaviour

G. the perspective that certain kinds of people are likely to emerge as leaders (or to be effective leaders) under one set of conditions, whereas other kinds of people are likely to emerge as leaders (or to be effective leaders) under a different set of conditions

H. actions to reduce conflict that one group takes without any request from the opponent and without any explicit demands for concessions from the opponent

I. an atmosphere of distrust and hatred that can develop in longstanding disputes

J. the process of cultural and psychological change that takes place as a result of contact between two or more cultural groups and their individual members

Answers to Test Your Knowledge

Multiple Choice Questions

1. D	6. D	11. C	16. D
2. A	7. B	12. A	
3. B	8. A	13. B	
4. C	9. D	14. C	
5. B	10. C	15. A	

Sentence Completion

1. improves, worsens
2. anonymity
3. external cues
4. additive, conjunctive, disjunctive
5. highly cohesive, directive
6. group polarization
7. confident, persistent (resolute)
8. productivity, satisfaction, impact
9. task, relationship, task, relationship
10. conflictive ethos, ethos of peace

Matching I – Key Terms

1. C	6. B
2. D	
3. F	
4. A	
5. E	

Matching II – Key Terms

7. C	12. F
8. G	13. H
9. D	14. E
10. A	15. I
11. B	

Matching III – Key Terms

16. C	21. F
17. D	22. B
18. G	23. I
19. A	24. F
20. J	25. H

Chapter 11
Aggression and Violence

Try It Yourself
Venting Your Rage

The textbook describes the catharsis effect in aggression, which is the idea that engaging in aggressive acts relieves the need for future aggression. Although some early research seemed to confirm the effect, most studies have not found the effect to be reliable. Despite this lack of supporting research, companies have embraced the idea of catharsis in developing products designed to help people vent their anger appropriately. An advertisement for one such product is reproduced below.

The Anger Works Kit™

Included in the *Anger Works Kit*™ is the Red Crab stuffed animal which represents their Mad Part which needs understanding and safe expression. The tearful Puppy represents the Sad Part which helps children get in touch with the hurt underneath their anger. The children use the Sponge Batika to pound the two Mad Face Sponges, squeeze the two Mad Face Balls and talk to the two Ugly Face Puppets while being encouraged by the therapist to "get their mads out." A canvas bag with our logo holds all the toys.

Fourteen Lesson Plans, included: IT'S OK TO BE MAD IF YOU ARE NICE ABOUT IT ... feeling comfortable about having an angry part. I GET MY MADS OUT ... learning the trigger points of anger and learning to release anger symbolically in safe ways. I CAN CHILL OUT! I CAN COOL DOWN! I DON'T HAVE TO BE A CRAB ALL OF THE TIME! ... learning to discriminate between the "LITTLE MADS AND BIG MADS," not getting angry when you don't get your own way and letting go of grudges. Plus many more!

Source: http://www.angriesout.com/catalog/

Similarly, popular magazines, newspapers, and self-help books often perpetuate the message that "letting off steam" in a safe way can reduce the likelihood that people will engage in destructive aggressive behaviour.

Find an example of such a product or article and answer the questions below. To get started, you may wish to do an Internet search for "venting your anger" and similar phrases. It will probably be harder to find an example of a product than to find an article in a magazine, newspaper, or self-help book.

Questions:

1. Describe any product you identified that is based on the catharsis effect.

2. Describe any message you identified in a magazine, newspaper, or self-help book that is based on the catharsis effect.

3. Do you think the claims made about the product or message you identified are scientifically valid? Why or why not?

Thinking Critically about Social Psychology
Girls and Aggression

The Story of Reena Virk

In 1997, a fourteen-year-old girl by the name of Reena Virk was killed in Victoria, British Columbia. The young girl was severely beaten by a group of teenagers and then drowned. In the months following the killing, six teenage girls (two 14 year-olds, two 15 year-olds, and two 16 year-olds) were found guilty of assault and two other teens were charged with second-degree murder (one 16 year-old girl and one 15 year-old boy).

Further information on the Reena Virk beating can be found online at:
http://www.cbc.ca/news/background/virk/

Questions:

1. The death of Reena Virk made national news at the time it took place, and prompted a response of shock and outrage. Consider the fact that most of Reena Virk's attackers were girls. How do you think the response would have differed if the participants had been boys? What if they had been black students from an inner-city neighborhood? Why does an incident like this garner national attention while other sorts of violence barely rate a mention in local newspapers?

2. Can you think of other more recent news events of girls acting in physically aggressive ways? Do you think these events are becoming more common, or have just begun to attract more media attention? What factors do you think could contribute to the increase?

3. Relational aggression is a psychological form of aggression intended to damage another person's peer relationships, and has traditionally been considered the domain of girls. It has only recently begun to attract media attention and study for its detrimental effects on the targets of such acts. Books such as *Odd Girl Out: The Hidden Culture of Aggression in Girls* (by Rachel Simmons), and *Queen Bees and Wannabes* (by Rosalind Wiseman) have brought this sort of behaviour to the attention of the general public. The effects of physical aggression, on the other hand, has been studied by psychologists for years. Why do you suppose relational aggression has been ignored (and perhaps implicitly condoned) for so many years?

4. The news reported that one of the girls found guilty of assault had witnessed the murder of her father when she was six years old. According to research presented in the text on social learning, why might this information be relevant in explaining what happened?

5. Interview one of your male friends and one of your female friends about their experiences in high school with physical and relational aggression, and summarize their responses below. Do your friends' responses support the notion that males are more likely to commit physical aggression and females are more likely to commit relational aggression?

Male Friend	
1. Were you the perpetrator of relational violence in high school? Were you a victim of it? If so, who was the perpetrator?	
2. Were you the perpetrator of physical violence in high school? Were you a victim of it? If so, who was the perpetrator?	
Female Friend	
3. Were you the perpetrator of relational violence in high school? Were you a victim of it? If so, who was the perpetrator?	
4. Were you the perpetrator of physical violence in high school? Were you a victim of it? If so, who was the perpetrator?	

Commentary:

When you think of aggression in school-age children, the classic image that most often comes to mind is that of two boys beating each other up, surrounded by a ring of cheering peers. Girls rarely enter the stereotypical picture of aggressive children. As you saw in the chapter, however, girls can be aggressive in their own way. Girls tend to engage in relational aggression whereas boys tend to engage in physical aggression. Even that stereotype, however, is just that—a stereotype. Recent events in the news have demonstrated that girls can be just as physically aggressive as boys can. The episode described in the above article is just one example of female aggression.

Your text describes aggressive behaviour in the context of social groups as mob violence, which can either be planned or more spontaneous. To some extent, the Reena Virk murder is an example of mob violence—a planned action in which a group of people acted aggressively towards a target. Several of the factors commonly associated with mob violence were present, including conformity (the pressure for the teenagers to conform to expectations), and social contagion (the spreading of the violence throughout the group).

Social Psychology Alive Journal
Violence and the Media

As the textbook describes, psychological research has found that long-term exposure to media violence is associated with aggressive behaviour. One study, for example, found that the more aggressive adults were ones who, as children, had watched more violence on television and identified more strongly with the aggressive characters.

Do you think you are exposed to a little or a lot of media violence? Over the next week, watch at least three television programs and record each instance of aggression that occurs in each program, using the table below. Pick three different types of programs to watch (i.e., cartoons, dramas, sitcoms, news, sporting events), with at least one program being one that you watch somewhat regularly. Look for examples of hostile aggression (i.e., acts motivated by anger, frustration, and hatred and intended to harm another), instrumental aggression (i.e., aggressive acts motivated by goals other than to directly hurt the target), physical aggression, relational aggression (i.e., acts to harm another's peer relationships), and displaced aggression (i.e., acts aimed at someone or something that was not the source of the frustration).

Name of program	Type of program (e.g., cartoons, dramas, sitcoms, news, sporting events)	Length of program (i.e., 30 minutes, one hour)	Number of aggressive acts	Examples of aggressive act

Questions:

1. Do the number and type of the aggressive acts vary by the type of program? What type of program do you think might have the most negative impact on viewers' aggressive behaviour? Why?

2. Ask a few friends to predict how many aggressive acts occur during a particular show or time period on television. Are their predictions accurate? Too high or too low? How might you explain these results?

Thinking Critically about Social Psychology
Violent Videogames and Aggressive Behaviour

Toy or Trojan Horse? Young Children Lured to Play Violent Games
By Daphne White

The action figure your preschooler is clamoring for looks innocent enough, as these things go: "Primagen" is a green creature with five tentacles plus one lobster-like claw and one three-fingered hand. Its blue face—a cross between that of a turtle and ET—looks a bit sad. The label on the package says Primagen is a Turok character—not that you know what Turok is—suitable for "ages 4 and up."

So maybe you buy one.

If you do, you will be bringing home a Trojan horse. For inside Primagen's box is a "game code," or tip sheet, for Turok 2: Seeds of Evil—which is, in fact, an explicitly gory, frighteningly violent video game that is industry-rated "M"—for "mature" players at least 17 years old.

Certainly there is a significant distance between the plastic doll in the toy store and the adrenaline-pumping interaction of the videogame. But there is no question that the cross-marketing of brands—in this case, the videogame developer Acclaim licensing its Turok characters to the kiddie-toy maker Playmates—is a way to get 4-year olds to bridge that distance, to make friends at an early age with characters most parents wouldn't want them to know. . . .

Game companies introduce children to a brand early in the hope that they will identify with it and grow up with it. . . .

The need for action was made clear . . . when four major public health groups – the American Medical Association, the American Psychological Association, the American Academy of Pediatrics, and the American Academy of Child and Adolescent Psychiatry—issued a joint statement to Congress saying that "viewing entertainment violence can lead to increases in aggressive attitudes, values and behavior, particularly in children. Its effects are measurable and long-lasting. Moreover, prolonged viewing of media violence can lead to emotional desensitization toward violence in real life."

Significantly, the statement noted: "Although less research has been done on the impact of violent interactive entertainment (such as video games) on young people, preliminary studies indicate that the negative impact may be significantly more severe than that wrought by television, movies, or music."

The Charlotte Observer (August 20, 2000) 1C, 6C.

Questions:

1. Based on what you have learned about the causes of aggression, why might interactive entertainment such as videogames lead to more real-life violence than passive entertainments such as television programs and movies?

2. Many videogames are "first-person shooter" games. That is, the player sees the world through the perpetrator's eyes and wields his weapons. Why might this type of videogame have an especially negative impact?

3. Indoor laser tag arenas and outdoor paintball courses move the level of interaction up another step. What effect do you think these types of activities have on a person's propensity towards violence? Why? Which of the two activities might have a more negative impact? Why?

Social Psychology Online Lab
Sentencing

In this online lab, you will be asked to recommend a sentence for a defendant who has been convicted of a crime. Its purpose is to show how the presence of aggressive cues elicits more aggressive responses to a situation. As you may recall from the textbook, according to the cognitive neoassociation model of aggression, aggression results from a process of spreading activation. Initially, an unpleasant event arouses negative affect (negative emotion). This negative affect then simultaneously activates two distinct schemas, or response tendencies. One is the tendency to *fight*—the type of responses we associate with aggression or harm-doing. The other is the tendency toward *flight*—the type of responses we associate with escape or avoidance. Through a process of spreading activation, these two schemas further activate *anger* (the emotion associated with fight) and *fear* (the emotion associated with flight). If other events or cues in the situation produce relatively greater activation of schemas related to anger, then aggression is more likely to be the result. If other cues are more likely to activate schemas related to fear, then flight is the more probable response.

Thinking Critically about Social Psychology
School Violence

On April 20, 1999, Eric Harris and Dylan Klebold killed 12 students and one teacher, and wounded 23 others at Columbine High School in Colorado before turning their guns on themselves. Columbine was the deadliest incident of school violence, but it was far from the only one. Marc Lepine killed 14 students at Ecole Polytechnique in Montreal, Quebec; Kimveer Gill killed 1 student and injured 19 others at Dawson College in Montreal, Quebec; Todd Cameron Smith killed one student at W. R. Myers High school in April, 1999; Luke Woodham killed 2 classmates and wounded 7 at Peal High School in Mississippi in October, 1997; Michael Carneal killed 3 students and wounded 5 at Heath High School in Kentucky in December 1997; Mitchell Johnson and Andrew Golden killed four students and one teacher, and wounded ten others at Westside Middle School in Jonesboro, Arkansas in March 1998; and Kip Kinkel killed two students and wounded 22 others at Thurston High School in Springfield, Oregon in May 1998. Donald R. Burt, Jr., a 17-year-old student who had been expelled from Lew Wallace High School in Gary, Indiana, killed another student in March 2001. John Jason McLaughlin, 15, killed two students at Rocori High School in Minnesota in September 2003.

The above list is just a sample of the some of the incidents of school violence in the past decade. In the aftermath of the Columbine and other tragedies, lay theories to explain the increase in school violence were unavoidable on television news programs, newspapers, and the Internet. Blame was placed on a wide variety of culprits, including bullies (Todd Cameron Smith was reportedly bullied at school), modern music (the Columbine shooters were acknowledged fans of controversial singer Marilyn Manson), violent television and movies (Kimveer Gill's web "blog" made reference to many violent movies), and violent videogames and gun control laws (Kimveer Gill's weapons were legally owned in accordance with Canadian gun laws).

Many of these lay theories have correlations to social psychological explanations for violence and aggression. For example, the frustration-aggression model maps nicely onto the lay explanation of bullying being at the root of the violence. Several of the shooters were acknowledged to have been bullied by more popular students and "jocks," which may have increased their levels of frustration. Also, research disconfirming the catharsis effect suggests that venting one's rage can actually serve to heighten subsequent aggression. This research may explain why the Columbine shooters continued their rampage for such an extended period of time—their aggressive urge actually increased as more people were killed.

Questions:

1. Violent videogames and television were also viewed as partially responsible for the shootings. How does this explanation map onto social psychological explanations for violence and aggression?

2. Another theory is that violent music may have triggered the assaults. What social psychological explanations for violence and aggression support this interpretation?

Learning Objectives

Definition and Varieties of Aggression

1. Define and distinguish the concepts "aggression" and "violence." (p. 419)

2. Compare and provide examples of hostile aggression, instrumental aggression, and relational aggression. (pp. 419–422)

3. Do you think the spanking of children is effective as a method of discipline? Why or why not? (p. 421)

4. Describe the gender differences and social consequences associated with relational aggression. (pp. 420–422)

Theories of Aggression

5. Briefly describe the general aggression model. (pp. 423–424)

6. Discuss two sources of evidence for the biological influences on aggression. (pp. 424–425)

7. What are the two basic principles of the frustration-aggression hypothesis? What relationships between frustration and aggression are demonstrated in the 1967 experiment by Russell Geen? What chief problem with the frustration-aggression hypothesis did this experiment identify? (pp. 425–426)

8. Describe the concepts of displaced aggression and provide a concrete example. (pp. 426–427)

9. What is meant by the catharsis effect? Is it generally supported by other existing research? Explain. (p. 427)

10. What is the concept of excitation transfer? (pp. 427–429)

11. What is the social learning theory of aggression? Briefly describe how the Bobo doll study supports it. (pp. 429–430)

12. According to the neoassociation model of aggression, what two response tendencies are activated by negative affect, and by what process are they thought to lead to the activation of anger and fear? What accounts for a person deciding to act upon anger or fear? (pp. 430–431)

Influences on Aggression

13. Discuss three individual difference dimensions that may explain why some people are more aggressive than others. (pp. 433–435)

14. What are two possible explanations for the fact that alcohol consumption causes an increase in aggressive behaviour? (pp. 435–436)

15. Why might heat cause an increase in aggressive behaviour? (pp. 436–437)

The Social Context of Aggression

16. Describe what is meant by a "culture of honour" and the correlational and experimental support for it. (pp. 438–439)

17. Are aggressive children disliked by their peers? (p. 440)

18. Into what three groups do violent husbands generally fall? Which group is generally more amenable to interventions that can curb their violence? How does domestic violence affect the children who witness it? (pp. 441–442)

19. What are two social psychological processes that might contribute to mob violence? (pp. 442–444)

Media Effects on Aggression

20. What are the basic findings about the impact of television violence on real-life aggressive behaviour? (pp. 445–447)

21. What are the basic findings about the impact of violent videogames on real-life aggressive behaviour? (pp. 447–448)

22. What is the demonstrated relationship between pornography and aggression? (pp. 448–450)

Controlling Aggression and Violence

23. Describe four approaches to controlling aggressive behaviour. (pp. 451–454)

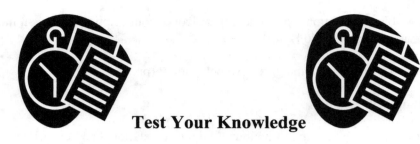

Test Your Knowledge

Multiple Choice Questions

1. What is the relationship between aggression and violence, according to social psychologists?
   A. Violence and aggression are interchangeable terms.
   B. Violence is any behaviour intended to injure; aggression is behaviour intended to cause extreme injury.
   C. Aggression is any behaviour intended to injure; violence is behaviour intended to cause extreme injury.
   D. All aggression is violence, but not all violence is aggression.

2. Ethan is a troubled student who rarely attends classes. He is told by his TA, who he has always suspected of resenting him, that he cannot miss any more classes without receiving a failing grade for the course. This news makes him furious, and he loudly insults the TA before storming out of the office. Ethan's behaviour is an example of
   A. hostile aggression.
   B. relational aggression.
   C. instrumental aggression.
   D. rational aggression.

3. Behaviour that is intended to damage another's peer relationships is known as
   A. hostile aggression.
   B. relational aggression.
   C. instrumental aggression.
   D. rational aggression.

4. In Nikki Crick's study of aggression in preschool boys and girls, she found that boys tended to exhibit
   A. relational aggression, whereas girls tended to exhibit instrumental aggression.
   B. relational aggression, whereas girls tended to exhibit physical aggression.
   C. physical aggression, whereas girls tended to exhibit relational aggression.
   D. general aggression, whereas girls tended to exhibit relational aggression.

5. Which of the following is the most accurate description of how frustration and aggression are related?
   A. Frustration always leads to aggression.
   B. Aggression is always the only result of frustration.
   C. When frustrated, people always aggress against the source of frustration.
   D. When frustrated, people may aggress against someone other than the source of frustration.

6. In the Zillmann et al. experiment demonstrating the excitation transfer theory of aggression, which experimental condition produced the highest level of aggression in participants?
   A. an anger-eliciting procedure, followed by non-strenuous activity
   B. an anger-eliciting procedure, followed by vigorous activity
   C. a non-anger-eliciting procedure, followed by non-strenuous activity
   D. a non-anger-eliciting procedure, followed by vigorous activity

7. The Bobo doll experiments in which children modeled the aggressive behaviour they observed adults engaging in is a classic example of which theory of aggression?
   A. social learning
   B. catharsis
   C. excitation transfer
   D. social perception

8. Which of the following would *not* be expected to be an aggression-related cue?
   A. a menorah
   B. a swastika
   C. a cross-bow
   D. a burning cross

9. The general aggression model encompasses elements of several theories of aggression. Which theory is best captured by the model's category of appraisal processes?
   A. frustration
   B. social learning
   C. cognitive neoassociation
   D. excitation transfer

10. Researchers (Santor et al., 2003) have found evidence to suggest that people with _____ may have difficulty processing multiple pieces of information simultaneously and fail to notice cues that would inhibit aggression.
   A. high blood alcohol levels
   B. poor executive functioning
   C. good executive functioning
   D. high body temperature

11. The anecdotal stories that there are more batters hit in the head by pitches in July and August than in other months of the baseball season would seem to support the influence of which factor on aggression?
   E. alcohol
   F. narcissism
   G. culture
   H. heat

12. Researchers have found higher homicide rates in the southern United States than in the northern United States. Nisbett and Cohen's research has speculated that this is due to southerners'
   A. culture of farming.
   B. culture of honour.
   C. culture of rage.
   D. culture of empathy.

13. Which of the following categories do school bullies tend to fall into?
   A. rejected by peers and non aggressive
   B. rejected by peers and aggressive
   C. not rejected by peers and non aggressive
   D. not rejected by peers and aggressive

14. Stephanie and Jeff have been married for four years. Jeff often comes home from work in a rage, insulting his female boss. He spends a great deal of time drinking in bars, and has been arrested several times for starting fights in the bars, and once for assaulting a passerby. When he gets home, he frequently hits Stephanie and their young son. Which of Holtzworth-Monroe's subgroups of batterers does Jeff fall into?
    A. family only
    B. dysphoric/borderline
    C. situational
    D. generally violent/antisocial

15. There has been a great deal of research on the effects of violent television programming on aggressive behaviour. Which two characteristics do aggressive adults tend to share, with respect to television violence?
    A. They watched a lot of television and identified strongly with violent characters.
    B. They watched a lot of television, but did not identify with violent characters.
    C. They watched very little television, but identified strongly with violent characters.
    D. They watched very little television and did not identify with violent characters.

16. In Donnerstein's study of pornography and violence, which type of pornography was found to increase aggression against women?
    A. erotica
    B. degrading pornography
    C. violent pornography
    D. degrading erotica

17. Which of the following strategies would be most effective in reducing instrumental aggression?
    A. controlling anger
    B. reducing the pain that leads to aggression
    C. teaching alternatives to aggression
    D. using cognitive relaxation training

Sentence Completion

1. The primary goal of _____ aggression is to hurt the target whereas _____ aggression is motivated by goals other than hurting the target.

2. Trying to get others to dislike a peer is an example of _____ aggression.

3. Research on children indicates that boys are more prone to _____ aggression whereas girls are more prone to _____ aggression.

4. According to the frustration-aggression hypothesis, _____ always leads to some form of _____, and _____ is the only cause of _____.

5. Your professor gives you a bad grade on a paper on which you had worked very hard. Later that day, you get angry with your roommate for no good reason. This is an example of _____ aggression.

6. The social learning theory of aggression proposes that people learn aggressive behaviour by _____ and _____ others.

7. According to the cognitive neoassociation model of aggression, an unpleasant event arouses negative emotion, which simultaneously activates the tendency to _____ and its associated emotion, _____ and the tendency toward _____ and the associate emotion, _____.

8. Husbands who engage in _____-_____ aggression are most amenable to interventions that can curb their violence and allow them to develop a healthier marital relationship.

9. Mob violence may be caused by _____ or _____ _____.

10. _____may not cause aggression, but they can increase the likelihood that aggressive impulses will have serious consequences like death or physical injury.

Matching I – Key Terms

_____ 1. aggression	A. harm-doing that is motivated by goals other than hurting the target, such as obtaining something of value
_____ 2. violence	B. a broad theory that conceptualizes aggression as the result of a chain of psychological processes, including situational events, aggressive thoughts and feelings, and interpretations of the situation
_____ 3. hostile aggression	C. harm-doing that is borne out of negative emotions like anger, frustration, or hatred
_____ 4. instrumental aggression	D. aggression that is intended to cause extreme injury
_____ 5. relational aggression	E. behaviour that is intended to injure someone physically or psychologically
_____ 6. general aggression model (GAM)	F. behaviour that is intended to damage another person's peer relationships
_____ 7. frustration-aggression hypothesis	G. the idea that aggressive behaviour releases people's pent-up frustration and reduces the likelihood of subsequent aggression
_____ 8. displaced aggression	H. harm-doing that is directed at someone or something that was not the actual source of frustration
_____ 9. catharsis	I. the twin propositions that frustration always leads to some form of aggression and frustration is the only cause of aggression
_____ 10. excitation transfer	J. the idea that physiological arousal from sources other than frustration or anger can be linked to anger-related thoughts and cognitions, thereby increasing aggression

Matching II – Key Terms

_____ 11. **social learning theory**

_____ 12. **cognitive neoassociation model of aggression**

_____ 13. **trait aggressiveness**

_____ 14. **aggression questionnaire (AQ)**

_____ 15. **executive functioning**

_____ 16. **culture of honour**

_____ 17. **mob**

_____ 18. **erotica**

_____ 19. **degrading pornography**

_____ 20. **violent pornography**

_____ 21. **cognitive-relaxation coping skills training (CRCS)**

_____ 22. **cognitive restructuring**

A. sexually explicit material that depicts aggressive, hostile sexual activity

B. sexually explicit material that debases or dehumanizes people, usually women

C. a scale that measures individual differences in trait aggressiveness

D. a disposition that represents how likely people are to respond to provocations with aggression

E. sexually explicit material that depicts nonviolent, consensual sexual activity

F. an approach proposing that humans learn many kinds of responses, including aggressive ones, by observing others; observation shows people both how to perform a behaviour and whether that behaviour will be rewarded or punished

G. an intervention program designed to reduce anger, which involves teaching people a set of relaxation techniques and ways to modify their anger-related thoughts

H. a social network in which men are taught from an early age to defend their reputation for strength by responding to insults or threats with aggression

I. a crowd acting under strong emotional conditions that often lead to violence or illegal acts

J. a theory of harm-doing proposing that aversive events activate the schemas for _fight_ and _flight_, which elicit the emotions of anger and fear; whether people respond with aggression or escape depends on the pattern of cues in the situation

K. recognizing and modifying anger-related thoughts and attributions; it forms part of CRCS training

L. higher-order cognitive processing that organizes and coordinates lower-level elements of behaviour such as planning and monitoring progress toward goals

Answers to Test Your Knowledge

Multiple Choice Questions

1. C	6. B	11. D	16. C
2. A	7. A	12. B	17. C
3. B	8. A	13. B	
4. C	9. C	14. D	
5. D	10. B	15. A	

Sentence Completion

1. hostile, instrumental
2. relational
3. physical, relational
4. frustration, aggression, frustration, aggression
5. displaced
6. observing, imitating
7. fight, anger, flight, fear
8. family-only
9. deindividuation, conformity pressure
10. guns

Matching I – Key Terms

1. E	6. B
2. D	7. I
3. C	8. H
4. A	9. G
5. F	10. J

Matching II – Key Terms

11. F	17. I
12. J	18. E
13. D	19. B
14. C	20. A
15. L	21. G
16. H	22. K

Chapter 12
Helpful Social Behaviour

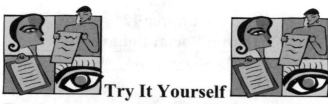 **Try It Yourself**
Can You Demonstrate the Social Norms of Casual Helping?

Experiment A
To demonstrate the norm of social responsibility:

This experiment requires you to approach at least ten strangers in a common area on campus. If you are at a small college or university or have limited time, it may be more practical for you to work with a partner.

For the experiment, ask five of the strangers "Can you give me a nickel?" and ask the other five people "Can you give me a nickel? I need to make an important phone call, and I am five cents short." The main point is to ask the first group of strangers for some help, without providing an explanation or elaboration. The same request is made of the second group of strangers, but an explanation or justification is added, in an effort to invoke the norm of social responsibility. That norm dictates that we should help people who need help.

To be sure extraneous factors such as your nonverbal behaviour and the time of day don't affect the results:
- Alternate which question you pose so that the 1st, 3rd, 5th (and so on) people are asked the first question, and the 2nd, 4th, 6th (and so on) are asked the second question;
- If you're working with a partner, be sure each of you poses each question the same number of times;
- Try to be sure no one you approach has seen you approach another person; and
- Try to devise a way to randomly select the strangers you approach (e.g., the tenth person that walks by). In any event, try to balance the number of males and females you approach.

Question:

1. Tally your responses. Did more people respond positively to the request when you gave a reason for needing five cents? Compare your results with those of your classmates.

Other ways to do this experiment:
- Each person in your social psychology class could ask one stranger the first question and another stranger the second question, and bring the responses to class for tabulation.
- Your instructor could randomly assign half the class to ask a stranger the first question and the other half to ask a stranger the second question. It is important that students not pick which question they want to ask as this could bias the results. Tally the results in class.

Experiment #2
To demonstrate the norm of reciprocity:

The norm of reciprocity suggests that people should help those who have helped them in the past. Bibb Latané and John Darley (1970) found that even telling a person your name increased the likelihood that the person would reciprocate and help you. You can try to demonstrate this norm yourself. Follow one of the procedures set out in Experiment A but use these questions: (1) "What's your name?" and (2) "My name is _____. What's your name?"

Question:

1. Tally your responses. Did more people respond positively to the second question, as the norm of reciprocity would predict? Compare your results with those of your classmates.

Try It Yourself
Why Do People Donate Blood?

The need for blood is constant and pressing. From accident victims to cancer patients, the demand for blood transfusions often outpaces the supply. In Canada and the United States, most blood is donated by volunteers. Because a relatively small percentage of the adult population actually volunteers to donate blood, understanding both what motivates people to donate blood and how to recruit and maintain new donors is an important public health issue. What motivates people to donate blood that will eventually be given to a stranger? Because the Red Cross cannot pay individuals for their blood donations, the motivation is not financial. Altruism may provide one explanation for their behaviour—individuals donate blood in order to help others. Egoism may provide another—individuals enjoy the positive emotions that result from blood donation. Motivation may also depend on an individual's prior experience with blood donation.

The vast majority of blood donors are repeat donors, people who continue to return to the donation centers several times a year, and have donated many litres of blood. Researchers generally acknowledge that as an individual's donations increase in number, his or her motivation for donating may change (Ferguson and Bibby, 2002). First-time donors are more likely to be influenced by external factors, such as the presence of a friend, persuasion by others, and the existence of a blood emergency, whereas repeat donors are more likely to cite internal, and more altruistic, motivations such as a general desire to help others (Piliavin and Callero, 1991). Indeed, one study by Paulhus, Shaffer, and Downing (1977) found that communications emphasizing altruistic reasons for giving blood increased the likelihood that repeat donors would return for future donations, but had no effect on first-time donors. However, altruism is not the only internal motivating factor for donors; as noted earlier, egoism may also play a crucial role. Researchers have found that giving blood produces an emotional high that can be addictive, much the same way that physical exercise can be addictive. In this sense, then, donation can also be egoistically motivated; donors give blood because they enjoy the feeling it brings them.

Hypotheses

This exercise is designed to test whether donors are motivated by altruism or egoism, and whether that motivation differs based on donation experience. Specifically, are experienced donors more motivated by altruism and novice donors more motivated by egoism? Altruism research suggests conflicting hypotheses. A study by Omoto and Snyder (1995), examining motivations for AIDS volunteers, indicated that people who had served as volunteers for the longest time cited egoistic reasons for their participation. Studies of blood donors, on the other hand, indicated just the opposite: repeat donors were more likely to cite altruism as their primary motivation.

Method

First, identify three or four friends or family members who have donated blood at least once. If you can, try to identify people who have donated once or twice and people who have donated more often. Ask them if they would help you with a simple study.

Ask each volunteer to indicate how many times he or she has donated blood. Record this information in the data sheet for this exercise. Enter an N (Novice) if the person has donated 1 or 2 times; E (Expert) if the person has donated between 3 and 8 times, and V (Veteran) if the person has donated more than 9 times.

Now, ask each volunteer to complete the "Reasons for Donating Blood" check sheet.[1] Instruct them to check all the reasons they donate blood and to place an asterisk (*) next to the most important reason. In the data sheet, record whether each volunteer's most important reason for donating blood is an egoistic or altruistic reason. The following table categorizes the reasons in the check sheet as altruistic and egoistic.

Altruistic Reasons:	Egoistic Reasons:
As a service to the community	It makes me feel good
It is a good thing to do	To help a friend or relative
To help an anonymous person	As repayment for blood received from a family member or self
Sense of duty to give blood	Peer pressure

Predictions

If the Omoto and Snyder (1995)'s AIDS volunteerism model is correct, experienced donors will be more likely to cite egoistic reasons for their donation (i.e., "it makes me feel good") than altruistic reasons (i.e., "to help an anonymous person"). If previous research on blood donation is correct, experienced donors will be more likely to cite altruistic reasons than egoistic reasons.

Data Analysis Suggestions

The data you collected yourself can provide some insight into the motivations of blood donors. But to more reliably determine which of the above studies is better supported, your instructor may collect your data sheet and combine your data with that collected by your classmates. The combined data can then be put into a contingency table, like that below. To complete the table, you add up the number of novice volunteers who gave an egotistic reason as most important, the number of novice volunteers who gave an altruistic reason, the number of expert volunteers who gave a egotistic reason, and so forth. Your instructor may provide direction for more formal analysis of the table using the chi-square statistic.

	Egoistic Reason is Most Important	Altruistic Reason
Novice		
Expert		
Veteran		

Questions:

1. Did the volunteers' most important reason for donating blood depend on their level of experience with blood donation? With respect to experienced donors, does the data support Omoto and Snyder (1995)'s AIDS volunteerism model or previous research on blood donation?

---

[1] The check list is based on a measure developed by Oswalt (1977).

2. Based on the results, how should agencies go about recruiting first-time donors? How could they retain expert and veteran donors? Which marketing appeals would more likely engage first-time donors, and which would engage experienced donors?

Data Sheet for Blood Donation Exercise

	Experience Level N (Novice) if the person has donated 1 or 2 times; E (Expert) if the person has donated between 3 and 8 times, and V (Veteran) if the person has donated more than 9 times.	Most Important Reason for Donating Blood (Egoistic or Altruistic)
1.		
2.		
3.		
4.		
5.		

Reasons for Donating Blood

Instructions. Check all the reasons you donate blood and then place an asterisk (*) next to the most important reason.

	To help a friend or relative
	To help an anonymous person
	Sense of duty to give blood
	As repayment for blood received from a family member or self
	As a service to the community
	It is a good thing to do
	It makes me feel good
	Peer pressure

Thinking Critically about Social Psychology
Relief Cowboy: What Motivates Professional Relief Workers?

Reading

Sri Lanka posting marks 16th mission for Canadian Red Cross nurse
Canadian Red Cross website (2005, November). Reprinted by permission of the Canadian Red Cross.

"Working internationally provides me with challenges," says Pauline Soucy, the Canadian Red Cross operating theatre nurse at the Kilinochchi Hospital in northern Sri Lanka. "Each mission, each day provides new challenges. I first became involved because I needed a change, something different."

Soucy's six month assignment in Killinochchi is her 16th international mission with the Red Cross. A native of Lac St. François near Edmundston, New Brunswick, her first international posting was in 1988 in the Cambodian refugee camps in Thailand. She has since worked in Rwanda, Sudan, Uganda, Angola, Sierra Leone, Kenya, Cambodia, Afghanistan and Pakistan, mostly with the International Committee of the Red Cross (ICRC).

Her enthusiasm for her work inspired her niece, Dr. Lyne Soucy to give up her medical practice in Edmundston, New Brunswick and also work with the International Committee of the Red Cross. She is presently on her second mission working in Kyrgyzstan managing an anti-tuberculosis campaign in the prisons visited by the ICRC.

Pauline Soucy says she was pleasantly surprised when she arrived in Kilinochchi at the end of September.

"The conditions in the operating theatre were relatively good and they are not understaffed as in the other wards of the hospital," she says. "I like working with the staff here, they are ready to work and are open and eager to learn."

Soucy says there is still a lot of work to be done and new sterilisation machines have been ordered for the hospital by the Canadian Red Cross.

"I will be teaching the staff how to properly sterilize and prepare tools and equipment for surgery," she says. "I hope the procedures I show them will stick at the end of my mission. We are in the business of planting seeds, and you have to hope some of those seeds eventually bear fruit."

At 62, Soucy says she has no regrets about the life she has chosen, although she does admit it has its difficult moments.

"Each time you leave on mission, you are torn away from your friends at home. Then at the end of the mission you are torn away from the new friends you made there. It creates a lot of instability in your life. But after so many missions you see the real need in these countries and how you can help."

Questions:

1. Does helping over a long period of time fall into one of the categories described by Ann McGuire (1994) (i.e., casual helping, substantial personal helping, emotional helping, or emergency helping)? Does another category need to be created to account for behaviour such as Pauline Soucy?

2. Is Pauline's helping an example of pure altruism? What other motivations may have influenced her choice of profession? How does the empathy-altruism model apply to Pauline's situation?

3. How would you explain the actions of Dr. Lyne Soucy, Pauline's niece, using the psychological theories and research findings presented in your textbook?

4. How might you expect the recipients of Pauline's aid to respond? What are some potential long-term consequences for the recipients of aid?

Further Reading:

Visit the following page on the Canadian Red Cross's website and read more "Stories from Canadian Relief Workers in Sri Lanka":

http://www.redcross.ca/article.asp?id=013342&tid=094

Thinking Critically about Social Psychology
Holocaust Rescuers and Bystanders

In describing Adolph Hitler's Nazi regime in Europe, social psychologist Eva Fogelman, wrote:

> It was a reign which, nearly half a century later, still challenges our understanding. Evil was rewarded and good acts were punished. Bullies were aggrandized and the meek trampled. In this mad world, most people lost their bearings. Fear disoriented them, and self-protection blinded them. A few, however, did not lose their way. A few took their direction from their own moral compass. Fogelman (1994), p. 38.

It is difficult to understand how so many people witnessed the horrors of the Holocaust and did not try to help its victims. Indeed, the inaction by German citizens and others has been the focus of many controversial articles and books. See, for example, Barnett (1999), Browning (2000), Hilberg (1992), Steinfeldt (2002). Although the term "bystander" was initially applied only to seemingly apathetic German citizens, recent scholarship suggests that it also describes other people and groups, including some sectors within the international Christian and Jewish communities, and perhaps the Allied governments themselves (Barnett, 1999).

An equally perplexing question is why a relatively few ordinary people chose to take action to help save thousands of Jewish lives. Although their helping behaviour took many forms, all the rescuers recognized a person's life or the lives of a group of people was endangered, and took responsibility for helping despite the grave risks of doing so.

Many non-Jews who helped Jews during the Holocaust are profiled in the websites and books listed below. Read five to ten of these profiles and then answer the following questions.

Questions:

1. What do you think motivated the rescuers to act? How do you think they would have scored on the Interpersonal Reactivity Index, which is described and partly reproduced in your textbook?

2. Conversely, how do the principles of **social validation** and **diffusion of responsibility** help explain why people did not help Holocaust victims? According to the **belief in a just world** theory, how do you think people who actively chose not to help viewed the victims in the ensuing years?

Websites

http://www.ushmm.org/wlc/en/
This link will take you to a page about rescuers in the Holocaust Encyclopedia, maintained by the United States Holocaust Memorial Museum. In addition to general information about how rescuers accomplished their goals, it includes personal accounts (some in audio and video) of people who were rescued and their rescuers, as well as links to other related material.

http://www.humboldt.edu/~altruism
This website contains a wealth of material on altruism and bystander inaction during the Holocaust, as well as links to information on such great altruistic personalities as Mohandas Gandhi, Mother Teresa, Elie Wiesel, and Nelson Mandela. It is maintained by Samuel P. Oliner, Professor of Sociology at Humboldt State University and Founder/Director of the Altruistic Personality and Prosocial Behaviour Institute who has authored many publications on the Holocaust and altruism and prosocial behaviour. Many of the sites listed below can be reached from Professor Oliner's site. (Hint: From the site's home page, select "altruistic links.")

http://www.ushmm.org/outreach/rescue.htm
This website maintained by the U.S. Holocaust Memorial Museum in Washington, D.C. provides general information about rescue efforts, and profiles some rescuers and rescuees.

http://www.pbs.org/wgbh/pages/frontline/shtetl/righteous/gentilesbios.html
This website contains profiles of five people who helped Jews during the Holocaust.

http://www.humboldt.edu/~rescuers/
To Save a Life: Stories of Holocaust Rescue, by Ellen Land-Weber (2004), is available on the Internet. It contains personal narratives of six rescuers and thirteen people whom they helped during the Nazi era in Europe.

http://fcit.coedu.usf.edu/holocaust/people/rescuer.htm
This website contains links to profiles of and first-hand narratives by holocaust rescuers.

http://www.holocaustcenter.org/oralin.shtml
This website maintained by the Holocaust Memorial Center of Detroit, Michigan has summaries of oral histories given by Holocaust survivors, witnesses, and rescuers.

Books

Barnett, V. J. (1999*). Bystanders: Conscience and complicity during the Holocaust.* Westport, Conn.: Greenwood Press.

Browning, C. R. (2000). *Nazi policy, jewish workers, German killers.* Cambridge, U.K.; New York: Cambridge University Press.

Fogelman, E. (1994). *Conscience and courage: The rescuers of the Jews during the Holocaust.* New York: Anchor Books.

Hilberg, Raul (1992). *Perpetrators victims bystanders: The Jewish catastrophe 1933-1945.* New York: Aaron Asher Books.

Keneally, T. 1982. *Schindler's List.* New York: Simon & Schuster.

Oliner, S. P. & Oliner, P. M. (1988). *The altruistic personality: Rescuers of Jews in Nazi Europe.* New York: Free Press.

Oliner, S. (2003). *Do unto others: Extraordinary acts of ordinary people.* Boulder, Colorado: Westview Press.

Steinfeldt, I. (2002). *How was it humanly possible? A study of perpetrators and bystanders during the Holocaust.* Jerusalem: International School for Holocaust Studies, Yad Vashem; Laxton, Newark, Nottinghamshire: Beth Shalom Holocaust Memorial Centre (available at the United States Holocaust Museum).

Thinking Critically about Social Psychology
Good Samaritan Laws

"A sees B, a blind man, about to step into the street in front of an approaching automobile. A could prevent B from doing so by a word or a touch without delaying his own progress. A does not do so, and B is run over and hurt. . . ." Restatement of Torts, Second, Sect. 314.

The common law that developed through the courts would impose no duty for Person A to help Person B. A bystander is not obligated to assist a stranger even if the stranger is in grave danger and the bystander could easily help the person in trouble. For example, a bystander would not be legally culpable if he or she stood on a riverbank and watched a stranger being swept to certain death, even though the bystander could have easily avoided the disastrous result by throwing out a nearby life-line.

Although the common law imposed no duty to come to the aid of a stranger, it held that a volunteer (i.e., the "Good Samaritan") who helps can be held legally liable if he or she does not use reasonable care in rendering aid. That is, the person who was helped may be able to successfully sue if the helper was negligent is some way. This created the anomalous, almost bizarre situation, in which people who witness an accident may ignore seriously injured persons without incurring the disfavour of the law. But if they attempt to assist the victims, they might be held liable if they make mistakes in doing so.

All fifty states in America and the District of Columbia have taken legislative action to remedy this situation by passing "Good Samaritan" statutes (Stewart, 1998, Sullivan, 1832). These laws, named after the New Testament parable set out in the textbook, encourage people to help at the scene of accidents by removing the fear that they will be held legally liable for doing so. The laws were initially aimed at medical providers, but have been extended to other would-be rescuers. Laws have also been enacted to impose a legal duty to help in the case of special relationships (e.g., an employer may be obligated to help an employee under certain situations).

The development of the law in the Canadian common law jurisdictions is similar to that in the United States (see Schwartz, 1995, 2004). Many of the provinces in Canada have passed "Good Samaratan" laws (e.g., The Good Samaritan Act in Ontario, The Emergency Medical Act in Alberta, The Good Samaritan Act in British Columbia, and the Volunteer Services Act in Nova Scotia). However, in Quebec, a civil rather than a common law jurisdiction, the law imposes a duty on everyone to help a person in peril. Despite this difference, there have been few lawsuits against people who have played the Good Samaritan.

Questions:

1. By not requiring people to help strangers in emergencies, the common law seems to recognize that human nature sometimes makes it difficult for them to do so. How does social psychology help explain why people are not as helpful in emergency situations as we would hope?

2. By imposing potential liability on those who actually do render aid, the common law actually discourages helping. What does social psychology say about people's reluctance to take responsibility in an ambiguous situation? How does the common law exacerbate their unwillingness? Under what situations might a person ignore the threat of potential liability and help a stranger?

3. How much do you think the "Good Samaritan" statutes actually encourage helping? What other obstacles may stand in the way of people rendering aid? Could other laws help eliminate these obstacles? Would such laws be fair, human nature being what it is?

On the Web
Vacationing as a Volunteer

Margot Page felt guilty raising her kids in what she calls Seattle's "toxic" environment, where people check their stock prices several times a day. She and her husband wanted to instill in their three children cores values, like "sharing their gifts," but rarely had time for community service. So they made time—on their vacation. Last April, Page, a software program manager, and her family went to Costa Rica to work with local people grooming rainforest trails. For two weeks they spent time with Costa Ricans, she says, whose "happiness did not rely on material things."

Excerpted from Klein, D. (2000, July 10). Hard-work holidays. *Newsweek*, 69–70.

Nice as it was, Pat Carnright's cruise to Alaska two years ago just wasn't quite enough. "It's so much more fun to go and learn about a country and the people," she says. This past summer, when she ventured from her home near Tacoma, Wash., it was not to Rome or Rio but to West Africa, where she did as much as six hours' worth of volunteer work each day for three weeks in a village named Ho, fifty miles north of Acra, Ghana. Under the auspices of the organization Cross-Cultural Solutions, Carnwright, a part-time real estate agent, assisted in a local nursery school, reading to children, teaching them songs, numbers and colors, and telling them about life in America.

Excerpted from Mitchell, E. (1999, October 18). Lending a helping hand. *Time, 154 (16)* (online at http://www.time.com/time/magazine/0,9263,7601991018,00.html).

Maybe you're one of those people whose conscience rears up if life becomes too pampered — like when you're lying by a resort pool being served a frothy cocktail by a uniformed waiter. Or maybe you can't justify the expense of an exotic trip simply for pleasure. We've got the solution: a guilt free vacation. When you sign on for a volunteer trip, not only does your fee help fund the project, but your time and sweat make it happen. Now, c'mon, isn't that better than a poolside pina colada?

Excerpted from Traveler's Almanac, 1999 Annual Travel Guide, *Outside Magazine* (online at http://outside.away.com/outside/magazine/travelguide99/99tgtavolunteer.html).

Go to http://www.globeaware.org/Content/ and click on "Alumni" to read other stories from Canadians and Americans who choose to go on volunteering vacations.

Are you tired of vacationing at crowded amusement parks? Does visiting an exotic place with nothing on the agenda but fun and sightseeing (even if it is educational) leave you unfulfilled? Do you feel guilty about finding no time for community service in your day-to-day life? Yes? Then an altruistic vacation may be just the break you need. Check out the following organizations for help in planning your trip. Although such trips are not free and may carry a price tag into the thousands, their cost may be tax-deductible as a charitable donation.

Cross-Cultural Solutions
www.crossculturalsolutions.org

Service Civil International
www.sci-ivs.org

Earthwatch Institute
www.earthwatch.org

Global Volunteers
www.globalvolunteers.org

Action Without Borders
www.idealist.org

International Medical Volunteers Association
www.imva.org

Globe Aware
http://www.globeaware.org/

Volunteer Abroad
http://www.volunteerabroad.ca/media.cfm

Questions:

1. As you browse the websites, read the testimonials and think about what factors drive people to vacation as a volunteer. Do people take these vacations for altruistic or egoistic reasons? Does one type of motivation seem to be stronger for certain kinds of people and in certain situations? Would you consider taking such a vacation? Why or why not?

2. How does "vacationing as a volunteer" fall along the three dimensions of helping behaviour identified by Philip Pearce and Paul Amato (1980) and described in the text: (1) planned or formal helping versus spontaneous or informal helping; (2) helping with a non-serious problem versus helping with a serious problem; and (3) helping by "giving what you have" versus helping by "doing what you can"? Does the third dimension seem valid for this type behaviour?

 **On the Web**
Social Psychology Online Lab
Cooperation versus Competition: Will You Choose to Compete?

In the textbook you read about the prisoner's dilemma game that forces people to choose between selfishness and cooperation. Visit this website, http://serendip.brynmawr.edu/playground/pd.html, to play an interactive prisoner's dilemma game. Gold coins instead of years in prison are at stake when you choose whether to cooperate or compete with your partner, Serendip. If you both choose to cooperate, you'll both receive 3 gold coins; if you both choose to compete, you'll both receive 1 gold coin; and if one of you competes while the other cooperates, the competitor will receive 5 gold coins, but the cooperator none. Will you choose to cooperate in an effort to maximize the common good, or will you try to come out ahead by competing? Try different strategies and see how you fare.

Question:

1. According to psychological research, which strategy, competition or cooperation, is the most common?

Online lab

The online lab also contains an interactive prisoner's dilemma game. Try the lab and see if you respond as research would predict.

***Social Psychology Alive* Journal**
The Story of Kitty Genovese

Bibb Latané and John Darley conducted an important series of studies in social psychology to investigate the dynamics of bystander intervention in emergencies. Their research was inspired by the story of Kitty Genovese, as reported in the following 1964 *New York Times* article. In the ensuing years, the accuracy of the Times account has been challenged, but its impact on the research about helping behaviour has endured.

Thirty-Seven Who Saw Murder Didn't Call the Police

Martin Gansberg
New York Times March 27, 1964 Copyright © 1964 by The New York Times Co. Reprinted with permission

For more than half an hour 38 respectable, law-abiding citizens in Queens watched a killer stalk and stab a woman in three separate attacks in Kew Gardens.

Twice their chatter and the sudden glow of their bedroom lights interrupted him and frightened him off. Each time he returned, sought her out, and stabbed her again. Not one person telephoned the police during the assault; one witness called after the woman was dead.

That was two weeks ago today.

Still shocked is Assistant Chief Inspector Frederick M. Lussen, in charge of the borough's detectives and a veteran of 25 years of homicide investigations. He can give a matter-of-fact recitation on many murders. But the Kew Gardens slaying baffles him—not because it is a murder, but because the "good people" failed to call the police.

"As we have reconstructed the crime," he said, "the assailant had three chances to kill this woman during a 35-minute period. He returned twice to complete the job. If we had been called when he first attacked, the woman might not be dead now."

This is what the police say happened at 3:20 a.m. in the staid, middle-class, tree-lined Austin Street area:

Twenty-eight-year-old Catherine Genovese, who was called Kitty by almost everyone in the neighborhood, was returning home from her job as manager of a bar in Hollis. She parked her red Fiat in a lot adjacent to the Kew Gardens Long Island Railroad Station, facing Mowbray Place. Like many residents of the neighborhood, she had parked there day after day since her arrival from Connecticut a year ago, although the railroad frowns on the practice.

She turned off the lights of her car, locked the door, and started to walk the 100 feet to the entrance of her apartment at 82-70 Austin Street, which is in a Tudor building, with stores in the first floor and apartments on the second.

The entrance to the apartment is in the rear of the building because the front is rented to retail stores. At night the quiet neighborhood is shrouded in the slumbering darkness that marks most residential areas.

Miss Genovese noticed a man at the far end of the lot, near a seven-story apartment house at 82-40 Austin Street. She halted. Then, nervously, she headed up Austin Street toward Lefferts Boulevard, where there is a call box to the 102nd Police Precinct in nearby Richmond Hill.

She got as far as a street light in front of a bookstore before the man grabbed her. She screamed. Lights went on in the 10-story apartment house at 82-67 Austin Street, which faces the bookstore. Windows slid open and voices punctuated the early-morning stillness.

Miss Genovese screamed: "Oh, my God, he stabbed me! Please help me! Please help me!"

From one of the upper windows in the apartment house, a man called down: "Let that girl alone!"

The assailant looked up at him, shrugged, and walked down Austin Street toward a white sedan parked a short distance away. Miss Genovese struggled to her feet.

Lights went out. The killer returned to Miss Genovese, now trying to make her way around the side of the building by the parking lot to get to her apartment. The assailant stabbed her again.

"I'm dying!" she shrieked. "I'm dying!"

Windows were opened again, and lights went on in many apartments. The assailant got into his car and drove away. Miss Genovese staggered to her feet. A city bus, 0-10, the Lefferts Boulevard line to Kennedy International Airport, passed. It was 3:35 a.m.

The assailant returned. By then, Miss Genovese had crawled to the back of the building, where the freshly painted brown doors to the apartment house held out hope for safety. The killer tried the first door; she wasn't there. At the second door, 82-62 Austin Street, he saw her slumped on the floor at the foot of the stairs. He stabbed her a third time—fatally.

It was 3:50 by the time the police received their first call, from a man who was a neighbor of Miss Genovese. In two minutes they were at the scene. The neighbor, a 70-year-old woman, and another woman were the only persons on the street. Nobody else came forward.

The man explained that he had called the police after much deliberation. He had phoned a friend in Nassau County for advice and then he had crossed the roof of the building to the apartment of the elderly woman to get her to make the call.

"I didn't want to get involved," he sheepishly told police.

Six days later, the police arrested Winston Moseley, a 29-year-old business machine operator, and charged him with homicide. Moseley had no previous record. He is married, has two children and owns a home at 133-19 Sutter Avenue, South Ozone Park, Queens. On Wednesday, a court committed him to Kings County Hospital for psychiatric observation.

When questioned by the police, Moseley also said he had slain Mrs. Annie May Johnson, 24, of 146-12 133rd Avenue, Jamaica, on Feb. 29 and Barbara Kralik, 15, of 174-17 140th Avenue, Springfield Gardens, last July. In the Kralik case, the police are holding Alvin L. Mitchell, who is said to have confessed to that slaying.

The police stressed how simple it would have been to have gotten in touch with them. "A phone call," said one of the detectives, "would have done it." The police may be reached by dialing "0" for operator or Spring 7-3100.

Today witnesses from the neighborhood, which is made up of one-family homes in the $35,000 to $60,000 range with the exception of the two apartment houses near the railroad station, find it difficult to explain why they didn't call the police.

A housewife, knowingly if quite casually, said, "We thought it was a lovers' quarrel." A husband and wife both said, "Frankly, we were afraid." They seemed aware of the fact that events might have been different. A distraught woman, wiping her hands in her apron, said, "I didn't want my husband to get involved."

One couple, now willing to talk about that night, said they heard the first screams. The husband looked thoughtfully at the bookstore where the killer first grabbed Miss Genovese.

"We went to the window to see what was happening," he said, "but the light from our bedroom made it difficult to see the street." The wife, still apprehensive, added: "I put out the light and we were able to see better."

Asked why they hadn't called the police, she shrugged and replied: "I don't know."

A man peeked out from a slight opening in the doorway to his apartment and rattled off an account of the killer's second attack. Why hadn't he called the police at the time? "I was tired," he said without emotion. "I went back to bed."

It was 4:25 a.m. when the ambulance arrived to take the body of Miss Genovese. It drove off. "Then," a solemn police detective said, "the people came out."

Questions:

1. If you had read the above article in the newspaper, what questions would it have raised in your mind? How have these questions been answered, at least, in part by subsequent social psychology research?

2. If you had been one of Kitty Genovese's neighbors in 1964, do you think you would have come to her aid? Now that you know the research on emergency intervention, do you think you would be more likely to help in such a situation?

3. Describe a situation in which you could have helped a stranger, and think about why you did or did not help. How do your reasons map onto the social psychology theories about bystander intervention?

On the Web
The Victoria Cross:
Heroes Do Exist!

The Candian military honour of the Victoria Cross is "Awarded for most conspicuous bravery or some daring or pre-eminent act of valour or self-sacrifice or extreme devotion to duty in the presence of the enemy."

Visit the Veterans Affairs Canada website and browse through the recipients of the Victoria Cross at: http://www.vac-acc.gc.ca/remembers/sub.cfm?source=collections/cmdp/mainmenu/group01/cdn_vc

Select five recipients of the Victoria Cross and ask yourself what motivated the awardees to act.

Brief description of the heroic act	What appeared to motivate the awardee to act?
1.	
2.	
3.	
4.	
5.	

Question:

1. How do the motivations of would-be rescuers differ in the military?

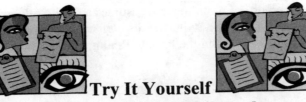

Try It Yourself

Thoughts on Helping by Authors, Philosophers, and Leaders

Authors, philosophers, and political and social leaders have made many statements about why people choose to help or not to help others, and the consequences of their choices. Pick five of the following quotes and describe how they relate to the social psychology theories and findings in the textbook.

1.	"Charity and personal force are the only investments worth anything." Walt Whitman, "Song of Prudence"
2.	"One will seldom go wrong if one attributes extreme actions to vanity, average ones to habit, and petty ones to fear." Nietzsche, *Human, All Too Human* (1878), 74, tr. Helen Zimmern
3.	"Not always actions show the man; we find/Who does a kindness is not therefore kind." Alexander Pope, *Moral Essays* (1731–35), I.109.
4.	"We do not quite forgive a giver. The hand that feeds us is in some danger of being bitten." Emerson, "Gifts," *Essays: Second Series* (1844).
5.	"It is more blessed to give than receive." *Bible*, James 1:17.

6.	"[G]oodness that comes out of hiding and assumes a public role is no longer good, but corrupt in its own terms and will carry its own corruption wherever it goes." Hannah Arendt, "The Public and the Private Realm," *The Human Condition* (1958).
7.	"Men that talk of their own benefits are not believed to talk of them because they have done them, but to have done them because they might talk of them." Ben Jonson, "Explorata," *Timber* (1640).
8.	"A large part of altruism, even when it is perfectly honest, is grounded upon the fact that is uncomfortable to have unhappy people about one." H. L. Mencken, *Prejudices: Fourth Series* (1924), 11.
9.	"If all alms were given only from pity, all beggars would have starved long ago." Nietzsche, *The Wanderer and His Shadow* (1880), 239, in *The Portable Nietzsche*, tr. Walter Kaufmann.
10.	"Human happiness and moral duty are inseparably connected." George Washington
11.	"Many persons have a wrong idea of what constitutes true happiness. It is not attained through self-gratification but through fidelity to a worthy cause." Helen Keller

Source: Quote # 1 through # 9 are taken from: *The International Thesaurus of Quotations* (2nd ed.) (1996). New York: Harper Collins.

Quote # 10 and #11 are taken from: Bruun, E. A. and Getzen, R. (eds.) (1996). *The Book of American Values and Virtues.* New York: Black Dog and Leventhal Publishers.

On the Web
How Can I Help?

Has all your reading and thinking about helping left you asking, "How can I pitch in?" If so, check out the following sites:

http://www.redcross.ca
This site describes the many services of the Canadian Red Cross and how people can go about making a donation.

http://www.unicef.org/index2.php
This site describes the work of UNICEF and how you can contribute towards it.

http://www.ushmm.org/conscience/
This site of the United States Holocaust Museum list ways college students can help promote awareness and prevent genocide in the Darfur region of Sudan.

www.hungersite.com
By visiting this website and clicking a button, you'll make a donation of food to one of the world's hunger hot-spots. It costs you nothing; all the food is paid for by the site's sponsors whose logos appear after you click, and the food is distributed by the United Nations World Food Programme. You can donate once a day, so to be of most help, become a regular visitor to the site.

www.therainforestsite.com
Another easy way to exhibit prosocial behaviour: This site works the same way as www.hungersite.com but the proceeds are used to purchase and otherwise protect rainforests.

http://www.thebreastcancersite.com/cgi-bin/WebObjects/CTDSites
When people visit this site, it funds mammograms for women who can't afford them.

Learning Objectives

Helping Behaviour

1. Distinguish helpful social behaviour and prosocial behaviour. (pp. 461–462)

2. Name the four basic categories of helping behaviour identified by Ann McGuire, and give examples of each. (pp. 462–463)

3. Phillip Pearce and Paul Amato identified three major dimensions of helping by examining the similarities and differences among 62 helping situations. Describe the dimensions and give examples of helping behaviour that fall at each end of the dimensions. (p. 463)

4. What is the helper's end goal when his or her motivation is altruistic? When it is egoistic? Why is it difficult to distinguish between egoistic and altruistic motivations for helping? (pp. 463–464)

5. Describe an evolutionary explanation for altruistic behaviour. (pp. 464–465)

6. Based on studies of the empathy-altruism hypothesis, Daniel Batson and his co-workers concluded that true altruism—behaviour that is truly aimed at helping another and not at gaining self-benefit—exists. Based on a similar study, Robert Cialdini challenged Batson's conclusion. Explain why. (pp. 465–468)

7. How do the norm of social responsibility and the norm of reciprocity help promote helping behaviour? How does the personal norms model help explain whether a person will or will not provide help? (pp. 468–469)

8. Despite the old saying, "do as I say, not as I do," intuition tells us that children may more often do as adults do, and not as they say when it comes to helping others. What does the research say about the validity of this intuition? How do the research findings extend to the helping behaviour of adults? (p. 469)

9. How does the hypothesis, Belief in a Just World, help explain when people will and will not help others? (pp. 469–470)

10. How does good mood affect a person's tendency to help? How does bad mood affect it? (p. 471)

11. Are people more likely to help another when they are the cause of a person's misfortune? Are they more likely to help a third-party who needs help? (p. 471)

12. What evidence exists for the existence of an altruistic personality—a personality type that is predisposed to help others? What childhood experiences might account for the development of such a personality? (pp. 471–472)

13. Based on research on AIDS and other types of volunteerism, what motivates people to become long-term volunteers? (pp. 474–478)

14. According to Latane and Darley, what five things must occur for a bystander to intervene in an emergency? (p. 479)

15. How does being in a hurry affect the likelihood that a person will help another in an emergency? (pp. 479–480)

16. How does the presence of someone who is seemingly unconcerned affect the likelihood that a person will interpret an event as an emergency? (pp. 480–481)

17. How does group size affect the likelihood that a person will accept personal responsibility for helping another person in an emergency? (pp. 481–482)

18. Explain how a victim might help a potential helper overcome obstacles to providing help. (p. 483–484)

19. Explain how pro-social behaviour differs across cultures, and how these differences might develop. (pp. 484–485)

20. How does the norm of reciprocity help explain why people may refuse help? Under what circumstances might accepting help threaten a person's self esteem, and make them feel worse rather than better? How does a helper's reason for helping affect a person's response to the help? How does dispositional gratitude affect a person's response? (pp. 485–489)

Social Dilemmas: Cooperating for the Common Good

21. What two features characterize all social dilemmas? Describe what is meant by a tragedy of the commons and provide an example. Describe the prisoner's dilemma and how it is used to study behaviour in social dilemmas. (pp. 490–492)

22. What factors influence whether people in social dilemmas decide to act selfishly or cooperatively? What strategies might be used to encourage cooperation rather than competition? (pp. 492–495)

23. How does social value orientation affect the likelihood that a person will cooperate in a social dilemma? (pp. 495–496)

Social Support

24. What are the two distinct functions of a social support network? Why is the metaphor "support banks" used to describe such networks? (pp. 496–498)

25. Describe four ways that social support might improve the recipients' mental or physical health? What is the effect of *perceived availability of social support* on a person's physical and mental well-being? What is the effect of *actual social support* on a person's physical and mental well-being? (pp. 498–501)

Test Your Knowledge

Multiple Choice Questions

1. Which of the following is *not* of one of the categories of helping, as described by McGuire?
   A. emergency helping
   B. emotional helping
   C. planned helping
   D. casual helping

2. What is the difference between egoistic and altruistic motivations for helping?
   A. In egoistic helping, the goal is to provide benefit to others; in altruistic helping, the goal is to gain benefit for the self.
   B. In egoistic helping, the goal is to gain benefit for the self; in altruistic helping, the goal is to provide benefit to others.
   C. In egoistic helping, the goal is to provide benefit to the greater society; in altruistic helping, the goal is to provide benefit to others.
   D. In egoistic helping, the goal is to benefit the self; in altruistic helping, the goal is to provide benefit to the greater society.

3. According to the theory of inclusive fitness, who would you be most likely to help in a life or death situation?
   A. your sibling
   B. your spouse
   C. your best friend
   D. your cousin

4. In Batson et al.'s study of the empathy-altruism hypothesis, students watched "Elaine" receive electric shocks and were given the opportunity to switch places with her. In that study, which best represents the altruistic motivation?
   A. Low levels of empathy and an easy opportunity to escape witnessing the distress.
   B. Low levels of empathy and no easy opportunity to escape witnessing the distress.
   C. High levels of empathy and no easy opportunity to escape witnessing the distress.
   D. High levels of empathy and an easy opportunity to escape witnessing the distress.

5. As you are walking past a crowded store, you notice a woman pushing a baby carriage and holding a toddler by the hand. As you pass, she asks you if you will hold the door open for her. You willingly oblige, the woman thanks you, and you continue on your way. Your helping behaviour can best be explained by
   A. guilt.
   B. social norms.
   C. good mood.
   D. modeling helpful behaviour.

6. According to the blame the victim explanation for helping, you are most likely to help someone in trouble when that person
   A. is not at fault for his or her trouble, and can be easily helped.
   B. is not at fault for his or her trouble, and whose suffering is expected to continue.
   C. is at fault for his or trouble, and can be easily helped.
   D. is at fault for his or her trouble, and whose suffering is expected to continue.

7. Recently researchers have begun to study the motives underlying volunteerism, with mixed results. The work of Davis, Hall, and Meyer, surveying volunteers in various organizations suggests an explanation of the seemingly conflicting findings of previous studies. According to their work, what is the most important predictor of satisfaction with a volunteer experience?
   A. The extent to which volunteers had other-oriented motives.
   B. The extent to which volunteers had egoistic motives.
   C. The extent to which volunteers' motives were fulfilled.
   D. The extent to which volunteers had multiple motives.

8. The researchers most closely associated with investigating the dynamics of bystander intervention are
   A. Latané and Darley.
   B. Omoto and Snyder.
   C. Cialdini and McGuire.
   D. Greenberg and Shapiro.

9. Which of the following is *not* one of the steps in the decision tree necessary to intervene in an emergency?
   A. accepting personal responsibility for helping
   B. interpreting the event as an emergency
   C. implementing an action for helping
   D. following the lead of other witnesses

10. Imagine you are walking down the street when you have a seizure. In which situation do you have the best chance of receiving help from those around you?
    A. You are in a large city like Ottawa or Calgary.
    B. You are surrounded by a group of seminary students.
    C. It is late at night and you are outside a bar.
    D. You are able to single out a person and ask directly for assistance.

11. In the cross-cultural investigation of children's helping behaviour, which type of socialization behaviours were found to be correlated with the fewest helpful behaviours?
    A. caring for younger siblings
    B. competing in school
    C. working on the family farm
    D. performing household chores

12. In Nadler et al.'s study of the effects of receiving help on self-esteem in which students played a game with a similar or dissimilar partner, in which condition was the participants' self-esteem most threatened?
    A. when the partner was similar to the participant and helped the participant
    B. when the partner was similar to the participant and did not help the participant
    C. when the partner was dissimilar to the participant and helped the participant
    D. when the partner was dissimilar to the participant and did not help the participant

13. According to the studies of Ames et al. (2004), which motivation for helping elicits the most positive response from the recipient of that help?
    A. cost-benefit motivation
    B. norm of reciprocity motivation
    C. liking/caring motivation
    D. role demands motivation

14. Which of the following was not correlated with high levels of dispositional gratitude, as demonstrated by the research of McCullough et al.?
    A. higher levels of empathy
    B. lower levels of optimism
    C. lower levels of anxiety
    D. higher incidence of helpful behaviours

15. What is the term used to describe a common methodology for studying social dilemmas?
    A. cooperation matrix
    B. tragedy of the commons
    C. prisoner's dilemma game
    D. cost-benefit decisional analysis

16. Which of the following strategies has been shown to increase cooperative responses in social dilemmas?
    A. priming a competitive schema
    B. reducing the impact of social norms
    C. modeling behaviour on dissimilar others
    D. communicating with other participants

17. Recent social psychological research has examined the role of social support and well-being. Which statement best reflects the findings?
    A. The perceived availability of social support and the actual receipt of social support are equally associated with well-being.
    B. The perceived availability of social support is more strongly associated with well-being than is the actual receipt of social support.
    C. The actual receipt of social support is more strongly associated with well-being than is the perceived availability of social support.
    D. The perceived availability of social support and the actual receipt of social support have no demonstrated effect on well-being.

Sentence Completion

1. Anne McGuire (1994) identified four major types of helping: _____ helping, _____ helping, _____ _____ helping, and _____ helping.

2. Two strangers, Ben and Ethan, were waiting in an airport for the same very delayed flight. As Ben stood and began to make his way to the snack bar, he asked Ethan whether he could bring him back a snack. Later, when Ethan went to the snack bar, he asked Ben the same question. This demonstrates the _____ of _____.

3. When victims cannot be easily helped, other people may protect their _____ in a _____ by _____ the victims for their plight.

4. People want to believe that the society in which they live is fair and through _____ _____ attempt to confirm this belief by derogating victims and enhancing people who are successful.

5. The bystander effect (both original and implicit) suggests that residents of big cities feel _____ responsible for the well-being of strangers and are _____ likely to interpret events as emergencies, compared to residents of small cities.

6. Compared to people in individualist cultures, people in collective cultures are _____ likely to help strangers and _____ likely to help in less serious situations.

7. According to the norm of reciprocity, Steve is _____ to ask for a needed ride to basketball practice from a friend who also sometimes needs a ride from another person than from a friend who never needs a ride from another person.

8. In social dilemmas, increased communication generally leads to increased _____.

9. According to the concept of social value orientation, _____ are primarily concerned with maximizing their own outcomes, _____ are primarily concerned with maximizing their own outcomes relative to others' outcomes, and _____ are primarily concerned with maximizing the total outcomes of everyone in the setting.

Matching I – Key Terms

_____ 1.	helping	A. a model proposing that humans need to believe that the world is a fair place where people generally get what they deserve
_____ 2.	prosocial behaviour	B. the principle that some social behaviours have been selected during the course of evolution because they increase the survival of our genes
_____ 3.	egoistic motivation	
_____ 4.	altruistic motivation	C. guidelines that have been internalized to become expectations for oneself in particular situations
_____ 5.	inclusive fitness	D. the idea that feelings of empathy for a person can lead to behaviour that is motivated solely by wanting to help that person
_____ 6.	empathy	
_____ 7.	empathy-altruism hypothesis	E. the rule or guideline that we should help those who need help, if possible
		F. any action that provides benefit to others
_____ 8.	norm of social responsibility	G. behaviour that is intended to help another person
		H. a motive for helping in order to obtain rewards or avoid punishments
_____ 9.	personal norms	I. a motive for helping purely for the sake of providing benefit to another person
_____ 10.	just world theory	J. the ability to comprehend how another person is experiencing a situation
_____ 11.	Interpersonal Reactivity Index (IRI)	K. a disposition reflecting the extent to which people feel empathy in response to others' experiences

Matching II – Key Terms

_____ 12. **volunteerism**	A. a table representing the outcomes for each player in a prisoner's dilemma game based on the players' combined choices
_____ 13. **decision tree**	B. a situation in which selfish choices produce better immediate outcomes for the individual than do cooperative choices, but long-term outcomes for everyone will suffer if everyone behaves selfishly
_____ 14. **bystander effect**	
_____ 15. **dispositional gratitude**	C. a set of five steps that must be completed before an individual will intervene in an emergency situation
_____ 16. **cooperation**	D. collaborative behaviour with other people that takes into account both one's own outcomes and the outcomes of the others
_____ 17. **social dilemma**	
_____ 18. **tragedy of the commons**	E. a simulated social dilemma that requires participants to make choices between acting selfishly and cooperatively when selfishness looks better initially but can damage long-term joint outcomes of the players
_____ 19. **prisoner's dilemma game**	
_____ 20. **payoff matrix**	F. the likelihood that an individual will intervene in an emergency goes down as the number of bystanders increases
_____ 21. **social value orientation**	G. people who can be called upon for help and who will provide help when needed, such as family, friends, and neighbors
_____ 22. **social support network**	
	H. the depletion of a communal resource, such as a shared cow pasture for a group of farmers, because each individual pursues selfish interests
	I. an individual differences variable reflecting the extent to which people feel thankful for receiving help from others
	J. unpaid helping behaviour that is given willingly to a worthwhile cause or organization
	K. a disposition that reflects individual differences in cooperativeness in social dilemmas; three orientations are typically distinguished: individualists, competitors, and prosocials

Answers to Test Your Knowledge

Multiple Choice Questions

1. C	6. A	11. B	16. D
2. B	7. C	12. A	17. B
3. A	8. A	13. C	
4. D	9. D	14. B	
5. B	10. D	15. C	

Sentence Completion

1. casual, emergency, substantial personal, emotional
2. norm of reciprocity
3. belief, just world, blaming
4. system justification
5. less, less
6. more, more
7. more likely
8. cooperation
9. individualists, competitors, prosocials

Matching I – Key Terms

1. G	6. J
2. F	7. D
3. H	8. E
4. I	9. C
5. B	10. A
	11. K

Matching II – Key Terms

12. J	18. H
13. C	19. E
14. F	20. A
15. I	21. K
16. D	22. G
17. B	

Chapter 13
Liking, Loving, and Close Relationships

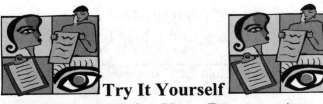

Try It Yourself
Do the Westgate Findings Hold for Your Dorm or Apartment Building?

For this exercise, first sketch out the arrangement of the rooms in your dormitory, the apartments in your building, or the houses in your neighbourhood. Second, measure or estimate the physical distance between each unit (room, apartment, or house), and put that information on the map. Then answer the questions found below.

Sketch and physical distances between units:

Questions:

1. How do the physical distances between units compare with your sense of how much the residents of each unit cross each other's paths?

2. We know from research on propinquity that functional distance is more important than physical distance in determining patterns of interaction. Recall from the text that functional distance is the closeness between two places in terms of opportunities for people to interact. Estimate the functional distance between several pairs of units as either short, medium, or long, and explain the reasoning behind your estimates.

3. Now, if possible, select one pair of units with a short functional distance but a moderate to long physical distance separating them, and select another pair with a moderate to long functional distance but a short physical distance separating them. Think about how the residents of each unit interact with one another. Which kind of distance—physical or functional—seems to be most strongly related to the frequency of contact?

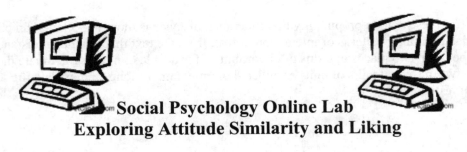

Social Psychology Online Lab
Exploring Attitude Similarity and Liking

Do birds of a feather flock together, or do opposites attract? Do people tend to like people who share their attitudes or do they tend to like people who have different attitudes, perhaps because they are more interesting?

The purpose of this online laboratory is to explore the relationship between attitude similarity and liking. You will answer some questions about your own attitudes and then rate how much you think you would enjoy working with a hypothetical person who is described. Participate in the lab and then answer the following questions.

Questions:

1. What is the expected pattern of results?

2. Did your responses fit into the expected pattern? If not, why do you think they deviated?

Try It Yourself
What Determines Physical Attractiveness?

In this chapter, you read about several studies that identified physical characteristics that make people appear more or less attractive, ranging from body type to body odour. The following exercise will allow you to replicate some of these experiments with friends and classmates, to see for yourself whether these characteristics are important determinants of physical attractiveness.

Because these exercises require the participation of a large number of people (at least 10 for Exercise A, 10 for Exercise B, and 12 for Exercise C), we suggest that you work on it in groups of two to five classmates. It is fine for one participant to take part in all three experiments. If you are working alone, an alternative procedure using five participants is suggested for Exercise C.

Experiment A: Body Type

This experiment should be conducted in two parts: one using five or more male participants and one using five or more female participants.

When you approach a person to participate in the experiment, tell them that you are collecting information for a social psychology project and that you would like to show them pictures of people they do not know and for them to rate the attractiveness of the people. Also tell them that you will not use their names when you report the results of your project, and be sure you follow through with this guarantee. You might also get more volunteers if you emphasize that the exercise takes just a few minutes to complete.

First, show the drawings of female figures on page 350 to the male participants. Ask them to tell you which figure they find the most attractive, and record their response. Then show the drawings of male figures on page 351 to five (or more) female participants, and record which one they find most attractive. After a participant has given his or her rating, explain what you expect the results of the exercise to be, and why.

Keep track of the number of times each body type is selected as the most attractive, and record it in the following tables.

Female Figures

	.7 Waist-to-Hip Ratio	.8 Waist-to-Hip Ratio	.9 Waist-to-Hip Ratio	1.0 Waist-to-Hip Ratio
Number of Responses				

Male Figures

	.7 Waist-to-Hip Ratio	.8 Waist-to-Hip Ratio	.9 Waist-to-Hip Ratio	1.0 Waist-to-Hip Ratio
Number of Responses				

Questions:

1. Which male body type do women find most attractive? Which female body type do men find most attractive?

2. Did you get the same results as Devendra Singh (1993, 1995)? That is, did you find that men prefer women whose waist is narrower than their hips, whereas women prefer men who have a relatively tapered look with hips and waist approximately the same circumference?

3. The studies that Devendra Singh conducted asked participants to rate the attractiveness of opposite sex body types. What do you think you would find if you asked women to rate the attractiveness of female body types? If you asked males to rate male body types? Do you think the results would be the same as Singh's? Why or why not?

Experiment B: Facial Averaging

This experiment is similar in method to the body type experiment. Show the photo array of mathematically averaged female faces on page 352 to 10 students, and ask them to select the one they find most attractive.[1] Then show them the photo array of male faces on page 353, again asking them to select the most attractive. Record their responses. When approaching people to participate in the exercise, use the same procedure described in the body type experiment.

Keep track of the number of times each face (both female and male) is selected as the most attractive, and record the total frequencies in the tables below.

Female Faces

	4-Face Composite	8-Face Composite	16-Face Composite	32-Face Composite
Number of Responses				

Male Faces

	4-Face Composite	8-Face Composite	16-Face Composite	32-Face Composite
Number of Responses				

Question:

1. Did you find that people found the 32-face composite the most attractive? Do you get the same results, regardless of the gender of the target face?

---

[1] The male and female faces were taken from a website maintained by J.H. Langlois. The same faces, but in a different format, are now posted at http://homepage.psy.utexas.edu/homepage/group/langloislab/newformat/morph.html

Experiment C: Body Odour

The following four vignettes each describe a hypothetical man with a severe body odour problem (adapted from Levine and McBurney, 1977). In the first vignette, the man is aware of the problem and able to control it, but chooses not to. In the second, he is unaware of the problem, but could control it if he were aware. In the third, he was aware of the problem but unable to control it, and in the fourth, he is both unaware of the problem and unable to control it.

To do this exercise, first copy each of the vignettes onto a separate sheet of paper.

- John Phillips is a first year student at McGill University who has a 3.0 average in his major, History. Unfortunately, he has a severe body odour problem due to poor personal hygiene. He is aware of the problem and could easily control it by bathing more frequently, but he is not doing so.

- John Phillips is a first year student at McGill University who has a 3.0 average in his major, History. Unfortunately, he has a severe body odour problem due to poor personal hygiene. He is not aware of the problem because, as with some people, he is not sensitive to his own body odour and no one has told him about it. However, if he were aware of the problem, he could easily control it by bathing more frequently.

- John Phillips is a first year student at McGill University who has a 3.0 average in his major, History. Unfortunately, he has a severe body odour problem due to a metabolic imbalance. He is aware of the problem, but cannot control it because there is no cure for this medical condition.

- John Phillips is a first year student at McGill University who has a 3.0 average in his major, History. Unfortunately, he has a severe body odour problem due to a metabolic imbalance. He is not aware of the problem because, as with some people, he is not sensitive to his own body odour and no one has told him about it. However, even if he were aware of the problem, he could not control it because there is no cure for this medical condition.

Now, try to recruit at least 12 people to participate. Tell them that you are collecting information for a social psychology project and that you would like to read a description of a person and rate the person's attractiveness. As before, tell them that you will not use their names when you report the results of your project and follow through with this guarantee.

Ask each participate to read the assigned vignette and afterwards, ask him or her to rate the attractiveness of the hypothetical man on a scale from 1–5, with 1 representing "Very Unattractive" and 5 representing "Very Attractive." Keep a record of which vignette each participant read, and the rating he or she gave the hypothetical man. After a participant has given his or her rating, explain what you expect the results of the exercise to be, and why.

Follow this procedure to determine which vignette a participant should read:
- On 4 small pieces of paper, write "Vignette 1" and do the same for the other three vignettes.
- Place the 12 small pieces of paper in an envelope.
- Determine which vignette a given participant will read by selecting a piece of paper from the envelope without looking at it.

This procedure will ensure that participants are randomly assigned in equal numbers to the four conditions of the experiment.

Add up the ratings for each vignette, and divide that by the number of participants who read it to get a mean attractiveness score for vignette. Enter the means into the table below, and look to see which hypothetical target person was rated as most attractive (remember than higher numbers represent greater attractiveness).

	Aware of Problem	Unaware of Problem
Able to Control Problem	Condition 1 Mean =	Condition 2 Mean =
Unable to Control Problem	Condition 3 Mean =	Condition 4 Mean =

Alternative Procedure (if you are working alone):

Make a copy of the four vignettes, all on one piece of paper. Ask five people to read the vignettes and then ask them which one of the four they find the most attractive.

Question:

1. How do your results compare to those reported in the text? In other words, did the participants find John Phillips more attractive when he was both aware of and able to control the problem?

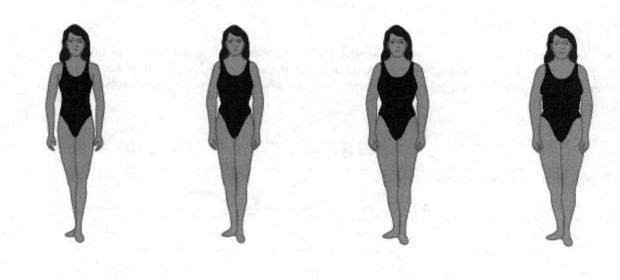

Based on Stunkard, Sorensen, and Schlusinger, 1980

350

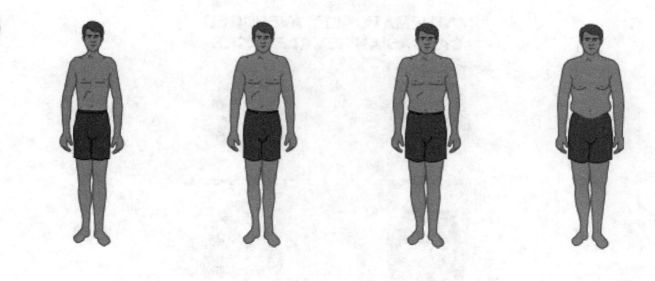

Based on Stunkard, Sorensen, and Schlusinger, 1980

MATHEMATICALLY AVERAGED
CAUCASIAN FEMALE FACES

4-FACE COMPOSITE

8-FACE COMPOSITE

16-FACE COMPOSITE

32-FACE COMPOSITE

Courtesy of Judith Langlois, University of Texas at Austin

MATHEMATICALLY AVERAGED
CAUCASIAN MALE FACES

4-FACE COMPOSITE

8-FACE COMPOSITE

16-FACE COMPOSITE

32-FACE COMPOSITE

Courtesy of Judith Langlois, University of Texas at Austin

Thinking Critically about Social Psychology
Are You Headed for Court? What You Need to Know

In the text, you read about a number of studies in which mock juries generally rate physically attractive defendants as less guilty and as deserving less punishment than unattractive defendants. But studies also show that being physically attractive can backfire on defendants who use their attractiveness to perpetuate a crime (for example, attractive defendants who swindle receive longer sentences than unattractive defendants).

Search the Internet for information and guidelines intended to assist people in preparing for court. Some examples of these guidelines can be found online at: http://www.courtprep.ca/; http://www.pimall.com/nais/n.testify.html; and http://www.njlawnet.com/njlawreview/testifyingincourt.html. Many guidelines include information on how to become knowledgeable on courtroom proceeding as well as information on how to behave and dress in court. This reflects an awareness of the paradoxical effect of attractiveness on credibility by highlighting the importance of being both attractive and substantively prepared. Read through several sets of guidelines and then answer the following questions.

Questions:

1. How do you think jurors would react to a witness who was very attractive, well-dressed, and immaculately groomed, but was unfamiliar with even the basics of the case and stumbled through the answers to straightforward questions?

2. How do you think jurors would react to a witness who obviously had taken no care with his or her appearance, but was very knowledgeable about the facts to which he or she was testifying?

3. Consider the guidelines that you have found in your search of the Internet. How would you explain the need for such guidelines based on your knowledge of social psychological concepts relating to social influence and persuasion.

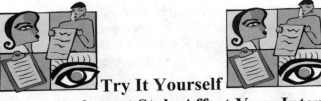

Try It Yourself
Does Your Attachment Style Affect Your Interactions
with Other People?

Studying adult attachment is one way of measuring close relationships among adults, and Hazan and Shaver (1987) translated the infant attachment styles of secure, anxious-ambivalent, and avoidant, into adult equivalents. In addition to helping adults describe their close relationships with other adults, these three attachment styles can influence how individuals interact on a daily basis. One way of investigating whether social interactions reflect attachment patterns is through event-sampling, in which individuals keep a record of daily interactions.

In Part A of this exercise, you can measure your own style of attachment, and in Part B, you can see whether that attachment style is reflected in your daily interactions with others. Remember, as with all the exercises in the workbook, one exercise does not tell the whole picture about you and others around you, and so you may find that you disagree with the results.

Part A: Determine Your Attachment Style

You can determine your attachment style in one or both of the following ways.

1. Read the following brief descriptions of the three attachment patterns and determine which best describes your style of interacting with others.

    Secure. I find it relatively easy to get close to others and am comfortable depending on them. I don't often worry about being abandoned or about someone getting too close to me.
    Anxious/Ambivalent. I find that others are reluctant to get as close as I would like. I often worry that my partner doesn't really love me or won't want to stay with me. I want to get very close to my partner, and this sometimes scares people away.
    Avoidant. I am somewhat uncomfortable being close to others; I find it difficult to trust them completely, difficult to allow myself to depend on them. I am nervous when anyone gets too close, and often, love partners want me to be more intimate than I feel comfortable being. (Shaver and Hazan, 1993, p. 35).

2. Complete the following Adult Attachment Scale on page 357 developed by Nancy Collins and Stephen Read (1990) to determine which attachment pattern best represents your style.

    Follow these steps to complete and score the scale.

    a. The scale consists of 18 items divided into three categories: Depend, Anxiety, and Close. Read each item and rate the extent that it describes your feelings on a scale ranging from 1 meaning "not at all characteristic" to 5 meaning "very characteristic."

b. Before you can calculate your scores for each subset of questions, you will need to reverse the value for some of the items. Use the following chart to do this. First, enter in the second column the number you circled above for items 3, 4, 8, 9, 10, 11, 12, 13, 14, and 17. For the remaining items (1, 2, 5, 6, 7, 15, 16, and 18), enter 5 if you circled 1, 4 if you circled 2, 3 if you circled 3, 2 if you circled 4, and 1 if you circled 5.

Depend	
• I find it difficult to allow myself to depend on others.	
• People are never there when you need them.	
• I am comfortable depending on others.	
• I know that others will be there when I need them.	
• I find it difficult to trust others completely.	
• I am not sure that I can always depend on others to be there when I need them.	
Anxiety	
• I do not often worry about being abandoned.	
• I often worry that my partner does not really love me.	
• I find others are reluctant to get as close as I would like.	
• I often worry that my partner will not want to stay with me.	
• I want to merge completely with another person.	
• My desire to merge sometimes scares people away.	
Close	
• I find it relatively easy to get close to others.	
• I do not often worry about someone getting too close to me.	
• I am somewhat uncomfortable being close to others.	
• I am nervous when anyone gets too close.	
• I am comfortable having others depend on me.	
• Often, love partners want me to be more intimate than I feel comfortable being.	

c. Now add up the values you entered for items 1–6 to get your score on the Depend subscale, add the values for items 7–12 to get your score on the Anxiety subscale, and add the values for items 13–18 to get your score for the Close subscale.

d. People with a more secure attachment style tend to score high on Close and Depend and low on Anxiety, people with an avoidant style tend to score low on all three sub-scales, and those with an anxious style tend to score high on Anxiety, regardless of their scores on the other two subscales.

Adult Attachment Scale[2]

	Not at all characteristic				Very characteristic
Depend					
• I find it difficult to allow myself to depend on others.	1	2	3	4	5
• People are never there when you need them.	1	2	3	4	5
• I am comfortable depending on others.	1	2	3	4	5
• I know that others will be there when I need them.	1	2	3	4	5
• I find it difficult to trust others completely.	1	2	3	4	5
• I am not sure that I can always depend on others to be there when I need them.	1	2	3	4	5
Anxiety					
• I do not often worry about being abandoned.	1	2	3	4	5
• I often worry that my partner does not really love me.	1	2	3	4	5
• I find others are reluctant to get as close as I would like.	1	2	3	4	5
• I often worry that my partner will not want to stay with me.	1	2	3	4	5
• I want to merge completely with another person.	1	2	3	4	5
• My desire to merge sometimes scares people away.	1	2	3	4	5
Close					
• I find it relatively easy to get close to others.	1	2	3	4	5
• I do not often worry about someone getting too close to me.	1	2	3	4	5
• I am somewhat uncomfortable being close to others.	1	2	3	4	5
• I am nervous when anyone gets too close.	1	2	3	4	5
• I am comfortable having others depend on me.	1	2	3	4	5
• Often, love partners want me to be more intimate than I feel comfortable being.	1	2	3	4	5

[2] Collins, N.L. & Read, S.J. (1990). Adult attachment, working models, and relationship quality in dating couples. *Journal of Personality and Social Psychology*, 58(4), 644–663. Copyright © 1990 by the American Psychological Association. Reprinted by permission.

Part B: Track Your Social Interactions

Track some of your social interactions for one or two consecutive days using the Social Interaction Diary on page 359. You will need to make additional copies of it for this purpose.

You should complete a form for at least five social interactions lasting more than ten minutes. Try to complete forms for a variety of social situations (i.e., class, extracurricular activities, parties, and weekend events). Keep several blank forms with you so throughout the day so you can complete it as soon after the interaction as possible.

The Social Interaction Diary sheets contain a great deal of information, but for this exercise, we will concentrate primarily on the emotions experienced during and immediately after the interaction. To summarize your diary, you will need to create a mean response for each of the emotions listed at the bottom of each sheet. For example, add up all the numbers that you circled for how happy/encouraged you felt after the interaction, and divide that by the number of interactions you recorded. That will provide you with a mean score for how happy you felt after all interactions. Do that for each of the 21 emotional responses listed. You may find it easiest to record the means on a new diary sheet.

Instead of calculating the means by hand, you may want to use a spreadsheet program such as Excel or Lotus 123 to record and analyze your responses. A layout of an Excel spreadsheet and instructions are found on page 379.

After you calculate the means for the emotional responses, look at which items have the highest scores. These represent the emotions you most commonly felt after interactions. Those emotions with the lowest means are the ones you are least likely to experience.

Interpreting Your Diary

Attachment research with adults has shown that individuals who have an avoidant attachment style are more likely to experience negative emotions following social interactions, whereas individuals with secure attachment styles are more likely to experience positive emotions following interactions. Thus, in this exercise, we would predict that individuals with avoidant attachment styles will feel more sadness, frustration, tension, worry and embarrassment when interacting socially, and that securely attached individuals will experience more positive emotions, such as happy, accepted, and stimulated. Additionally, individuals with anxious-ambivalent attachment styles may be more likely to feel anxious during social interactions.

Questions:

1. Which emotions were you most likely to experience and which emotions were you least likely to experience in your social interactions?

2. Do your emotional responses to social interactions correspond to what you would have predicted, based on your attachment style, as determined in Part A?

The Social Interaction Diary
(adapted from Tidwell, Reis, and Shaver, 1996)[3]

Date: _____

Time: _____ a.m. or p.m.

Length of interaction: _____ hours _____ minutes

Who initiated the interaction? ____ I did ____ Other did ____ It was mutual

Was this a phone call? ____ Yes ____ No

Initials of other(s): _____ _____ _____

Sex of others(s): _____ _____ _____

If more than three others, number of males _____ and females _____

Nature of interaction: ___ Job ___ Task ___Conversation ___Leisure Activity ____ Other

Briefly describe the content of the interaction (what you were doing and talking about):

_____

_____

_____

During the interaction (or immediately after it), how much did you feel . . .

	Not at All						A Great Deal
happy/encouraged	1	2	3	4	5	5	7
sad/disappointed	1	2	3	4	5	5	7
frustrated/irritated	1	2	3	4	5	5	7
rejected/left out	1	2	3	4	5	5	7
comfortable/relaxed	1	2	3	4	5	5	7
needed/appreciated	1	2	3	4	5	5	7
bored/distant	1	2	3	4	5	5	7
caring/warm	1	2	3	4	5	5	7
hurt/treated badly	1	2	3	4	5	5	7
worried/anxious	1	2	3	4	5	5	7
stimulated/invigorated	1	2	3	4	5	5	7
tense/ill at ease	1	2	3	4	5	5	7
successful/productive	1	2	3	4	5	5	7
sexually interested/aroused	1	2	3	4	5	5	7
envious/jealous	1	2	3	4	5	5	7
accepted/like you belong	1	2	3	4	5	5	7
embarrassed/self-conscious	1	2	3	4	5	5	7
disgusted/disapproving	1	2	3	4	5	5	7
ashamed/guilty	1	2	3	4	5	5	7
imposed upon/intruded upon	1	2	3	4	5	5	7
tired/low in energy	1	2	3	4	5	5	7

[3] Tidwell, M.-C.O., Reis, H.T., & Shaver, P.R. (1996). Attachment, attractiveness, and social interaction: A diary study. *Journal of Personality and Social Psychology*, 71(4), 729–745. Copyright © 1990 by the American Psychological Association. Reprinted by permission.

Social Interaction Spread Sheet Using Microsoft Excel

Below is an example of an Excel spreadsheet containing data from 12 fictional social interactions. Because of space constraints, only 6 of the 21 emotions are listed here. You may download a copy of the complete spreadsheet from the textbook website.

Int. Number	Type of Interaction	Happy	Sad	Frustrated	Rejected	Comfortable	Needed
1.00	Job	2.00	5.00	3.00	3.00	6.00	1.00
2.00	Conversation	6.00	1.00	2.00	2.00	4.00	3.00
3.00	Job	3.00	5.00	7.00	3.00	5.00	3.00
4.00	Task	5.00	4.00	2.00	2.00	5.00	1.00
5.00	Leisure	7.00	2.00	1.00	1.00	7.00	5.00
6.00	Conversation	6.00	2.00	2.00	1.00	4.00	2.00
7.00	Other	1.00	3.00	4.00	4.00	1.00	1.00
8.00	Job	3.00	2.00	5.00	2.00	3.00	1.00
9.00	Conversation	5.00	3.00	1.00	1.00	6.00	4.00
10.00	Leisure	6.00	2.00	1.00	1.00	7.00	6.00
11.00	Task	2.00	4.00	3.00	1.00	2.00	2.00
12.00	Job	4.00	2.00	3.00	2.00	3.00	5.00
Means		4.17	2.92	2.83	1.92	4.42	2.83

Calculating means across all types of interactions. In this example, the means for each emotion across all of the types of interactions were calculated by the Excel program. The generic formula used in Excel to calculate the average for a column is "=Average(column heading). So, to calculate the mean for "Happy", type "=Average(Happy)" in the blank means cell. Excel will provide the mean. You can do this for each column, making sure to insert the appropriate column heading.

Thinking Critically about Social Psychology
Can You Find True Love in Cyberspace?

Internet relationships are on the rise. From a social psychological perspective, these relationships offer new questions regarding how people meet, date, and fall in love. Relationships develop through e-mail, chat rooms, and even through organized Internet dating services.

Consider "Lavalife," which claims to be Canada's #1 Internet dating site. Lavalife offers singles a choice of browsing for dates in three different categories: dating, relationship, or intimate encounters. This offers people the choice to pre-select the type of relationship they expect and, theoretically, ensures that they will meet other singles who desire the same type of relationship. A picture and profile of each single is available to Lavalife members and prospective relationships start by sending a "smile" to another single and waiting to find out if the "smile" is returned. Further communication between interested parties is either through email or instant messaging (with or without a video). There is even a "backstage" collection of pictures that a single may choose to share with another single.

Although these connections between singles may eventually end up with a face-to-face meeting, all of the initial communication and dating practices are done online.

Questions:

1. One of the most noticeable characteristics of an Internet relationship is that individuals are exposed to each other's personality before they are aware of all of their physical characteristics. How does this affect the way in which people judge whether they are attracted to the other person? What roles do the key determinants of attractiveness described in your textbook (such as height, weight, and body type) play in relationships where the participants are able to choose what to share with each other?

2. Visit http://www.lavalife.ca/ and browse through some "success stories." How would a social psychologist explain why enabling people to meet in this way might lead to a successful relationship? (Hint: consider research on attitude-similarity, equity theory, etc.)

3. Your textbook emphasizes the importance of proximity in forming relationships—people who live near each other are more likely to form a relationship than people who do not. Over the Internet, however, physical distance is not an issue. How important do you think proximity is to Internet relationships? Is proximity important only because it makes it easier for two people to communicate regularly? Are Internet partners who happen to live close together more likely to have a long-term relationship than Internet partners who live far from each other?

4. Knowing what you do about attachment styles and their importance in adult relationships, do you think that one particular attachment style would to be more likely to get involved in an Internet relationship? Which one? Why? How would you design a social psychological study to answer this question?

5. Do you think an Internet dating service would be popular on your campus? Why or why not? Talk to one or two of your friends about this issue. Do they agree with you?

Commentary:

Cyber-relationships are becoming increasingly common as more households have access to the Internet. In chat rooms and through e-mail, people are able to interact with others without ever meeting them face-to-face. While some of these cyber-relationships lead to friendships, others may lead to romantic involvements based on exchanged e-mails and private chat room conversations that can progress from "dating" to "marriage."

The nature of attraction is an interesting issue raised by Internet relationships. In traditional relationships, many physical factors including height, weight, facial features, and body type influence a person's assessment of another person's attractiveness. People tend to pursue relationships with people that they find attractive, discovering internal qualities such as personality and sense of humor only after external qualities have been assessed. In Internet relationships, however, internal qualities become more important. Indeed, physical characteristics play less role in initial attraction. There are both positive and negative aspects to this reversal: on one hand, people who may not be traditionally considered physically attractive may have a chance to shine in an relationship that begins on the Internet, when his or her partner has a chance to know the internal qualities first. Relationships based on shared values and morals may be stronger than those based on looks alone. On the other hand, not knowing basic facts about a person may make it difficult to carry on a relationship, and again, the potential for deception increases.

These issues are only a small fraction of the many that arise about the nature of Internet relationships. Although research on traditional relationships can help researchers begin to understand cyber-relationships, specific studies are beginning to address this phenomenon.

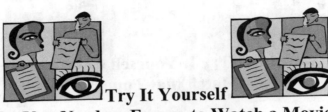

Try It Yourself
Do You Need an Excuse to Watch a Movie?

In the Warner Brothers movie, *You've Got Mail*, a superstore book chain magnate and the owner of a small children's book store build a strong friendship and fall in love, all by anonymous e-mail messages. Unbeknownst to them, they actually know each other and are business rivals. Rent the movie and find out what happens when their cyber-selves and actual selves meet.

Question:

1. Based on what you know about the psychology of attraction, do you think the ending of the movie is realistic? Why or why not?

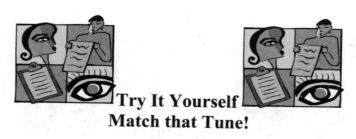

Try It Yourself
Match that Tune!

When you tune your radio to your favourite station, what do you hear? Whether it is opera, jazz, country, blue-grass, rhythm and blues, folk, rap, pop, hard rock, soft rock, heavy metal, or some of other type of music, it's almost certain that before long you'll hear a song about love. These songs are so varied, it's hard to believe they are all about the same thing—love. But love takes many forms.

Can you match the songs to one of the styles of six love styles set out below? If you're not familiar with the song, use the Internet to do a search on the lyrics to help provide more insight. How do your matches compare to those of your classmates? If you have trouble with this exercise, see the hint at the end.

Song	What is the Love Style?
1. "Lover Boy", Supertramp	
2. "Give a Little Bit", Supertramp	
3. "Soft and Gentle", Chick Corea	
4. "Every Breath You Take", The Police	
5. "Paradise by the Dashboard Lights", Meat Loaf	
6. "Hold On", Sarah McLachlan	
7. "The Ground Beneath Her Feet", U2	
8. "I'm on Fire", Bruce Springsteen	
9. "Why Don't We Get Drunk", Jimmy Buffett	
10. "Jealousy", Liz Phair	
11. "Two Out of Three Ain't Bad", Meat Loaf	
12. "I Could Write a Book", Harry Connick, Jr.	

Love Styles

Eros is an erotic style of loving that begins with a powerful physical attraction. The intensity may lessen over time, and ultimately develop into a more relaxed style.	**Storge** (pronounced store-gay) is the kind of love that develops when people enjoy similar activities, start up a friendship, and then slowly build an affection and sense of commitment.	**Ludus** is Latin for game or play; people with this style of loving tend to bounce from lover to lover, preferring not to settle down in any single long-term close relationship.
Mania is a style similar to ludus, but without the confidence. A manic lover is preoccupied with his or her lover and can be intensely jealous. At the same, he or she is insecure and needs repeated assurances he or she is loved in return. Manic lovers are in love with the idea of being in love, rather than in love with a particular person.	**Pragma.** Compatibility is the goal here. It's as if the person keeps an informal list of qualities they desire in a lover and the closer the match, the greater the love.	**Agape.** This style is selfless, giving, and altruistic. The agapic lover considers it a duty to love another who is in need of love, even in the absence of emotional attachment or eros.

Now try to identify a few other lyrics that match one of the love styles. Record them in the following table and share them with your classmates. Then answer the questions that follow.

Lyric and Song Title	What is the Love Style?
1.	
2.	
3.	
4.	
5.	

Questions:

1. For what love style or styles is it easiest to find examples? For what style is it hardest?

2. Do many lyrics reflect more than one style? Do different types of music typically reflect different love styles?

3. What does our music have to say about the values of our society?

Hint: The matches made by eight social psychologists (including two of this book's authors) are set out below. At least a majority of us, and for most songs, almost all of us, agreed with the indicated style. We found that it was easier to match songs we knew with a style, probably because the music itself provided clues about a song's intent.

Song	Love Style
"Lover Boy," Supertramp	Ludus
"Give a Little Bit," Supertramp	Agape
"Soft and Gentle," Chick Corea	Pragma
"Every Breath You Take," The Police	Mania
"Paradise by the Dashboard Lights," Meat Loaf	Mania
"Hold On," Sarah McLachlan	Storge
"The Ground Beneath Her Feet," U2	Eros
"I'm on Fire," Bruce Springsteen	Eros
"Why Don't We Get Drunk," Jimmy Buffett	Ludus
"Jealousy," Liz Phair	Mania
"Two Out of Three Ain't Bad," Meat Loaf	Ludus
"I Could Write a Book," Harry Connick, Jr.	Storge

Social Psychology Alive Journal
Dress for Success!

Study after study has found that attractive people are judged as more socially competent and socially skilled than unattractive people.

Does this finding translate into success in business? At least some business consultants think it does. *Professional Presence: Tips on Image, Wardrobe, and Body Language*, a training video developed by the Professional Image, Inc., offers practical tips for men and women on creating a winning professional presence. Among the advice is to wear classic clothing and accessories that exude credibility and power; to make strong eye contact and offer an immediate, firm and friendly handshake; and not to enter a room apologetically and with a defeated attitude but instead enter with a sense of confidence and authority. Says Susan Bixler, President of The Professional Image, Inc., "Professional Presence is a visible means of showing competence and credibility in business. Make it a part of your continuing success."[4]

Visit the job placement office on your campus, and search the Internet to find additional tips about creating a successful professional appearance, whether you are applying for a job or have already landed one. Attach the tips you find to this page or summarize them under question 1 below, and then answer the other questions.

Questions:

1. What tips for creating a professional appearance did you find in your campus job placement office or on the Internet?

2. How do the tips you identified compare to those described above?

3. What psychological findings about liking do they reflect?

---

[4] [Video issued by American Media Incorporated, Inc., 4900 University Avenue, West Des Moines, IA 50266-6769; 1-800-262-2557]

Learning Objectives

Attraction

1. Using the results of the studies conducted at Westgate and Westgate West, explain how the actual and functional distance between people is related to whether they become friends. Does actual and functional distance always lead to liking? (pp. 507–508)

2. According to the attitude-similarity effect, do "opposites attract" or do "birds of a feather flock together"? (pp. 509–510)

3. How does a person's willingness to disclose information about him or herself affect the degree to which the person is liked by others? Miller, Berg, and Archer (1983) designed the Opener Scale to measure individual differences in people's ability to get other people to "open up" and to disclose information about themselves. Describe the communication styles of high and low disclosers and how they interact with high and low openers. (p. 510)

4. What is facialmetrics and what does it tell us about how people rate facial beauty? (pp. 511–513)

5. Judith Langlois and Lori Roggman (1990) have shown that faces are judged as more attractive the closer they are to the average face. Explain the details of their study and provide an evolutionary and a development explanation of the effect. (pp. 511–513)

6. Describe the relationship of waist-to-hip ratio and the rated attractiveness of men and women. Provide an evolutionary explanation for this relationship and why it differs for men and women. (pp. 513–515)

7. Describe the relationship between weight and rated attractiveness and provide a cultural and an evolutionary explanation of the effect. (p. 515)

8. Describe the relationship between height and rated attractiveness. (p. 515)

9. What is the relationship between body odour and attractiveness? How does a person's ability to control an odour problem affect his or her attractiveness? (p. 516)

10. Explain the social psychology findings underlying the saying "what is beautiful is good." Why might a more accurate saying be "what is beautiful is culturally good"? (pp. 517–519)

11. How does the attractiveness of criminal defendants affect the degree to which they are believed to be guilty? (p. 518)

Friendships

12. What is a sociometric rating procedure? Based on the procedure, what people are considered to be friends and what people are considered to be popular? What most strongly determines whether an acquaintance develops into a closer friendship, and continues to grow? (p. 520)

13. What are the characteristics of popular children and the two forms of unpopular children (rejected-aggressive children and rejected-withdrawn children)? (pp. 520–521)

14. What effect do peers have on a child's willingness to engage in antisocial (but conforming) behaviour, and how does this change with age? (pp. 521–522)

15. In the study conducted by Robert Hays (1985), what factor predicted whether a potential friend developed into a close relationship? How did personal exchanges of information change as a friendship developed? (pp. 522–523)

Attachment

16. Bowlby's attachment theory emphasizes an ethological approach—what does this mean? (p. 524)

17. Explain how an infant with a secure attachment to his mother responds in the strange situation procedure developed by Mary Ainsworth. How does an infant with a resistant insecure attachment responds? How does an infant with an avoidant insecure attachment responds? (pp. 524–526)

18. Around the world, the secure pattern of attachment is clearly the most frequently observed pattern, but the insecure patterns are more culture specific. Describe the cultural variations and explain why they may exist. (pp. 526–527)

19. How does an infant's early attachment style carry over to preschool and grade-school years? How does the concept of a working model or schema help explain these findings? (p. 527)

20. Shaver and Hazan (1993) translated the infant attachment patterns (secure, anxious/ambivalent, avoidant) into their adult counterparts—what are the corresponding adult characteristics? (p. 528)

21. How do secure and insecure adults differ in their approach to work? How do they differ in their daily social interactions, as recorded with a method called event-sampling? (pp. 529–531)

22. What did the study by Simpson, Rholes, and Nelligan (1992) reveal about the role of secure versus insecure attachment in the propensity of couples to seek and give emotional support? What did the Kirkpatrick and Davis (1994) study reveal about the role of attachment in the maintenance of, and satisfaction with, serious dating relationships? (pp. 532–533)

Close Relationships in Adulthood

23. According to Harold Kelley (1983), what four properties indicate a high degree of interdependence between two people? (p. 534)

24. Describe the characteristics of exchange and communal relationships. How does equity affect satisfaction in a relationship? (pp. 534–536)

25. Describe the Inclusion of Other in Self (IOS) Scale—how would an intimate relationship be depicted on the scale and how would a non-intimate relationship be depicted? (p. 536)

26. Briefly describe how the investment model of close relationships helps explain which relationships last and why a person might stay in an abusive relationship. (pp. 536–537)

27. Define commitment. Discuss the role of commitment in close relationships. (p. 538)

28. Discuss both enhancing versus verifying appraisals. Under which conditions would people prefer each kind of appraisal. (p. 538)

29. Social psychologists have developed various typologies and definitions to help describe and explain the varieties of love. Be able to describe:
    - passionate versus companionate love;
    - the three primary love styles identified by Lee (1988)—eros, storge, ludus—and three secondary love styles—mania, pragma, and agape; and
    - Sternberg's triangular theory of love.
    What cultural similarities and differences in love styles have been documented? What gender differences in conceptions of love have been found? (pp. 538–542)

30. How does *perceived regard* predict people's reactions to minor conflict. Discuss how self-esteem and trust correlate with perceived regard. (pp. 543–544)

31. In general, how does the quality of the relationships of gay couples, lesbian couples, married heterosexual couples, and co-habitating heterosexual couples compare? What factors contribute to satisfaction in the relationships and does this differ according to the type of couple? (pp. 544–546)

Test Your Knowledge

Multiple Choice Questions

1. The first dyadic relationship is formed between a(n)
   A. infant and its primary caregiver.
   B. toddler and his/her baby sibling.
   C. preteen and his/her best friend.
   D. teenager and his/her first love.

2. The term that best describes the nearness in physical space which creates opportunities to meet other people is
   A. prosperity.
   B. prolixity.
   C. propinquity.
   D. propriety.

3. You are a first-year student living in a dormitory. When you moved in, you knew no one. According to the studies on spatial ecology, what is your relationship likely to be with your next-door neighbour?
   A. You will become best friends.
   B. You will not like each other at all.
   C. You will have very little interaction with each other.
   D. You may become best friends or may dislike each other.

4. Which of the following statements is most accurate with regard to facial beauty and attraction?
   A. Faces that are closest to the population average are seen as most attractive.
   B. Standards of beauty are culture specific.
   C. Infants show no preference for attractive faces.
   D. Asymmetrical faces are seen as most attractive.

5. Which of the following characteristics has not been found to influence judgments of attractiveness?
   A. Height
   B. Eye colour
   C. Body type
   D. Body odour

6. According to jury research, attractive defendants receive harsher sentences than unattractive defendants when charged with which type of crime?
   A. Burglary
   B. Swindling
   C. Arson
   D. Assault

7. In Dodge's observations of the origins of popularity among second grade boys, what characteristics did the popular children exhibit?
   A. Physical attractiveness, frequent social conversation and frequent aggression.
   B. Physical attractiveness, infrequent social conversation and infrequent aggression.
   C. Physical attractiveness, frequent social conversation and infrequent aggression.
   D. Physical attractiveness, infrequent social conversation and frequent aggression.

8. The researcher most associated with developing attachment theory is
   A. Ellen Berscheid.
   B. Robert Sternberg.
   C. Cindy Hazan.
   D. John Bowlby.

9. Ainsworth's studies of infant/mother behaviour when placed in a strange situation identified several categories of attachment. Which attachment pattern is characterized by the baby becoming very upset when the mother leaves, but resisting physical contact with her upon her return?
   A. Secure attachment
   B. Ambivalent secure attachment
   C. Resistant insecure attachment
   D. Avoidant insecure attachment

10. In the three-year longitudinal study of serious dating relationships, how did insecure attachments predict relationship stability?
    A. Anxious men were more likely than avoidant men to have broken up after three years, whereas avoidant women were more likely than anxious women to have broken up.
    B. Avoidant men were more likely than anxious men to have broken up after three years, and avoidant women were more likely than anxious women to have broken up.
    C. Anxious men were more likely than avoidant men to have broken up after three years, and anxious women were more likely than avoidant women to have broken up.
    D. Avoidant men were more likely than anxious men to have broken up after three years, whereas anxious women were more likely than avoidant women to have broken up.

11. According to Clark and Mills, a relationship in which you and a partner provide a favour or good deed for another of similar value is called a(n)
    A. exchange relationship.
    B. beneficial relationship.
    C. communal relationship.
    D. fraternal relationship.

12. In sexual relationships, which category of people report being more satisfied?
    A. Those who are under benefited
    B. Those who are equitably treated
    C. Those who are over benefited
    D. There is no difference in satisfaction.

13. According to research conducted by Lydon and his colleagues (2003; 1999) individuals who are highly committed to a romantic relationship usually evaluate an attractive alternative partner
    A. less positively.
    B. more positively.
    C. similarly to their current partner.
    D. neutrally

14. Josh and Alison met in first-year university and were close friends for several years before beginning to date each other after graduation. After five years of dating, the two are engaged and very happy. This is an example of which love style?
    A. ludus
    B. agape
    C. storge
    D. mania

15. In Kurdek and Schmitt's survey of four groups of couples, which group experienced lower relationship quality?
    A. married heterosexuals
    B. cohabitating heterosexuals
    C. cohabitating lesbians
    D. cohabitating gays

16. In which of the following situations may a close network of social support *not* be beneficial?
    A. before a final exam
    B. before a job interview
    C. after a romantic breakup
    D. when suffering from coronary heart disease

Sentence Completion

1. A dyadic relationship involves _____ people.

2. In the Westgate study, _____ proximity was more important than _____ proximity in determining mutual friendships.

3. Faces are judged as more _____ the closer they are to the _____ of the population of faces.

4. Men tend to find women with a waist-to-hip ratio _____ than 1.0 more attractive, whereas women tend to find men with a waist-to-hip ratio _____ to 1.0 more attractive.

5. Peer influence _____ from the 3rd to the 9th grades, and _____ in the 11th and 12th grades.

6. Around the world, the _____ pattern of attachment is clearly the most frequently observed pattern. The _____ patterns, however, are more culture-specific—the _____ pattern occurs with greater frequency in Western European countries, whereas the _____ pattern is more common in Israel and Japan.

7. In a(n) _____ relationship, partners tend to keep track of what they have given and what they have received, and strive to keep the books balanced.

8. In a(n) _____ relationship, the receipt of a benefit creates no specific obligation to return that benefit.

9. One of the most important predictors of whether people escalate minor conflicts into major ones seems to be the _____ of their partner's _____ for them.

Matching I – Key Terms

_____ 1. dyadic relationships

_____ 2. interpersonal attraction

_____ 3. propinquity

_C_ 4. spatial ecology

_____ 5. functional distance

_L_ 6. attitude-similarity effect.

_____ 7. repulsion hypothesis

_____ 8. self-disclosure

_____ 9. what is beautiful is good

_____ 10. friendships

_A_ 11. sociometric rating procedure

_____ 12. popular children

A. within a group of acquaintances, each person is asked to name everyone whom he or she considers a friend. Two peers within that social network are then considered to be friends if each nominates the other as a friend

B. people revealing to one another increasingly personal and intimate details about themselves

C. the physical layout of buildings and the distance separating different buildings, rooms, and other spaces

D. relationships that develop between two people

E. the idea that people find others less attractive and less likeable if they differ substantially in their attitudes, beliefs, and preferences

F. nearness or proximity in physical space which creates the opportunity to meet another person

G. dyadic relationships involving mutual liking

H. people regularly make this inference: attractive people possess other desirable traits and abilities in addition to their good looks

I. the study of attraction or liking between two or more people

J. compared to physical distance, the closeness between two places in terms of the opportunities for interaction

K. children who are named frequently by others in a sociometric rating procedure

L. the idea that people find others more attractive and likeable the more similar they are in their attitudes, beliefs, and preferences

Matching II – Key Terms

_____ 13. **rejected-aggressive children**

_____ 14. **rejected-withdrawn children**

_____ 15. **attachment theory**

_____ 16. **strange situation**

_____ 17. **secure attachment**

_____ 18. **insecure attachment**

_____ 19. **resistant insecure attachment**

_____ 20. **avoidant insecure attachment**

_____ 21. **adult attachment**

_____ 22. **working model of a close relationship**

_____ 23. **interdependence**

_____ 24. **event-sampling**

A. a pattern seen in the strange situation in which the baby prefers to stay close to mother rather than actively explore the room, becomes very upset when mother leaves the room, and appears to be upset or angry when mother returns. During the reunion episodes, these babies try to remain near their mothers, yet they usually resist any physical contact initiated by her. It seems that these infants want to cling to their mothers, but they clearly have become angry with her. Because of the vacillation between the baby's approach to and avoidance of the mother, the pattern is sometimes called ambivalent or anxious-ambivalent insecure attachment

B. Bowlby's theory concerning the development and the effects of the emotional bond between an infant and its caregiver; also used to account for the relationships that develop between close friends and lovers throughout the life span.

C. the most common pattern seen in the strange situation procedure in which the baby actively explores the room when left alone with mother, gets upset when mother leaves the room, is clearly happy when mother returns, and may even seek close physical proximity with her in an effort to relieve distress; the baby uses his or her mother as a safe haven and a secure base from which he or she feels safe to explore a novel situation.

D. the concept of attachment is used to describe and understand close relationships in adulthood by translating each of the three major patterns of attachment found among infants—secure, anxious/ambivalent, and avoidant—into their adult forms

E. a sharing of contributions and outcomes by two people. The idea of a close, dyadic relationship is that two people see themselves as a unit – sharing in both the costs and the rewards of one another's outcomes

F. children who are unpopular because they commonly engage in disruptive aggressive behaviours

G. from his or her early attachments, the infant develops a mental representation, schema, or working model of what a close relationship is all about—the feelings, thoughts, beliefs, and expectations learned during the course of those first close relationships

H. a pattern of insecure attachment is seen among babies who basically ignore their mothers, and usually show no strong signs of disturbance when she leaves the room. These babies are often observed to avoid their mothers during reunion episodes, or at least to greet her return rather casually

I. children who are spurned by their peers because of their social awkwardness and immaturity

J. developed by Mary Ainsworth, a procedure involving several brief episodes during which experimenters observe a baby's responses to strangers, separation from mother, and reunions with mother

K. a method used to study adult attachment that involves the recording of information about a person's social interactions over a period of time

L. a pattern seen in the strange situation in which the baby does not use its mother as a safe haven and secure base from which to explore a novel situation

Matching III – Key Terms

_____ 25. **exchange relationship**	A. the motivation to maintain and sustain a relationship even in the face of adversity
_____ 26. **communal relationship**	B. the idea that people differ in their styles of love; the three primary styles are eros, storge, and ludus. People may change their preferred style over their lifetimes, and some people may even prefer more than one style at a time – two or three styles may be blended, or perhaps different styles may be used with different partners
_____ 27. **equity theory**	C. this theory was developed to help formalize the idea of perceived fairness or balance in interpersonal relationships, including close dyadic relationships. An equitable relationship is one in which both partners perceive that they are receiving relatively equal outcomes
_____ 28. **passionate love**	D. the kind of love that involves strong and intense feelings, infatuation, arousal, and a deep sense of passion
_____ 29. **companionate love**	E. according to this model, satisfaction and stability in a relationship depend on the degree to which its partners feel committed to the relationship. Commitment is determined by the balance or trade-off between the positive and negative aspects of the relationship, with the idea that people compare the value of their current relationship with the value of available alternatives
_____ 30. **love-styles**	F. the kind of love that develops in a close and intimate relationship; the affection we feel for those with whom our lives are deeply entwined
_____ 31. **triangular theory of love**	G. Robert Sternberg (1986) proposed that a large variety of love experiences could be understood as combinations of three components: intimacy, passion, and commitment. Intimacy is the sense of closeness or connectedness you experience when you feel understood and cared for by another. Passion is the intense physical and sexual attraction you may feel for another. Commitment in the short term is a decision to love someone, and in the long term a dedication to maintain that love
_____ 32. **investment model of close relationships**	H. partners in an exchange relationship tend to keep track of what they have given and what they have received, and they strive to keep the books balanced
_____ 33. **commitment**	I. responding to the needs of your partner is the benefit in a communal relationship; the receipt of a benefit creates no specific obligation to return that benefit

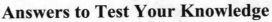

Answers to Test Your Knowledge

Multiple Choice Questions

1. A	6. B	11. A	16. D
2. C	7. C	12. B	
3. D	8. D	13. D	
4. A	9. C	14. C	
5. B	10 A	15. B	

Sentence Completion

1. two
2. functional, physical
3. attractive, average
4. less, close
5. increases, decreases

6. secure, insecure, avoidant, resistant
7. exchange
8. communal
9. perceptions, regard

Matching I – Key Terms

1. D
2. I
3. F
4. C
5. J
6. L

7. E
8. B
9. H
10. G
11. A
12. K

Matching II – Key Terms

13. F
14. I
15. B
16. J
17. C
18. L

19. A
20. H
21. D
22. G
23. E
24. K

Matching III – Key Terms

25. H
26. I
27. C
28. D
29. F
30. B

31. G
32. E
33. A

Chapter 14
Social Psychology in Your Life

On the Web
Name that Job

In the text, we explained how knowledge of social psychology could be put to use in one's career, and provided examples for careers in business and organizations, government, law, health and medicine, education, basic research, and college or university teaching. We also highlighted the interesting careers of Rod Hancock (president of an insurance company), Joy Stapp (who started her own trial consulting firm), and Louis Gliksman (director of the Social, Prevention and Health Policy Research Department at the Centre for Addiction and Mental Health).

To learn more career possibilities in psychology, visit the Careers in Psychology website maintained by the American Psychological Association: http://www.apa.org/science/careers.html. This website provides valuable advice and links relating to academic and non-academic careers. One link takes you to a library of Interesting Career articles: http://www.apa.org/science/nonacad_careers.html, where you will find dozens of interesting careers as described by those who have actually pursued them. For links to academic and non-academic careers in Canada, visit the website of the Canadian Psychological Association: http://www.cpa.ca/.

Additional perspectives on the field of social psychology, including career options and advice on graduate study, can be found at these two websites:

- Society for Personality and Social Psychology: http://www.spsp.org/index.html
- Social Psychology Network: http://www.socialpsychology.org, which includes an entire section devoted to psychology careers: http://www.socialpsychology.org/career.htm

Questions:

1. Some jobs and careers make very good use of the methods of social psychology. The ability to understand experiments, design surveys, and to critically analyze results can be key. Using the website resources described above, identify one or two careers or jobs in which the methods of social psychology would be especially valuable.

2. Some jobs and careers relate to one or more theories of social psychology. Understanding the nature of social behaviour, and appreciating the various influences in peoples' lives, can be very beneficial in many job settings. Using the website resources described above, identify one or two careers or jobs in which the theories of social psychology would be especially valuable.

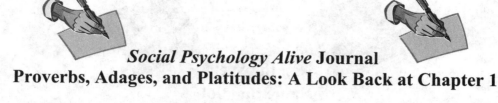

Social Psychology Alive **Journal**
Proverbs, Adages, and Platitudes: A Look Back at Chapter 1

An exercise in Chapter 1 asked you to record five sayings about human nature and social interaction that you had heard. Then, as the semester progressed, if you learned of a psychological concept or finding that supported or disabused the saying, you were to go back the exercise and briefly describe what you had learned.

Pick three of those sayings (or three new ones) and describe the related social psychology concept or finding.

Saying	Related Social Psychology Concept or Finding

Thinking Critically about Social Psychology
The Practical Relevance of Social Psychology

In Chapter 1, we defined social psychology as the scientific study of how individuals' thoughts, feelings, and behaviours are influenced by other people. We suggested that social psychology is really the *science* of social behaviour. Now that you have learned more about social psychology, we hope that you can appreciate how social psychologists use the methods of science to answer important questions about social behaviour.

To say that social psychology is a *science* means that the goal is to achieve some fundamental understanding—to understand cause and effect, to test hypotheses, and to explain why people behave the way they do. A common stereotype about science is that it can be far removed from practical application. We tend to conjure up images of people in white coats labouring deep into the night in crowded laboratories. We think of data and graphs and complex terminology. We sometimes hear the *ivory tower* criticism—that science is insulated from the reality of day-to-day life.

Very often, a distinction is made between basic research and applied research. This view supports the common stereotype that science involves a trade-off: as we move more toward application we must move farther from basic theory and research; as we move more toward fundamental understanding, we must move farther from practical relevance. To put it succinctly, scientific research is typically portrayed along a continuum:

Fundamental Understanding < ------------------------------------ > Practical Relevance

Yet, social psychology seems to blend the two ends of the continuum. Most of what you have read about in *Social Psychology Alive* was simultaneously motivated by wanting to solve a practical problem and the desire to uncover fundamental truths of human behaviour. Social psychology would appear to be struggling with its own identity! Is it a basic science or is it an applied science? How can we claim that social psychology is a science, when it seems to be so connected to the goal of informing and solving problems of great practical relevance?

The answer is that science—including the science of social behaviour—can be both rigorous and offer practical relevance. The tension between basic research and applied research need not exist. We can, in fact, have it both ways. Donald Stokes (1997), a philosopher of science, suggested that we think about scientific research in two distinct ways. One way is to focus on whether or not the research is motivated by a quest for fundamental understanding. Typically, we think of pure basic science as being driven by such a quest. It is the kind of scientific motivation that we often attribute to the white-clad, bench scientist.

But Stokes calls our attention to a second important way of thinking about scientific research—to focus, in addition, on whether or not the research is inspired by a consideration of its practical use or application. Rather than being driven by a need to know, this other way of thinking about science takes into consideration whether or not the research was driven by the need to solve a practical problem.

To understand the relationship between these two distinct ways of thinking about science, Stokes created a *quadrant model* of scientific research, which is depicted on the next page:

	A consideration of use?	
Research is inspired by:	No	Yes
A quest for fundamental understanding? Yes	Pure basic research (Bohr)	Use-inspired basic research (Pasteur)
No		Pure applied research (Edison)

According to this view, pure basic research is inspired by a quest for fundamental understanding, without necessarily being *inspired* by a particular use. A good example is the work of Niels Bohr, the great physicist who won a Nobel Prize for his theories of atomic structure. Bohr's work resolved fundamental theoretical problems having to do with the behaviour of electrons and the nature of their energy. Although Bohr's work was not motivated out of a need to solve a particular practical problem, it is interesting and important to point out that his insights were ultimately put to very practical use – splitting the atom and creating the atomic bomb. That is not, however, what inspired the original research. Indeed, Bohr was ultimately dismayed by the application (atom bombs) of his pioneering work.

The contrast to basic research is pure applied research, which is motivated only by the need to solve a specific practical problem. The great inventor Thomas Edison devoted his life to pure applied research—solving practical problems and inventing devices that could enjoy popular use. Edison liked to tinker with things, always with a practical goal in mind—to create safe and inexpensive lamps (the lightbulb), to store and retrieve sound recordings (the phonograph), to transmit voices and sounds over great distances (the telephone), and to capture and replay moving scenes (the motion picture projector). Edison did research to discover and invent, but his research was not inspired by a need to understand the fundamental nature of things. His research was driven by a need to invent.

When pure basic research and pure applied research come together, a fascinating and important third possibility is created—the upper right hand quadrant in Stokes' model. This is *use-inspired basic research*—the case in which research is simultaneously motivated by a practical need to know and a more basic quest for fundamental understanding. Stokes calls this Pasteur's quadrant, because it best describes the kind of science for which Louis Pasteur is well known. Pasteur was inspired by very practical and applied goals—to learn how to prevent the spoilage of food, to improve the technology of fermentation, such as that involved in making beer and wine, and to treat and cure diseases. Pasteur's work led to the process of "pasteurization," which prevents the kind of fermentation that leads to milk going bad. But Pasteur recognized that achieving these goals depended on a deeper and more fundamental understanding of chemistry, biology, and the nature of life. Pasteur ultimately discovered that microscopic organisms led food to spoil, produced fermentation, and caused diseases. Indeed, his research gave birth to the field of microbiology and much of modern medicine. In his quest to solve practical problems, Pasteur also discovered fundamental principles.

Questions:

1. Looking back over all of the experiments reviewed in *Social Psychology Alive,* identify one or two good examples of social psychological research that falls into Pasteur's quadrant.

2. Looking back over all of the experiments reviewed in *Social Psychology Alive*, identify one or two good examples of social psychological research that falls into Edison's quadrant.

3. Looking back over all of the experiments reviewed in *Social Psychology Alive*, identify one or two good examples of social psychological research that falls into Bohr's quadrant.

4. One quadrant represents the case when research is neither inspired by a quest for fundamental understanding, nor by a consideration of its use. This quadrant was left empty in the figure on the previous page. Why do you think this is? Do you think any worthwhile research could fall into this quadrant? What would you call it?

 **Learning Objectives**

1. Describe how social psychology might be useful in a business setting. What are three important differences between doing research in a corporate setting compared to an academic setting? (p. 554)

2. What drives research in government research institutions? How does its impact differ from research conducted in academic settings and how does this affect the research hypotheses and methods? What is the major role of government funding agencies with regard to social psychology? How might social psychologists contribute to the work of regulatory agencies? (pp. 554–556)

3. Explain how social psychology research and methods can be used to help lawyers prepare their cases for trial. (pp. 556–558)

4. Describe three examples of interconnections between social psychology and health. (pp. 558–560)

5. Describe three ways social psychology provides insight into academic achievement. (pp. 560–561)

6. Describe the education path to becoming a social psychology professor. (pp. 562–563)

7. Explain how functional Magnetic Resonance Imaging is used to study racial prejudice. (pp. 564)

8. Using the theory of cognitive dissonance, explain how psychologists rely on people with brain-related cognitive disorders to study psychological phenomena. (pp. 564–565)

9. Describe how immersive environments can be used to conduct experiments that need a "plant" or confederate of the researcher. What is nanotechnology? (p. 566–568)

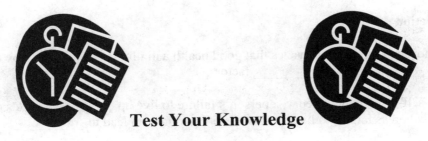

Test Your Knowledge

Multiple Choice Questions

1. Social psychology makes a contribution in the Canadian and United States government agencies that involve
   A. taxation, representation, or elections.
   B. agriculture, land, or water management.
   C. research, funding, or regulation.
   D. inventions, patents, or copyrights.

2. The model of good health and illness that guides health psychology is
   A. compliance-oriented intervention model.
   B. persuasion-laden preventive model.
   C. biopsychosocial model.
   D. ethos-psychosocial model.

3. Which of the following statements most clearly states what we know about the relationship between the social support a person actually receives and his or her health?
   A. Receipt of social support improves recovery from physical illness, but has no effect on reducing depression.
   B. Receipt of social support does not improve recovery from physical illness but it does reduce depression.
   C. Receipt of social support improves recovery from physical illness and reduces depression.
   D. It is unclear whether the actual receipt of social support helps or hurts a person's health.

4. Research with people suffering from anterograde amnesia indicates that people who do not remember engaging in attitude-discrepant behaviours do
   A. not engage in dissonance-reducing attitude change.
   B. engage in dissonance-reducing attitude change.
   C. engage in dissonance-reducing attitude change, but only if the researcher reminds them of their discrepant behaviour.
   D. not engage in dissonance-reducing behaviour, unless the researcher reminds them of their discrepant behaviour.

5. Research about the use of the Internet found that soon after the Internet was accessible in their houses, families experienced
   A. negative effects (e.g., decreased communication, smaller social circle, increased loneliness and depression), but after several years, the effects were positive (e.g., increased communication, larger social circle, decreased loneliness and depression).
   B. positive effects, but after several years, the effects were negative.
   C. negative effects, and after several years, the effects were still negative.
   D. positive effects, and after several years, the effects were still positive.

Sentence Completion

1. The biopsychosocial model emphasizes that good health and illness is determined by a combination of _____, _____, _____ factors.

2. According to self-discrepancy theory, a person's failure to live up to his or her ideals can lead to _____, whereas failure to live up to one's obligations can lead to _____.

3. According to the _____ model, a person's decisions about engaging in risky sexual behaviour are influenced by the information a person possesses, the person's motivation to perform risky or safer behaviours, and their skill at performing preventive behaviour correctly.

4. Children achieve more when they are _____ motivated rather than _____ motivated.

5. Portions of the _____ _____ area of the brain are activated when racially biased White participants are exposed to Black faces, indicating that they are engaging in much _____ _____ to control their responses.

Matching I – Key Terms

_____ 1. **biopsychosocial model**	A. the set of advanced cognitive processes involved in cognitive control, attention, judgment, and critical thinking
_____ 2. **social neuroscience**	B. model that emphasizes that good health and illness are determined by a combination of biological, social, and psychological factors
_____ 3. **executive function**	C. an emerging new area of research combining the perspectives of social psychology and neuroscience to understand the relationship between the brain and social behaviour

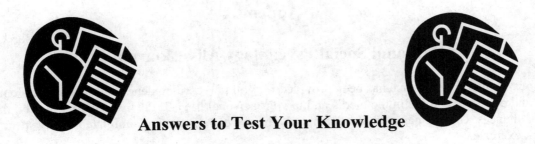

Answers to Test Your Knowledge

Multiple Choice Questions

1. C
2. C
3. D
4. B
5. A

Sentence Completion

1. biological, social, psychological
2. depression, anxiety
3. IMB
4. intrinsically, extrinsically
5. prefrontal cortex, cognitive effort

Matching I – Key Terms

1. B
2. C
3. A

Appendix A

Additional Social Psychology Alive Journal Entries

Throughout the workbook, space has been provided for you to record evidence of social psychological findings and concepts you see in the media and in your personal life and the lives of your family, friends, and acquaintances. Use the pages in this appendix to record entries that are not related to any specific workbook exercise.

Appendix B

Table of Contents from Textbooks from Social Psychology, Other Areas of Psychology, and Related Disciplines
(To be used in conjunction with Chapter 1)

Social Psychology

Olson, J. M., Breckler, S. J., & Wiggins, E. C. (2008). *Social psychology alive* (1st Canadian edition). Toronto, ON: Thomson Nelson.

Chapter 1: Introducing Social Psychology
Chapter 2: The Methods of Social Psychology
Chapter 3: Social Cognition: Thinking About People
Chapter 4: Social Perception: Perceiving the Self and Others
Chapter 5: The Person in the Situation: Self-Concept, Gender, and Dispositions
Chapter 6: Attitudes and Social Behaviour
Chapter 7: Attitude Change
Chapter 8: Conformity, Compliance, and Obedience
Chapter 9: Stereotypes, Prejudice, and Discrimination
Chapter 10: Group Dynamics and Intergroup Relations
Chapter 11: Aggression and Violence
Chapter 12: Helpful Social Behaviour
Chapter 13: Liking, Loving, and Close Relationships
Chapter 14: Social Psychology in Your Life

Social and Personality Development

Shaffer, D. R. (2005). *Social and personality development* (5th ed.). Belmont, CA: Wadsworth.

1. Introduction
   The universal parenting machine—a thought experiment; social-personality development in historical perspective; questions and controversies about human development; research methods; detecting relationships: correlational and experimental designs; designs for studying development; cross-cultural comparisons; postscript: on becoming a wise consumer of developmental research

2. Classical Theories of Social and Personality Development
   The psychoanalytic viewpoint; behaviourist viewpoint; Piaget's cognitive-developmental viewpoint

3. Recent Perspectives on Social and Personality Development
   Modern evolutionary perspectives; behavioural genetics: biological bases for individual differences; ecological systems theory: a modern environmentalist perspective; modern cognitive perspectives; theories and worldviews

4. Emotional Development and Temperament
   An overview of emotions and emotional development; appearance and development of discrete emotions; identifying and understanding others' emotions; learning to regulate emotions; emotional competence, social competence, and personal adjustment; temperament and development

5. Establishment of Intimate Relationships and Their Implications for Future Development
   What are emotional attachments?; how do infants become attached?; individual differences in attachment security; factors that influence attachment security; fathers as attachment objects; attachment and later development; the unattached infant; maternal employment, day care, and early emotional development

6. Development of the Self and Social Cognition
   Development of the self-concept; self-esteem: the evaluative component of the self; who am I to be? forging an identify; the other side of social cognition: knowing about others

7. Achievement
   The concept of achievement motivation; early reactions to one's accomplishments: from mastery to self-evaluation; theories of achievement motivation and achievement behaviour; cultural and subcultural influences on achievement; home and family influences on achievement; creativity and special talents

8. Sex Differences, Gender-Role Development, and Sexuality
   Categorizing males and females: gender-role standards; some facts and fictions about sex differences; developmental trends in gender typing; theories of gender typing and gender-role development; psychological androgyny: a prescription for the twenty-first century?; sexuality and sexual behaviour

9. Aggression and Antisocial Conduct
   What is aggression?; theories of aggression; developmental trends in aggression; sex differences in aggression; cultural and subcultural influences on aggression; family influences on aggression; methods of controlling aggression and antisocial conduct

10. Altruism and Moral Development
    What are altruism and prosocial behaviour?; theories of altruism and prosocial development; developmental trends in altruism; cognitive and affective contributions to altruism; cultural and social influences on altruism; what is morality?; psychoanalytic explanations of moral development; cognitive-developmental theory: the child as a moral philosopher; morality as a product of social learning (and social information processing); who raises morally mature children?

Abnormal Psychology

Barlow, D. H., Durand, V. M., & Stewart, S. H. (2006). *Abnormal psychology: An integrative approach* (1st Canadian ed.). Toronto, ON: Thomson Nelson.

1. Abnormal Behaviour in Historical Context
   Science of psychopathology; the supernatural tradition; the biological tradition; the psychological tradition; the scientific method
2. An Integrative Approach to Psychopathology
   One-dimensional vs. multidimensional models; genetic contributions to psychopathology; neuroscience; behavioural and cognitive science; emotions; cultural, social, and interpersonal factors; life-span development
3. Clinical Assessment and Diagnosis
   Assessing psychological disorders; diagnosing psychological disorders
4. Research Methods
   Studying individual cases; correlational research; experimental research; single-case experimental designs; studying genetics; studying behaviour over time; studying behaviour across cultures; the power of a research program; research ethics
5. Anxiety Disorders
   Anxiety, fear, and panic; generalized anxiety disorder; panic disorder; specific phobia; social phobia; posttraumatic stress disorder; obsessive-compulsive disorder
6. Somatoform and Dissociative Disorders
   Somatoform disorders (hypochondriasis, conversion disorder, pain disorder); dissociative disorders (depersonalization, amnesia, fugue, trance, identity, suggestibility)
7. Mood Disorders
   Depressive disorders; bipolar disorders; prevalence of mood disorders; anxiety and depression; causes; treatment
8. Eating and Sleep Disorders
   Bulimia; anorexia; binge-eating; statistics; causes; treatment; dyssomnias; treatment of dyssomnias; parasomnias
9. Physical Disorders and Health Psychology
   Psychological and social factors that influence biology; immune system and physical disorders; cardiovascular problems; chronic pain; chronic fatigue syndrome; psychosocial treatment of physical disorders
10. Sexual and Gender Identity Disorders
    What is normal?; gender identity disorders; sexual dysfunctions; assessing sexual behaviour; causes of sexual dysfunction; treatment; paraphilia (causes, assessing, treating)
11. Substance-Related Disorders
    Depressants; stimulants; opioids; hallucinogens; causes; integrative model; treatment
12. Personality Disorders
    Specific personality disorders; cluster A disorders (paranoid personality, schizoid personality, schizotypal personality); cluster B disorders (antisocial personality, borderline personality, histrionic personality, narcissistic personality); cluster C disorders (avoidant personality, dependent personality, obsessive-compulsive personality)
13. Schizophrenia and Other Psychotic Disorders
    The concept of schizophrenia; clinical description; causes; treatment
14. Developmental Disorders
    Attention deficit/hyperactivity disorder; learning disorders; autistic disorder; mental retardation
15. Cognitive Disorders
    Delirium; dementia; amnestic disorder

16. Mental Health Services: Legal and Ethical Issues
Civil commitment; criminal commitment; patients' rights

Sociology

Brym, R. J., Lie, J., & Nelson, A. (2005). *Sociology: Your compass for a new world* (Brief ed., 1st Canadian ed.). Toronto, ON: Thomson Nelson.

I. Foundations
   1. A Sociological Compass
      The sociological perspective; theoretical traditions; the research cycle; research methods, a sociological compass

II. Basic Social Processes
   2. Culture
      Culture as problem solving; culture from the inside and outside; culture as freedom and constraint
   3. Socialization
      Social isolation and socialization; theories of childhood socialization; agents of socialization; dilemmas of childhood and adolescent socialization
   4. Interaction and Organization
      What is social interaction?; what shapes social interaction?; modes of social interaction; micro, meso, macro, and global structures; bureaucracies and networks
   5. Deviance and Crime
      Social definition of deviance and crime; explaining deviance and crime; social control and punishment

III. Inequality
   6. Social Stratification
      Patterns of social inequality; is stratification inevitable? Three theories; social mobility; prestige and taste; politics and the perception of class inequality
   7. Race and Ethnicity
      Defining race and ethnicity; race and ethnic relations; theories of race and ethnic relations; the future of race and ethnicity in Canada
   8. Sexuality and Gender
      Sex versus gender; theories of gender; gender inequality; toward 2050; the women's movement

IV. Institutions
   9. Work and the Economy
      The promise and history of work; "good" versus "bad" jobs; the problem of markets (globalization, capitalism, communism and social democracy)
   10. Politics
      Free trade and democracy; what is politics?; theories of democracy; the future of democracy
   11. Families
      Functionalism and the nuclear ideal; conflict and feminist theories; power and families; family diversity; family policy
   12. Religion and Education
      Classical approaches to the sociology of religion; the rise, decline, and partial revival of religion; religion in Canada; education; rise of mass schooling; functions of education; school standards; dealing with the public school crisis
   13. Health, Medicine and Aging

Health and inequality; health and politics; aging as a social problem; medicine and society

V. Social Change

Cultural Anthropology

Haviland, W. A., Fedorak, S. A., Crawford, G. W., & Lee, R. B. (2005). *Cultural anthropology* (2nd Canadian ed.). Toronto, ON: Thomson Nelson.

I. Anthropology and the Study of Culture
    1. The nature of anthropology
        Development of anthropology; the discipline of anthropology; anthropology and science; anthropology and the humanities; anthrogy's contributions to other disciplines; questions of ethics; relevance of anthropology in contemporary life
    2. The nature of culture
        Concept of culture; characteristics of culture; studying culture in the field; culture and adaptation; culture, society, and the individual; evaluation of culture
    3. The beginnings of human culture
        Humans and other primates; human ancestors

II. Culture and Survival: Communicating and Staying Alive
    4. Language and communication
        Nature of language; gesture-call system; linguistic change; language in its cultural setting; origins of language; from speech to writing
    5. Making a living
        Adaptation; the food-foraging way of life; the food-producing way of life; mechanized agriculture
    6. Economic systems
        Economic anthropology; resources; distribution and exchange; consumption; economics, culture, and the world of business

III. The Formation of Groups: Solving the Problem of Cooperation
    7. Sex and marriage
        Human sexuality; control of sexual relations; forms of marriage; divorce
    8. Family and household
        The family defined; functions of the family; family and household; forms of the family; residence patterns; problems of family and household organization
    9. Kinship and descent
        Why we study kinship; urban kinship in Canada; descent groups; forms and functions of descent groups; kinship terminology and kinship groups
    10. Social stratification and groupings
        Grouping by gender; age grouping; common-interest associations; social stratification

IV. Search for Order: Solving the Problem Disorder
    11. Political Organization and the Maintenance of Order
        Kinds of political systems; political organization and the maintenance of order; social control through law; political organization and external affairs; political systems and the question of legitimacy; religion and politics

402

Political Science

Dyck, R. (2008). *Studying politics* (2nd ed). Toronto, ON: Thomson Nelson.

Political Development and Change

References

(References in the textbook list are excluded here.)

American Psychological Association. (2001). *Resolution on the death penalty in the United States.* Online at http://www.apa.org/pi/deathpenalty.html.

The Anger Kit. Online at http://www.angriesout.com/catalog/.

Atran, S. (2002). *In Gods we trust: The evolutionary landscape of religion.* Oxford University Press.

Atran, S. (2003). Genesis of suicide terrorism. *Science*, 299, 1534–1539.

Baldus, D. C, Woodworth, G., & Pulaski, C.A., Jr. (1990). *Equal justice and the death penalty: A legal and empirical analysis.* Boston: Northeastern University Press.

Ballew v. Georgia, 435 U.S. 223 (1978).

Barlow, D. H., Durand, V. M., & Stewart, S. H. (2006). *Abnormal psychology: An integrative pproach* (1st Canadian ed.). Toronto, ON: Thomson Nelson.

Barnett, V. J. (1999). *Bystanders: Conscience and complicity during the Holocaust.* Westport, Conn.: Greenwood Press.

Browning, C. R. (2000). *Nazi policy, Jewish workers, German killers.* Cambridge, U.K.; New York: Cambridge University Press.

Bruun, E. A. and Getzen, R. (Eds.) (1996). *The book of American values and virtues.* New York: Black Dog and Leventhal Publishers.

Brym, R. J., Lie, J., & Nelson, A. (2005). *Sociology: Your compass for a new world* (Brief Edition, 1st Canadian Edition).Toronto, ON: Thomson Nelson.

Canadian Broadcasting Company. Online at http://www.cbc.ca/ontariotoday/rings.html.

Canadian Institutes of Health Research, Natural Sciences and Engineering Research Council of Canada, Social Sciences and Humanities Research Council of Canada, *Tri-Council Policy Statement: Ethical Conduct for Research Involving Humans.* 1998 (with 2000, 2002 and 2005 amendments).

Canadian Red Cross (2005). *Sri Lanka posting marks 16th mission for Canadian Red Cross nurse.* Online at http://www.redcross.ca/article.asp?id=015443&tid=094

Center for Disease Control. (n.d.) *The Tuskegee syphilis study: A hard lesson learned.* Retrieved May 25, 2005, from http://www.cdc.gov/nchstp/od/tuskegee/time.htm.

Delano, J. (2004, March 12). After serving time, Martha may clean up once again. *Pittsburgh Business Times.* Online at http://pittsburgh.bizjournals.com/site_map/ pittsburgh_sitemap_100.html.

R. K., & Harackiewicz (1996). Self-handicapping and intrinsic motivation: Buffering ...ic motivation from the threat of failure. *Journal of Personality and Social Psychology, 70,* ...876.

...yck, R. (2008). *Studying Politics* (2nd ed). Toronto, ON: Thomson Nelson.

Ehrlich, E. (1995). *Veni, Vidi, Vici.* New York: HarperCollins.

Fenigstein, A., Scheier, M. F., & Buss, A. H. (1975). Public and private self-consciousness: Assessment and theory. *Journal of Consulting and Clinical Psychology, 43,* 522–527.

Ferguson, E. & Bibby, P. A. (2002). Predicting future blood donor returns: Past behavior, intentions, and observer effects. *Health Psychology, 21,* 513–518.

Fogelman, E. (1994). *Conscience and courage: The rescuers of the Jews during the Holocaust.* New York: Anchor Books.

Furman v. Georgia, 408 U.S. 238 (1972).

Gansberg, M. (1964, March 27). Thirty-seven who saw murder didn't call the police. *New York Times*, p. 1.

Hafer, C. L., & Olson, J. M. (1993). Beliefs in a just world, discontent, and assertive actions by working women. *Personality and Social Psychology Bulletin, 19,* 30–38.

Haslam, S. A. & Reicher, S. Beyond Stanford: Questioning a role-based explanation of tyranny. *Dialogue*, 2003, 18, 22–25. (Bulletin of the Society for Personality and Social Psychology).

Haviland, W. A., Fedorak, S., Crawford, G., & Lee, R. (2005). *Cultural anthropology* (2nd Canadian ed.). Toronto, ON: Thomson Nelson.

Heat-Mood, W. L. (1982). *Blue highways: A journey into America.* Boston: Little, Brown, and Company.

Hilberg, Raul. (1992). *Perpetrators victims bystanders: The Jewish catastrophe 1933-1945.* New York: Aaron Asher Books.

Hull, J. G., Slone, L. B., Meteyer, K. B., & Matthews, A. R. (2002). The nonconsciousness of self-consciousness. *Journal of Personality and Social Psychology, 83,* 406–424.

Inbau, F. E., Reid, J. E., Buckley, J. P., & Jayne, B. C. (2001). *Criminal interrogations and confessions* (4th ed.). Gaithersberg, MD: Aspen.

Interagency Advisory Panel on Research Ethics' (PRE) on-line Introductory Tutorial for the *Tri-Council Policy Statement: Ethical Conduct for Research Involving Humans* (TCPS). Online tutorial at http://www.pre.ethics.gc.ca/english/tutorial/. Ottawa: Interagency Advisory Panel on Research Ethics.

The International Thesaurus of Quotations (2nd ed.) (1996). New York: Harper Collins.